# Christmas Gifts FOR Everyone

# Christmas Gifts for Everyone

Edited by
Barbara Fimbel

Rodale Press, Inc.
Emmaus, Pennsylvania

A FRIEDMAN GROUP BOOK



Published in 1995 by Rodale Press, Inc.



The editors who compiled this book have tried to make all of the contents as accurate and as correct as possible. Illustrations, photographs, and text have all been carefully checked and cross-checked. However, due to the variability of materials, personal skill, and so on, neither the editors nor Rodale Press assumes any responsibility for any injuries suffered or for damages or other losses incurred that result from the material presented herein. All instructions should be carefully studied and clearly understood before beginning a project.

The editors at Rodale Press hope you will join with us in preserving nature's beauty so that others may share in the enjoyment of nature crafting. Unless you are certain that the plants or plant materials you are collecting—including leaves, stems, bark, flowers, fruits, seeds, or roots—are very common in your area, or over a wide geographic area, please do not collect them. Do not disturb or collect any plants or plant materials from parks, natural areas, or private lands without the permission of the owner. To the best of our knowledge, the plants and plant materials recommended in this book are common natural materials that can be grown and collected without harm to the environment.

Printed in the United States of America

**Library of Congress Cataloging-in-Publication Data**

Christmas gifts for everyone / edited by Barbara Fimbel.
p. cm.
"A Friedman Group book"—T.p. verso.
ISBN 0-87596-659-4 paperback (alk. paper)
1. Handicraft. 2. Gifts. 3. Christmas. I. Fimbel, Barbara.
TT157.C474 1995
745.5—dc20 95-9489

**Distributed in the book trade by St. Martin's Press**

2 4 6 8 10 9 7 5 3 1 paperback

If you have any questions or comments concerning this book, please write to:
Rodale Press, Inc.
Book Readers' Service
33 East Minor Street
Emmaus, PA 18098

*CHRISTMAS GIFTS FOR EVERYONE* was prepared and produced by
Michael Friedman Publishing Group, Inc.
15 West 26th Street
New York, New York 10010

**Michael Friedman Publishing Group Editorial Staff:**
*Project Editor:* Barbara Fimbel
*Technical Editor:* Kathleen Berlew
*Instructions Editor:* Charlotte J. Biro
*Copy Editor:* Loretta Mowat
*Editorial Director:* Sharyn Rosart
*Designer:* Andrea Karman
*Layout:* Robbi J. Oppermann
*Illustrator:* Barbara Hennig
*Art Director:* Jeff Batzli
*Photographer:* James Kozyra
*Photo Stylists:* Lynn McMahill and Sharon Ryan
*Photography Director:* Christopher C. Bain

**Rodale Press Editorial Staff:**
*Editor:* Karen Bolesta
*Cover Designer:* Lisa Palmer
*Interior Layout:* Robin M. Hepler
*Illustrator:* Glenn Hughes (Stitch diagrams on pp. 87, 115, 161)
*Copy Editor:* Maria Kasprenski Zator
*Manufacturing Coordinator:* Melinda B. Rizzo
*Editorial Director, Home and Garden:* Margaret Lydic Balitas
*Senior Editor, Craft Books:* Cheryl Winters Tetreau
*Art Director, Home and Garden:* Michael Mandarano
*Copy Director, Home and Garden:* Dolores Plikaitis
*Editor-in-Chief, Rodale Books:* William Gottlieb

**Contributors**
Julia Bernstein
Amy Albert Bloom
Jack Champlin
Michelle Filon
Barbara Fimbel
David Galt
Dale Joe
Patricia Richards
Lynne Shipp
Jacquelyn Smyth
Marinda Stewart

# CONTENTS

## *Gifts for Friends*

## *Secret Santa Gifts*

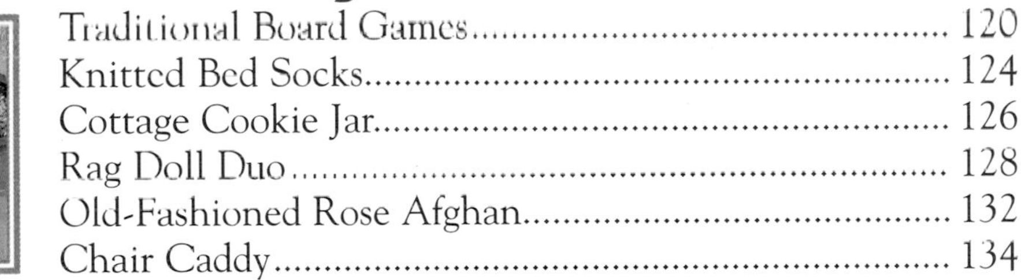



## *Gifts for VIPs*

## *Favor-ite Gifts*



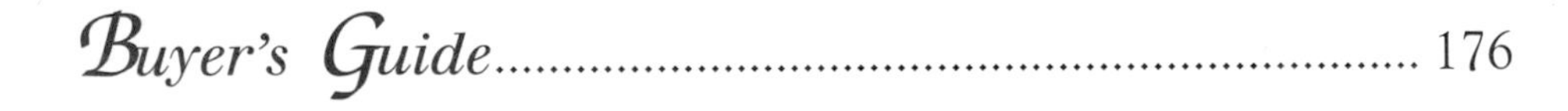

# INTRODUCTION

A handmade gift is like a hug. It wraps the recipient in a moment of affection—a moment that can be recalled with pleasure over and over, bringing on a smile each time. Like that loving squeeze, a handmade remembrance contains a little bit of yourself. Your fondness, concern, and

warm thoughts become a part of the finished product as surely as the time spent making it. At Christmas, we express our feelings for all of those around us—for our family, for our friends and neighbors, for people who make our lives easier during the year, and for people who can use our helping hand.

As you flip through the pages of *Christmas Gifts for Everyone*, you will come across projects selected and created for people in each group. We've given a lot of thought to these suggestions; we think these gifts will be ideally suited to those on your list. Many of the projects would be appropriate for other situations as well. Your baby-sitter, for example, might not be a teenager, but a retired schoolteacher who would prefer a lap robe or an evening bag. Your sitter might even be a young man who would be pleased by a video game rack.

While the collection of remembrances on the following pages covers a broad scope—from newborns to grandparents and delivery persons to friends far away—each of these diverse projects has one thing in common: it has been made as simple to complete as possible, including thorough, step-by-step instructions, with carefully thought-out diagrams and illustrations to help you duplicate the professional results shown.

We've even chosen gifts that are easy enough for kids to do—either by themselves or with a little assistance from Mom or Dad. Some will require adult supervision, but the actual crafting is geared to young fingers and quick results.

May the peace and joy of the Christmas season be yours as you craft gifts for those you love.

*Chapter One*

# Gifts for Children & Teens

*From the tiniest tot to the tallest teenager, children almost always top our Christmas gift lists. Delight a new baby with colorful booties, a young boy with a play mat for his cars, or a special girl with a topsy-turvy doll. Some of these gifts, like the duplicate-stitched sweater, can be completed in a wink; others, like the planet mobile, take a bit longer. The techniques and skill levels vary, but all of these gifts were created with very special young people in mind.*

# GOLDILOCKS AND THE THREE BEARS CARRY-ALONG HOUSE

*Your favorite little girl will be able to take along the whole cast of characters, the furniture, and even the porridge! And it's all packed up in a magical traveling cottage. Sheets of plastic canvas inside the lightly padded walls and roof define the shape of the house and the sweet, stitched details make it like home.*

**Sizes:** 8¼ × 10½ × 10½-inch house; 4½- to 5-inch figures

## MATERIALS

- Pencil
- Tracing paper
- Scissors
- Fabrics: 1 yard of yellow solid, ½ yard of blue print, ⅓ yard of red check, 12-inch square each of red print and white print
- 1 yard of fusible fleece
- Iron
- Two 12-inch squares of paper-backed fusible web
- Matching sewing thread
- Sewing machine
- Eight 10¾ × 13¾-inch sheets of plastic canvas
- Ribbons: 20-inch length of 1½-inch-wide red grosgrain; 48-inch length of ⅛-inch-wide red satin
- Two 1 inch red buttons
- 9 ×12-inch squares of felt: 3 pieces of turquoise; 2 pieces each of tan, red, green, and yellow; 1 piece each of peach, pink, white, and black
- 8 ounces of polyester fiberfill
- Paper punch
- Thick white craft glue
- Black, fine-point, permanent marker
- Ruler
- Blond curly wool doll hair
- Large-eyed needle
- 3½-inch-diameter wooden box with lid
- 5-inch-diameter white doily
- Small, pointed artist's brush
- Acrylic paints: black, red, yellow, and green
- 3 wooden candle cups
- 2-inch-high wooden pot with lid

## DIRECTIONS

### PREPARING THE PATTERNS

Enlarge the pattern pieces on page 19 as indicated. Trace the pattern pieces on pages 15 through 18 onto the tracing paper. Each pattern includes a ¼-inch seam allowance where needed. Cut out the pattern pieces.

### MAKING THE HOUSE

**1** From the yellow fabric, cut five straight walls (two will be used for the floor) and two side walls. From the blue fabric, cut one straight wall and two side walls. From the fusible fleece, cut three straight walls and two side walls.

2 Following the manufacturer's directions, fuse the paper-backed web to the wrong sides of the 12-inch squares of fabric. Mark one door and five windows on the paper side of the red print piece. Mark three windows and one heart for the door on the paper side of the white print piece. Cut out the shapes and peel away the paper.

3 Fuse the wrong side of one red print window to the right side of each of the yellow side walls, two red print windows to one yellow straight wall, and one red print window to one yellow straight wall, leaving space for the door on this wall. Place the door on this last yellow wall, then place the heart in position on the door. Fuse these two pieces to the wall. Fuse a white print window to each of the two side and one straight blue walls. Referring to the photograph, use blue or red thread and a medium-width zigzag stitch to machine appliqué along the edges of the windows, door, and heart. Appliqué straight lines across the center of the windows in each direction for the windowpane details.

4 Following the manufacturer's directions, fuse a piece of the fusible fleece to the wrong side of each of the four yellow walls with window and door appliqués, and to one of the yellow floor pieces.

5 With the right sides together, sew the plain yellow floor piece and the fleece-backed yellow floor piece together along the outer edges, leaving one short edge open. Turn right side out. Press, turning in ¼ inch along the open edges. Cut one piece of plastic canvas ¼ inch smaller all around than the floor size. Slide the canvas into the floor section and topstitch the opening closed, as shown in **Diagram 1.**

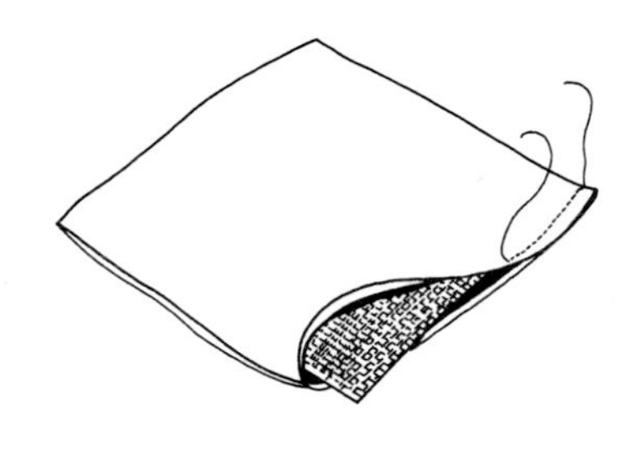

**Diagram 1**

6 Construct each of the walls in the same way as the floor. Sew the wall with the door and a yellow wall together. Sew each of the yellow side walls to a blue side wall. Sew the remaining yellow and blue windowed wall pieces together.

7 From the red check, cut two roof pieces. Fuse fleece to the wrong side of one piece. With right sides together, sew the pieces together along three edges. Turn right side out, turn under ¼ inch along the open edges and press. Topstitch ¾ inch from the short edge opposite the opening, as shown in **Diagram 2.**

**Diagram 2**

8 Cut a 5 × 10-inch piece of plastic canvas. Insert this piece into the roof and against the topstitching. Topstitch across the center of the roof, encasing the canvas piece, as shown in **Diagram 3.** Cut a second 5 × 10-inch piece of plastic canvas and insert this into the roof. Topstitch ¾ inch from the open edge of the roof, encasing the second piece of canvas. Topstitch the opening closed.

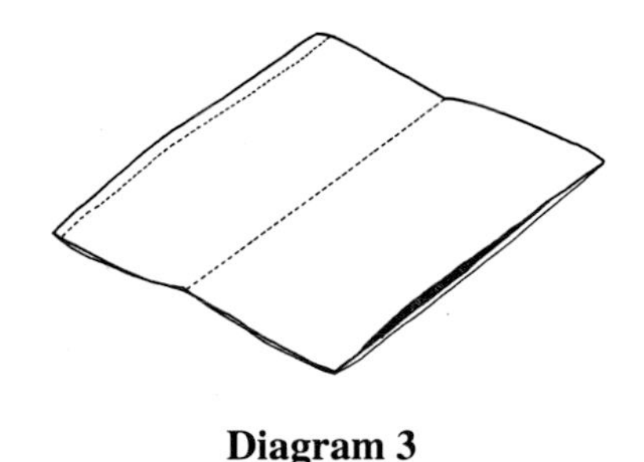

**Diagram 3**

9 Sew the walls to the floor, stitching close to the edge of the pieces. Sew the side walls to the back wall. Leave the front wall free on the sides. Slip stitch the roof in place, sewing only the back half of the roof to the back peak of the side walls; leave the ¾-inch "eave" at the back free.

10 Knot the grosgrain ribbon 1 inch from each end. Sew each knot to the outside of the house at the roof peak for a handle. Sew a button to each front edge of a side wall, 1½ inches from the corner (see the photograph on page 12). Sew the center of a 12-inch length of the satin ribbon to one side of the front wall to match the button. Knot the ends of the ribbon together to create a loop that fits over the button. Repeat on the other side of the front wall. (*Optional*: Make the button loops with narrow elastic cord instead. The stretch makes fitting the loop over the button easier.)

## Making the Figures

1 Using the tan felt for the bears' bodies and the peach felt for Goldilocks' body, cut two rectangles of felt slightly larger than the patterns. Mark the body on one piece of felt. Place the two felt pieces together and sew about ⅛ inch inside the marked outline, leaving an opening for stuffing where marked. Cut the figure out of the felt, being sure to cut away all marked lines. Stuff each figure lightly, then sew the opening closed.

2 Cut a peach muzzle for each of the bears. Use the paper punch to cut two pink cheeks and one black nose for each bear from the felt. Use the craft glue to glue the nose and cheeks to the muzzle, then glue the muzzle in place. Use the marker to draw the mouth onto the muzzle and two eyes on the face above the muzzle, as shown in the photograph on page 12.

3 Use the paper punch to cut one red mouth, two pink cheeks, and two turquoise eyes from the felt. Glue these in place on Goldilocks' face. Use the marker to draw eyelashes and the sides of the smile. Cut two stretched 12-inch lengths of doll hair. Slightly part the center of each length and glue them to the top and back of the head. Fluff the ends of the hair. Thread a 7-inch length of the ⅛-inch-wide ribbon through the large-eyed needle and sew it through the side of the head. Tie the ends of the ribbon around the hair and into a bow. Repeat for the other side of the head.

4 Cut one apron from the yellow felt for the mama bear, then one apron from the red felt for Goldilocks. Place an apron on each figure, overlapping and gluing the edges together in the back. Cut two overalls from the green felt for the papa bear and two overalls from the turquoise felt for the baby bear. Trim the back overall pieces where marked. Topstitch the front and back overall pieces together about ⅛ inch along each leg edge. Place the overalls on the figures, overlapping and gluing the straps together in the back.

## Making the Table and Dishes

1 Cut a circle of red felt to fit the top of the round box lid, then glue the felt to the lid top. Glue the doily to the box bottom for a rug.

2 Referring to the photograph on page 12, paint the wooden candle cups with a phrase and a flower. Use black to paint "TOO HOT" on the first, "JUST RIGHT" on the second, and "TOO COLD" on the third. Paint four flowers and "HONEY" on the side of the wooden pot.

## Making the Beds

1 Cut two 5⅛ × 6⅞-inch pieces each of red, turquoise, and pink felt for the mattresses. Using a ¼-inch seam allowance, sew the pairs of mattress pieces together along the outer edges, leaving an opening at the center of one short edge for turning.

2 Refold a corner so the seams meet. Sew across the corner about ½ inch from the point to miter the corner, as shown in **Diagram 4.** Repeat on the three remaining corners. Turn right side out. Stuff and slip stitch the opening closed.

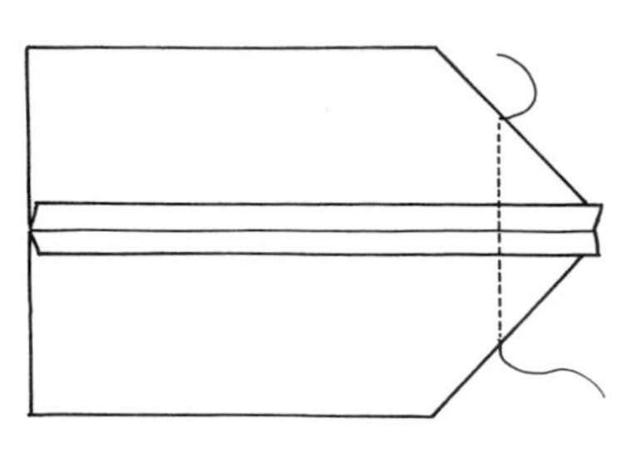

**Diagram 4**

3 Using the white felt for two headboards and the red felt for one headboard, cut two rectangles of felt slightly larger than the pattern for each headboard. Mark the headboard on one felt rectangle. Place the two felt pieces together and sew about ⅛ inch inside the marked outline, leaving the bottom edge open. Cut the headboard out of the felt. Cut a piece of plastic canvas about ¼ inch smaller all around than the pattern for each headboard. Insert the canvas into the headboard and topstitch the opening closed. Cut and glue a heart of a contrasting color to each mattress and each headboard. Glue the white headboards to the pink and red mattresses, and the red headboard to the turquoise mattress.

## Making the Chairs

1 Using the green felt for the large chair, the turquoise felt for the medium chair, and the yellow felt for the small chair, cut two pieces of felt for each chair, slightly larger than the pattern. Mark the pattern on one piece of felt. Then sew the two felt pieces together inside the marked outline, leaving the bottom edge open. Topstitch a straight line from the corner of each arm to the bottom edge, as marked on the pattern by the dashed lines.

2 Cut a piece of plastic canvas to fit inside each of the three sec-

tions of the chair. Insert the plastic canvas piece into each chair section, then topstitch the bottom edge closed, as shown in **Diagram 5.**

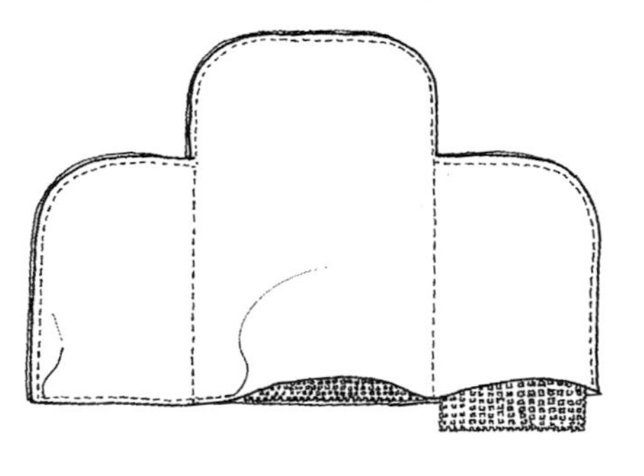

**Diagram 5**

3 Cut two squares of felt in the same color as the chair for each chair seat: 3-inch squares for the small chair, 4-inch squares for the medium chair, and 4¾-inch squares for the large chair. Using a ¼-inch seam allowance, sew the two pieces together along the outer edges, leaving an opening at the center of one short edge. Use the same method as for the mattress to miter the corners, sewing across each corner ½ inch from the point for the small seat, ¾ inch from the point for the medium seat, and 1 inch from the point for the large seat. Turn right side out and stuff. Sew the opening closed.

4 Cut and glue a large heart of a contrasting color to the inside top of the medium and large chairs. Cut and glue a small heart of a contrasting color to the inside top of the small chair. Glue the chair to the seat, gluing the arms to the sides of the seat.

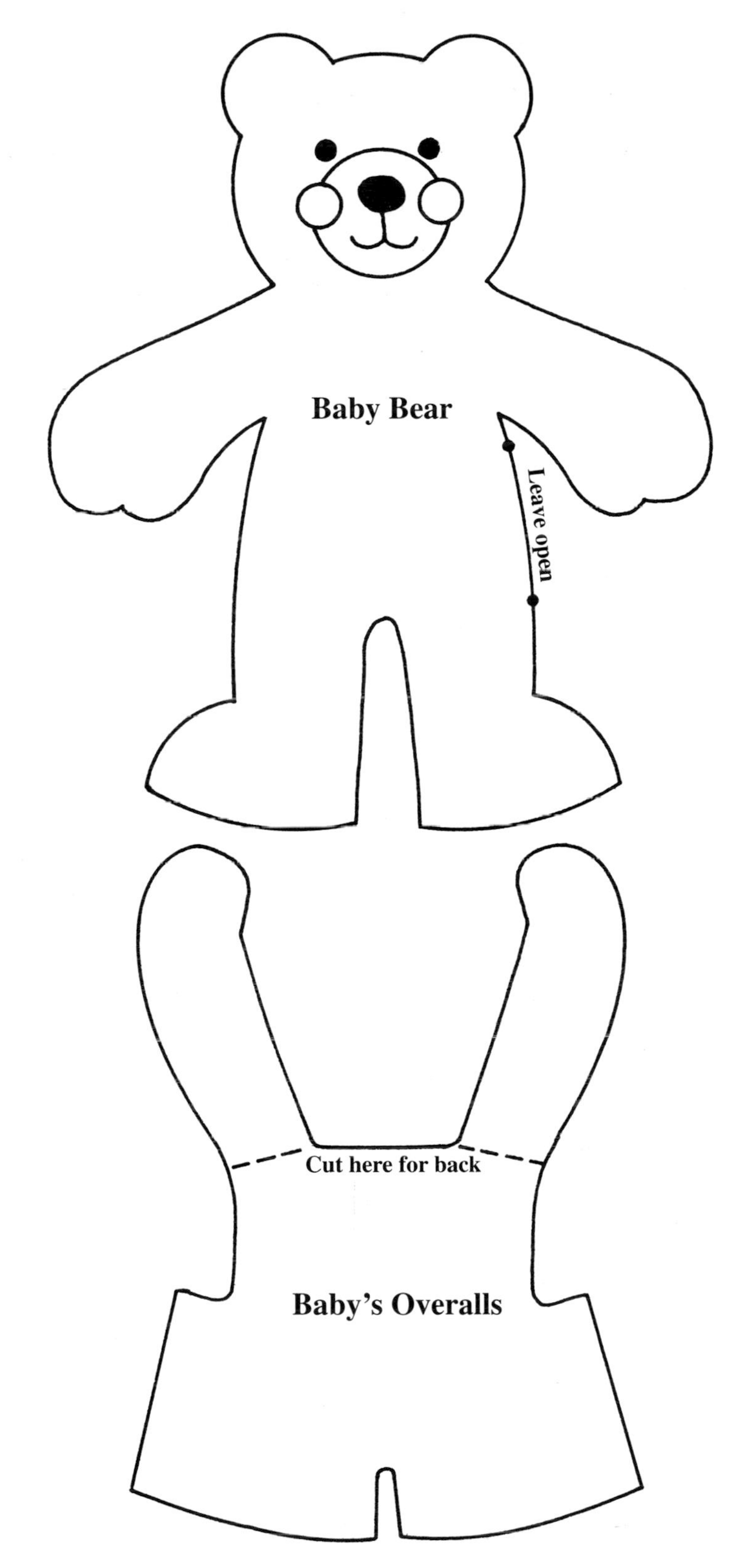

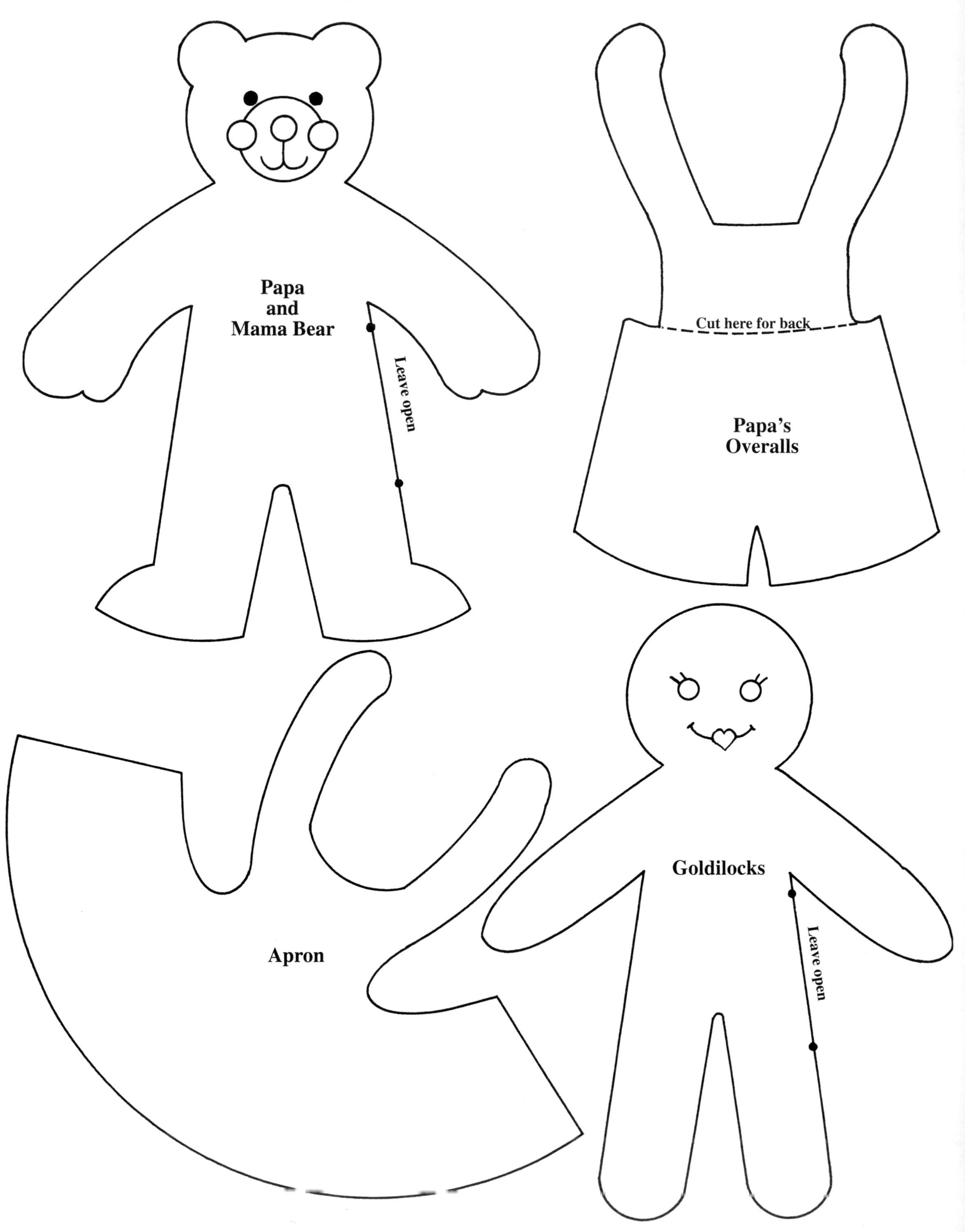
Papa
and
Mama Bear
Leave open
Cut here for back
Papa's
Overalls
Apron
Goldilocks
Leave open

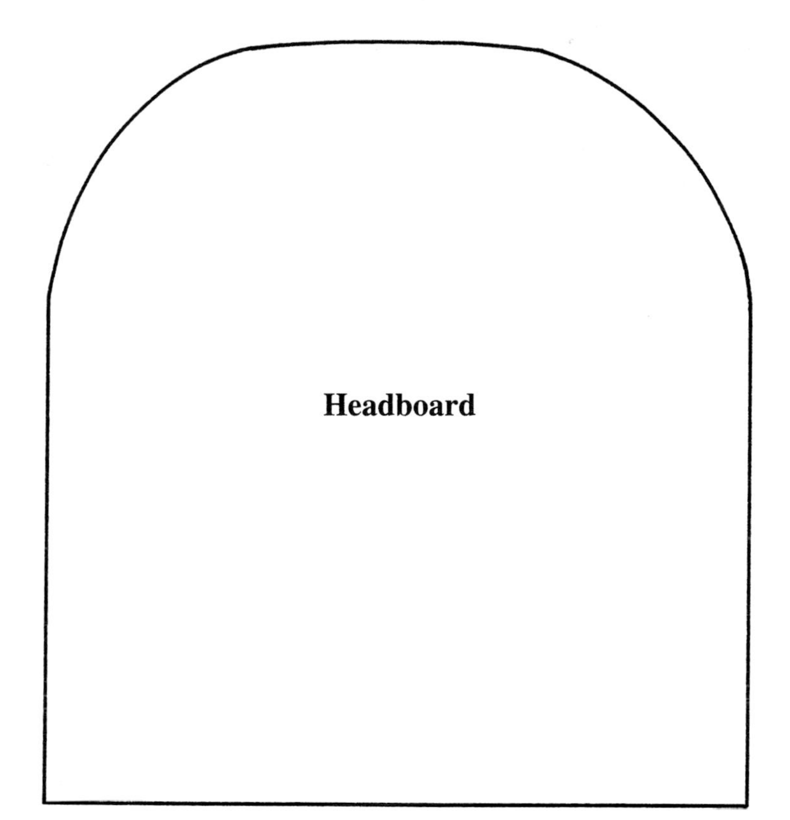
Headboard

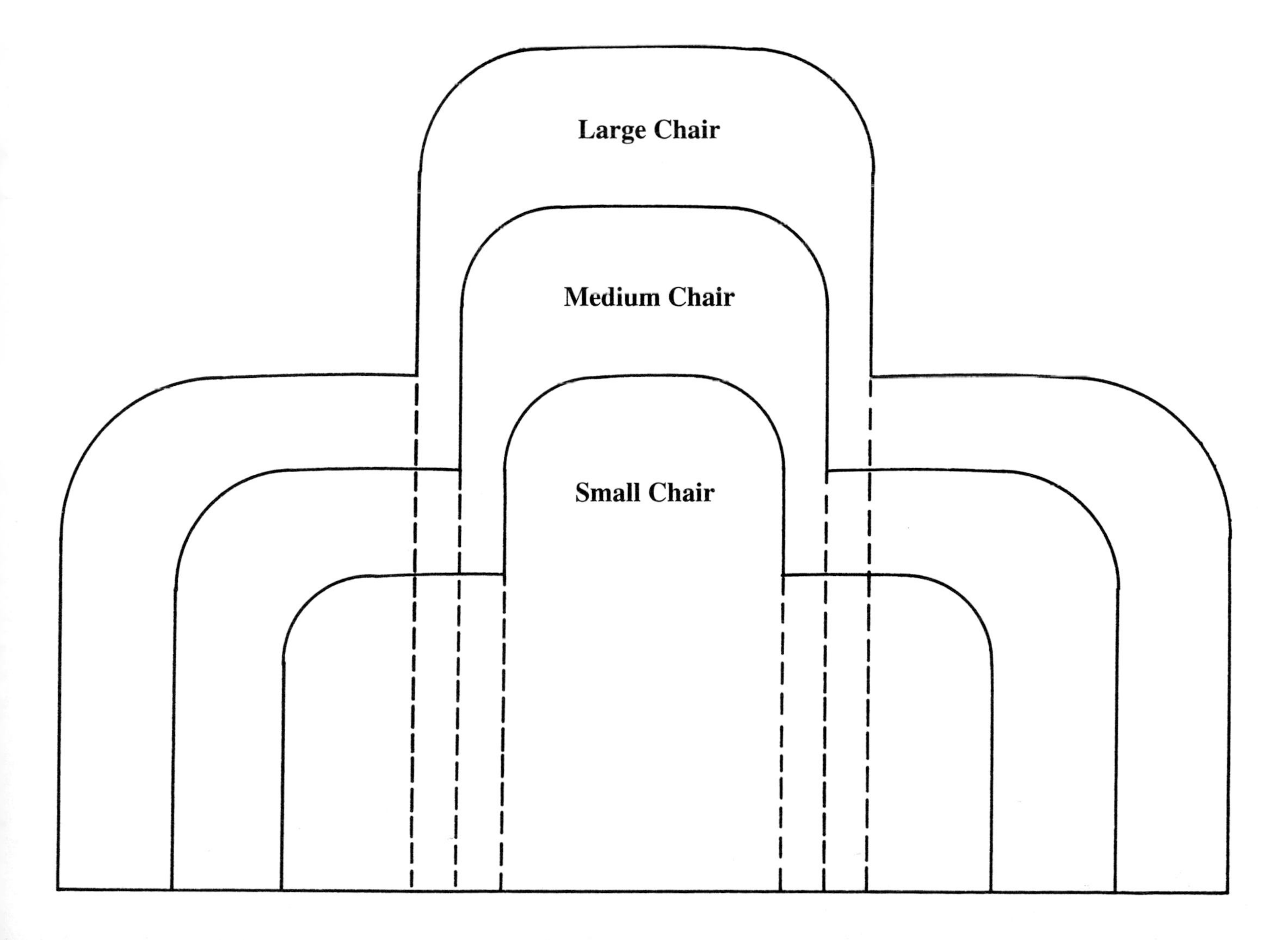
Large Chair
Medium Chair
Small Chair

Large Heart
Door

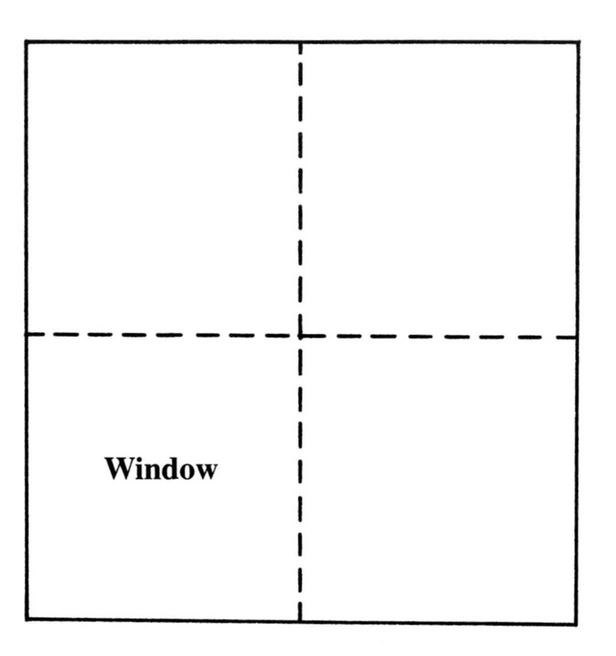
Window

Small Heart

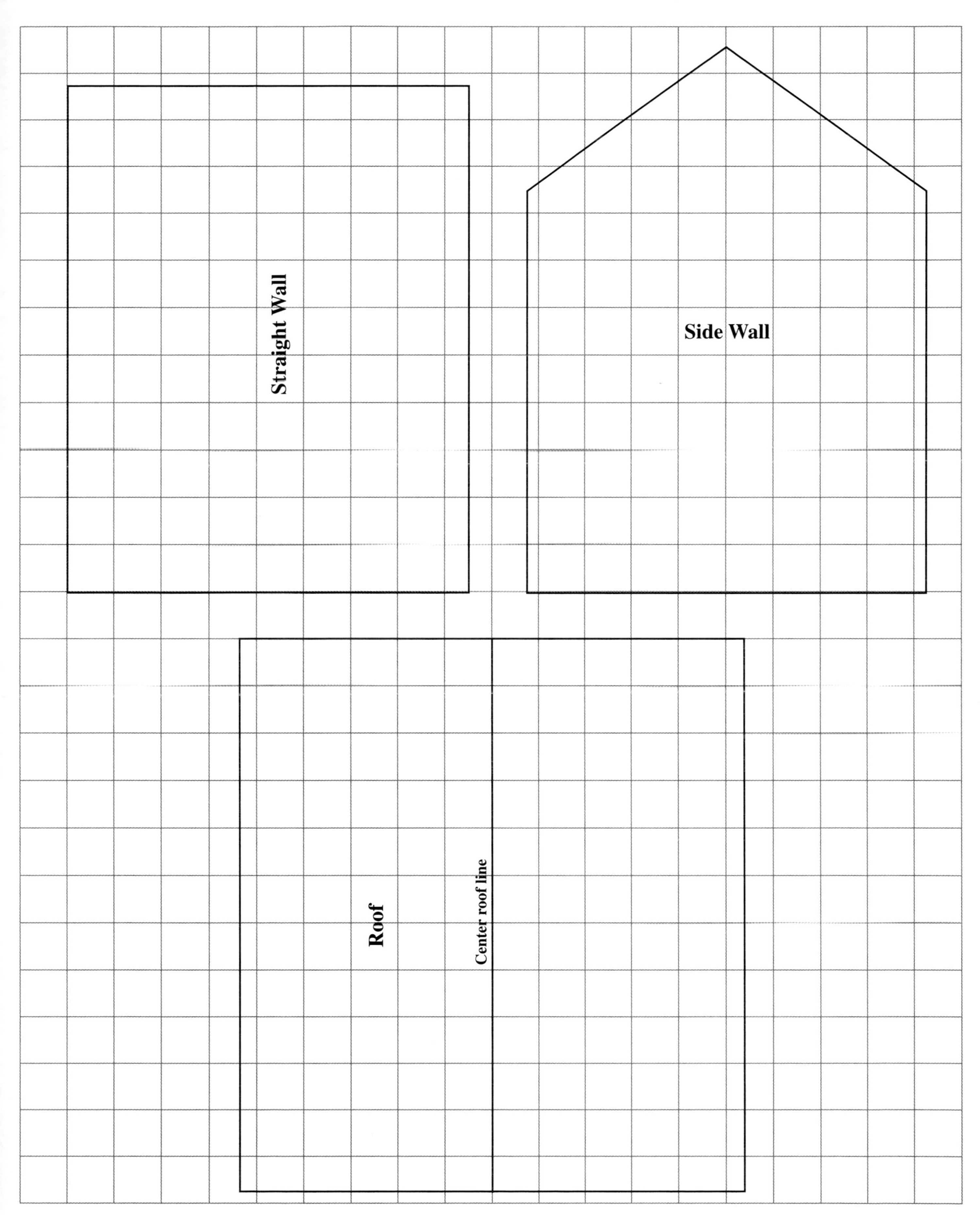


1 square = 1 inch

Enlarge 267%

# PLANET AND STARS MOBILE

*A budding astronaut will dream of other worlds with this mobile as inspiration. A combination of soft sculpture and glow-in-the-dark clay stars creates a colorful galaxy. Bright prints and metallic fabric scraps re-create a space shuttle and satellite as well as a variety of planets. Your young scientist will experience the thrill of space travel with this dramatic accent.*

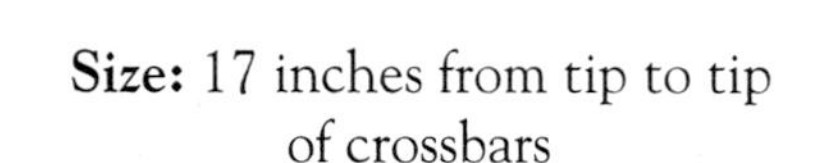

**Size:** 17 inches from tip to tip of crossbars

## Materials

- Sandpaper
- Inner ring of a 12-inch wooden embroidery hoop
- Water-soluble marking pen
- Thick white craft glue
- Two ⅛-inch-diameter wooden dowels, each 17 inches long
- Paintbrush
- White acrylic paint, or paint color to blend with ceiling color
- Paint sealer
- Lightweight iron-on interfacing to stabilize woven lamé fabrics
- Assorted lamé scraps, including silver, textured gold, copper, and gold
- Pencil
- Tracing paper
- Scissors
- Assorted calico fabrics, including 4 blues, 1 purple, 1 red, and 1 brown
- Sewing machine
- Matching sewing thread, including metallic thread
- Polyester fiberfill
- Hand-sewing needle
- Toothpicks
- Black fabric paint
- Compass
- Ruler
- Pins
- 18-gauge floral wire
- Polymer clay, such as Fimo Night Glow*
- Monofilament thread
- Large-eyed, sharp needle

*See the "Buyer's Guide" on page 176.

## Directions

### Preparing the Wooden Pieces

1 Sand the surface of the embroidery hoop smooth, if necessary, to remove any splinters. Referring to **Diagram 1** and using the marking pen, mark the outer edge of the hoop in quarters, placing two marks opposite each other on the top edge of the hoop, and the other two marks opposite each other on the bottom edge of the hoop. These marks will position one length of the wooden dowel across the top of the hoop and the other length of the

wooden dowel as a crossbar across the bottom of the hoop.

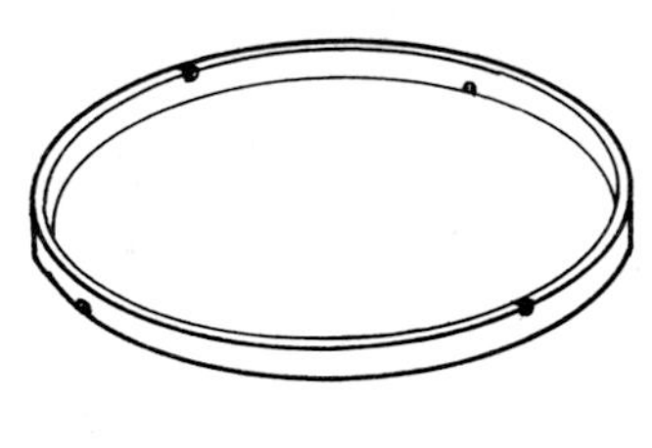

Diagram 1

2 Use the sandpaper to sand a notch into the hoop edge at each mark. Make the notches deep enough to hold the ⅛-inch dowels securely.

3 Glue the dowels into the sanded notches, as shown in **Diagram 2,** centering the dowels across the hoop. Add a dot of glue to the dowels where they cross.

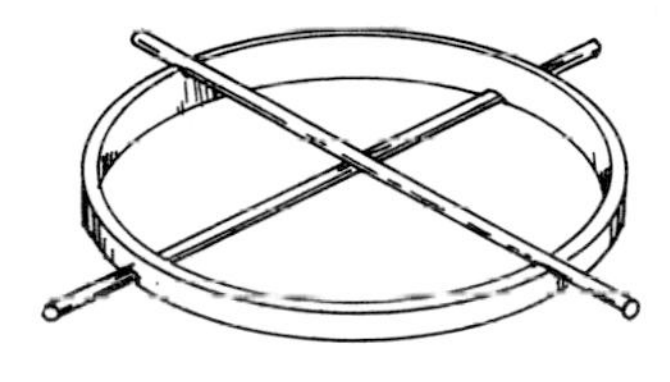

Diagram 2

4 Apply a coat of white paint (or ceiling color) to the hoop and wooden dowels. Let the paint dry thoroughly. Paint a second coat if necessary. Apply a coat of paint sealer to these wooden pieces and let them dry thoroughly.

## Preparing the Fabric

Woven lamé fabrics fray easily and should be stabilized with fusible interfacing to make the fabric easier to work with. Following the manufacturer's directions, use a low steam setting to fuse the lightweight interfacing to the wrong side of the woven lamé pieces before cutting the pattern shapes.

## Making the Planets

1 Trace the planet segment patterns on pages 23 and 24 onto the tracing paper. Trace the planet ring patterns onto paper. Add ¼-inch seam allowances to all the pattern edges before cutting out each pattern piece.

2 Use the patterns to cut four pieces from the same calico fabric for each planet, making one A planet in red, one B planet in purple, one C planet each in blue and brown, and one D planet in blue. With right sides facing, sew the four segments of each planet together, leaving about a 1½-inch opening on one seam for turning, as shown in **Diagram 3.** Clip the seams and turn right side out. Stuff the planet firmly and slip stitch the opening closed.

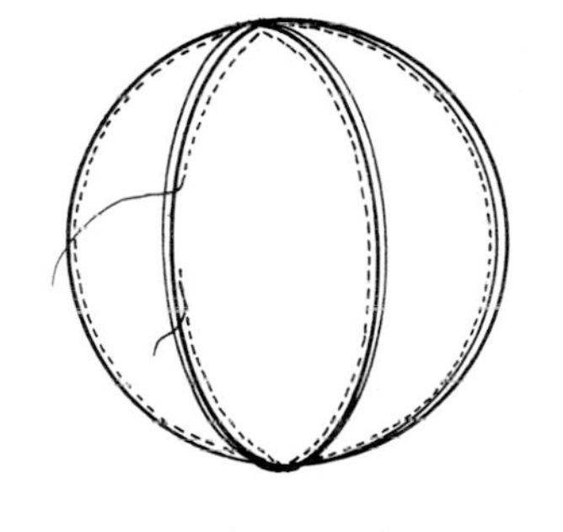

Diagram 3

3 For each of the C and D planet rings, cut two pieces each from the remaining two blue fabrics. Sew a line of stay stitching along the inner edge of each ring piece. With right sides facing, sew the matching ring pieces together along the outer edge. Clip the outer seam edges and turn right side out. Stuff the rings very lightly. Turn under the seam allowance along the inner edge of each ring piece, and sew the inner edges together. Place the rings on the corresponding planet at the desired angle, and tack in place, sewing the tacking stitches on opposite sides of the planet.

## Making the Space Shuttle

1 Trace the space shuttle pattern pieces on page 23 onto paper, adding 3/16-inch seam allowances to all edges. From the silver lamé, cut the space shuttle body, base, and tail.

2 With right sides facing, sew the nose seam of the body. With right sides facing, sew the body and base together, sewing from marked point A around the shuttle wing, nose, and other wing to marked point B, as shown in **Diagram 4.** (The shorter space between A and B remains open for turning.) Clip the curves and turn right side out.

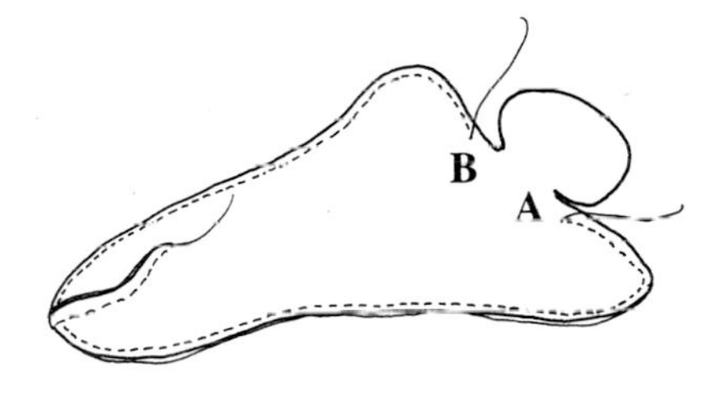


Diagram 4

3 Stuff the wings very lightly. Sew a line of top stitching through both fabric layers and along the inner edge of each wing to the nose, as marked on the **Space Shuttle Body** pattern by the dashed lines. Firmly stuff the remaining body of the shuttle. Fold down the rear flap of the body piece, turn under the seam allowance, and slip stitch the flap in place to close the shuttle body, as shown in **Diagram 5.**

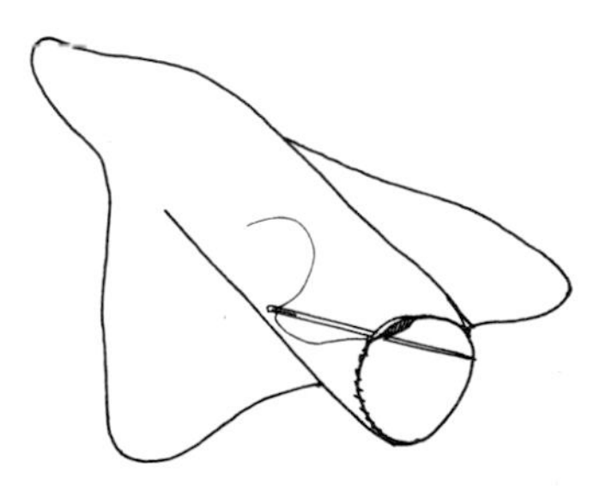

Diagram 5

4 With right sides facing, sew the two tail pieces together, leaving the bottom edge open. Clip the curves and turn right side out. Turn under the remaining seam allowance at the bottom and slip stitch the tail in position on the back of the shuttle, as shown in the photograph on page 20.

5 Use toothpicks to apply black paint "windows" to the front of the shuttle; refer to the photograph for placement.

## Making the Satellite

1 Use the compass to draw a 2⅜-inch circle on the tracing paper for the base cylinder pattern and a 1⅛-inch circle for the upper cylinder pattern.

2 For the satellite base, cut two 2⅜-inch circles and one 1½ × 4¾-inch rectangle from the textured gold lamé. For the upper cylinder, cut one 1⅛-inch circle and one ⅞ × 3-inch rectangle from the copper lamé. Also cut three gold and one copper lamé pieces, each 1¼ × 5 inches, for the solar panels. Each fabric piece includes a 3⁄16-inch seam allowance.

3 With right sides facing, fold each solar panel piece in half crosswise. Sew each long edge of each panel, leaving the short edge opposite the fold open for turning. Turn each panel right side out and turn under the seam allowance at the open edge. Pin in place.

4 To topstitch the grid pattern on each panel, begin by sewing two lines lengthwise on the panel, dividing the piece into thirds. Sew cross lines every ¼ inch along the length of the panel to complete the grid.

5 Cut two 5-inch lengths of wire. Slide a panel onto each end of each wire length, slipping the wire between and through the topstitching all the way to the end of the panel and having the open ends of the panels facing each other at the center of the wire, as shown in **Diagram 6.**

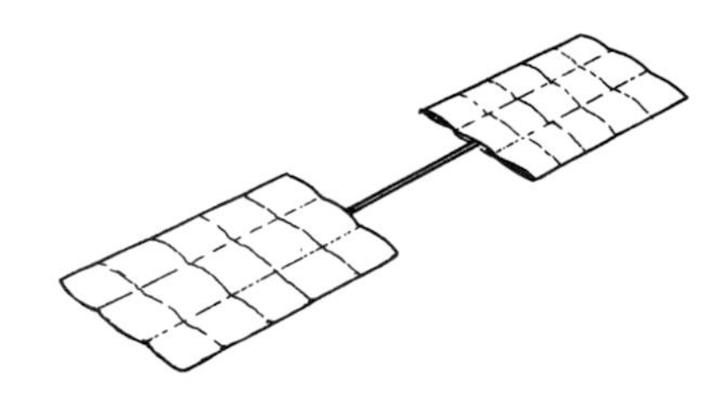

**Diagram 6**

6 Place the panel pairs together, crossing them at the center. Wrap thread around the crossed wires to secure the panels, as shown in **Diagram 7.** Cut a ½-inch square of gold lamé and glue it in place to cover the crossed wires or, if desired, wrap metallic thread around each exposed wire to cover it.

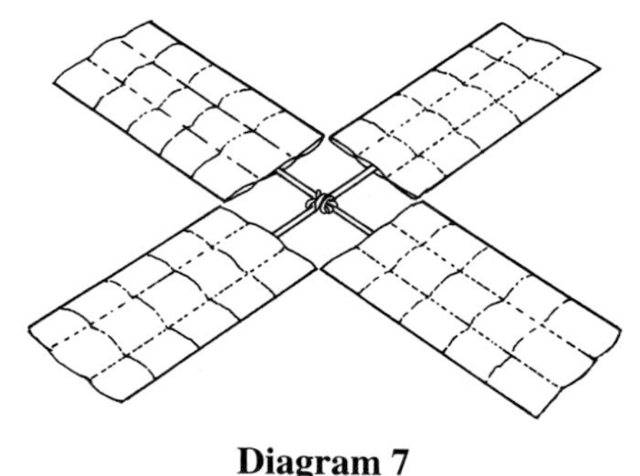

**Diagram 7**

7 With right sides facing, fold the satellite base rectangle in half and sew the narrow ends of the rectangle together to form a tube, leaving a small opening for turning. Sew a 2⅜-inch fabric circle to each end of the tube. Clip the curves and turn the satellite base right side out. Stuff the base and sew the opening closed.

8 Fold in half and sew the narrow ends of the upper cylinder together to form a tube. Hand sew the 1⅛-inch fabric circle to one end of the tube. Clip the curves and turn right side out. Lightly stuff the upper cylinder, turn under the seam allowances at the open edge, and slip stitch the cylinder in the center of one end of the base cylinder, as shown in **Diagram 8.** Center the crossed solar panels on top of the upper cylinder and tack in place, adding a dab of glue to hold them securely.

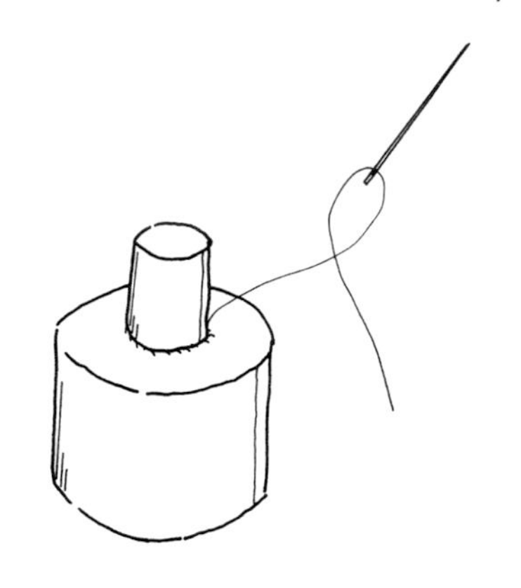

**Diagram 8**

9 To make the stars, begin by kneading the clay until it is malleable. Roll out the clay to about ⅛ inch thick. Draw eight free-hand stars of different sizes on paper. Cut these out and use them for star patterns. Place the patterns on the clay and use a pin or toothpick to mark the inner and outer points of each star. Use a knife or scissors to cut out each star shape from the clay. Poke a hanging hole in the top point of each star. Bake the clay stars, following the manufacturer's directions.

## Assembling the Mobile

1 Cut two 28-inch lengths of monofilament. Tie each monofilament end to opposite ends of a dowel at the hoop edge, adjusting the ties so that the hoop is balanced

when the monofilaments are held in the center, as shown in **Diagram 9.** Use another piece of monofilament to tie a hanging loop at the center of the dowel filaments.

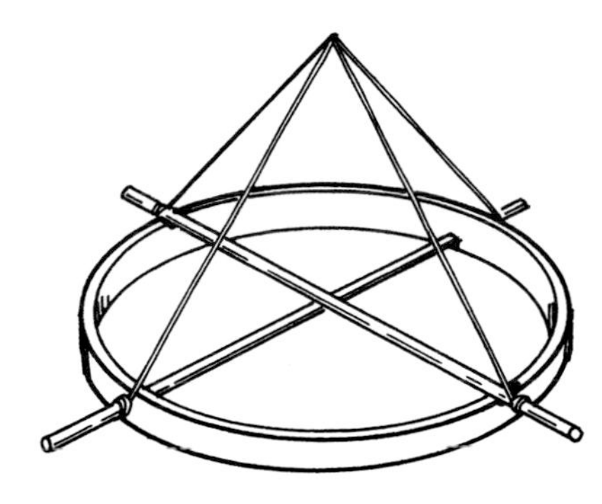

**Diagram 9**

**2** Thread monofilament through a large-eyed needle and sew a generous length of monofilament to the top of each planet, the shuttle, and the satellite. Tie a length of monofilament through the hole in each star. Use a double knot to secure each monofilament, adding a dab of glue to seal each knot.

**3** Tie the fabric shapes to the hoop and dowels, as shown in the photograph on page 20, or as desired. Vary the lengths at which the shapes hang, taking care to keep the mobile balanced. Attach the stars last.

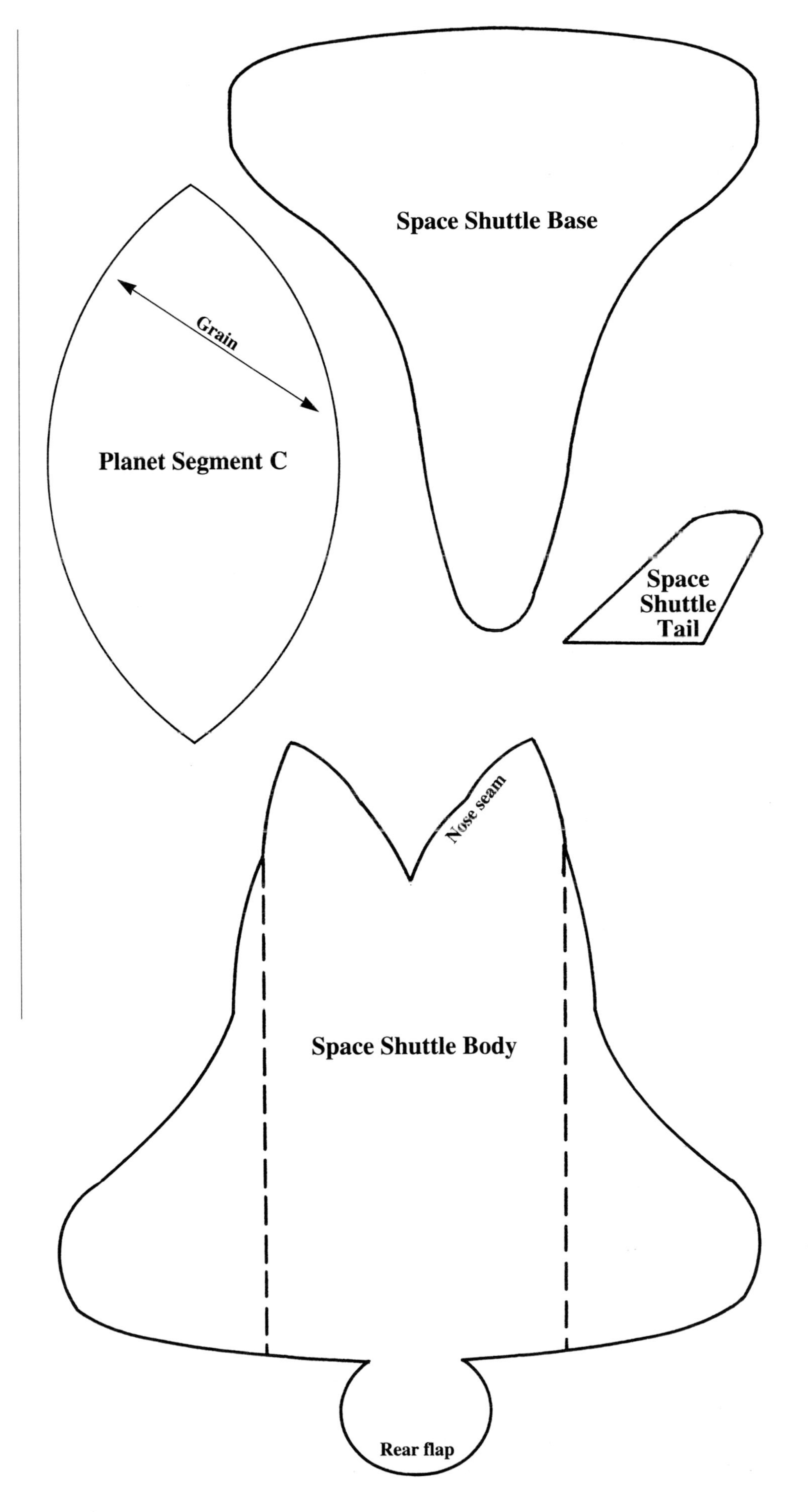

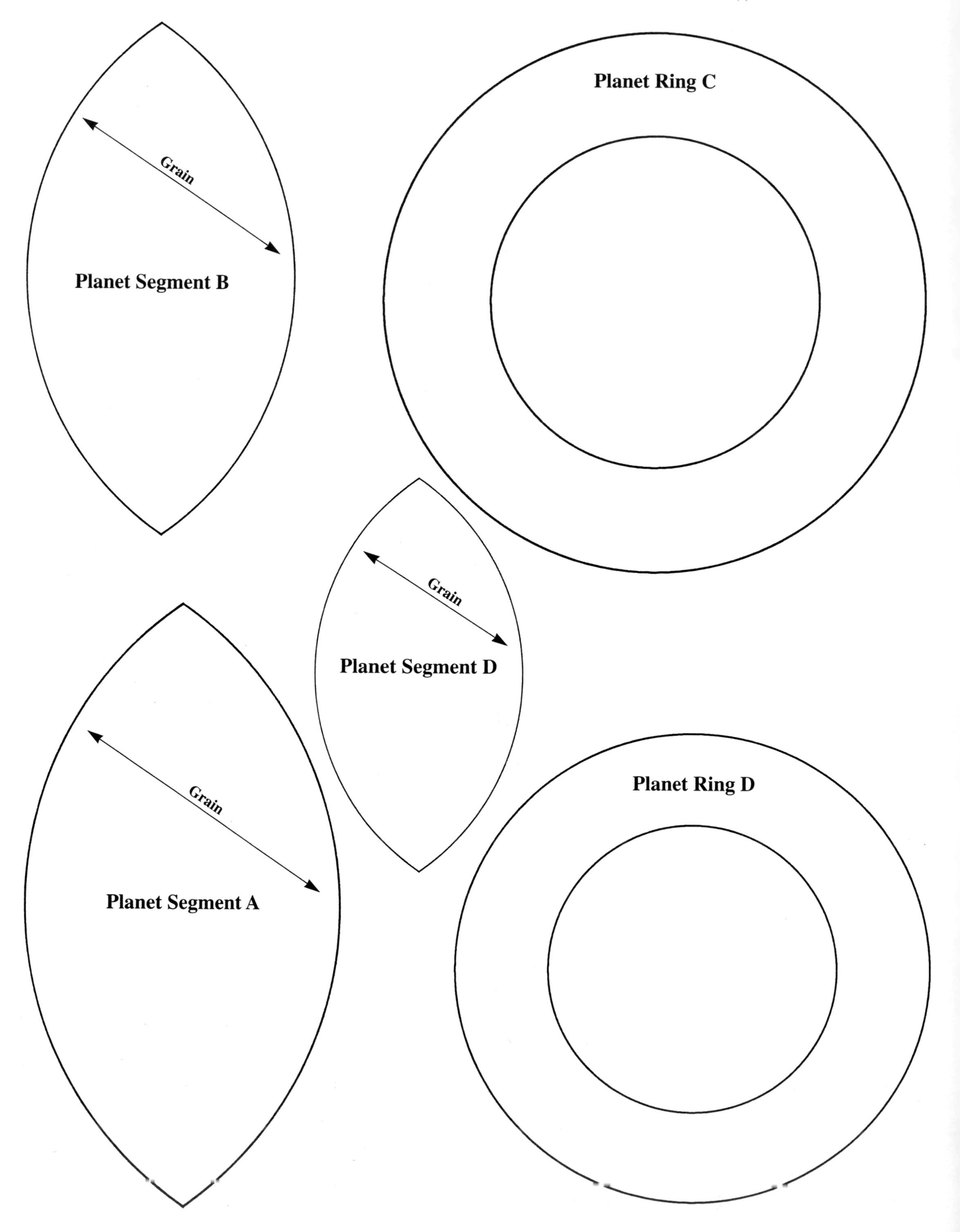
Planet Segment B
Grain
Planet Ring C
Grain
Planet Segment D
Planet Segment A
Grain
Planet Ring D

# LITTLE RED RIDING HOOD TOPSY-TURVY DOLL

*Telling this favorite old tale will be brand-new fun for a child, when you illustrate it with all three of the story's characters. Little Red Riding Hood highlights this whimsical topsy-turvy design. A quick flip of the calico skirt will reveal either Granny or the Big Bad Wolf, depending on the placement of the nightcap.*

**Size:** About 14 inches tall

## Materials

- ❄ Pencil
- ❄ Tracing paper
- ❄ Pinking shears and scissors
- ❄ ¼ yard of peach fabric
- ❄ 12-inch square of gray solid fabric to match the felt
- ❄ ½ yard each of red print, blue check, and blue print fabrics
- ❄ 9 × 12-inch pieces of felt: 2 red, 1 gray, and small scrap of white
- ❄ Water-soluble marking pen
- ❄ Straight pins
- ❄ Matching sewing thread
- ❄ Sewing machine
- ❄ Iron
- ❄ Large-eyed needle, hand-sewing needle, and embroidery needle
- ❄ Polyester fiberfill
- ❄ ⅜-inch pink pom-pom
- ❄ Six-strand embroidery floss: red, dark blue, brown, and black
- ❄ Pink crayon or cosmetic blush
- ❄ 2 yards of 1-inch-wide white ruffled eyelet
- ❄ Worsted-weight yarns: 1 skein of black, and short lengths of red to tie braids together
- ❄ 13-inch-long piece of cardboard
- ❄ Safety pin for threading elastic through casing
- ❄ 24-inch length of ⅜-inch-wide elastic
- ❄ 1 yard of narrow yellow rickrack
- ❄ 24-inch length of ⅛-inch-wide red ribbon
- ❄ 1 yard of narrow white bias binding
- ❄ Small straw basket
- ❄ 6-inch square of red calico
- ❄ Miniature fruits and vegetables

## Directions

**1** Trace the pattern pieces on pages 28 through 30, including markings, onto the tracing paper. Each pattern includes a ¼-inch seam allowance, except where noted. Cut out the pattern pieces.

**2** From the peach fabric, cut three heads and six hands. From the gray fabric, cut one head and two hands. From the red print and blue check, cut two bodies each. From the gray felt, cut one nose and two ears. Transfer pattern markings to the fabrics with the marking pen.

**3** With right sides facing, pin and sew a peach head to the neck of each red body piece, and sew a peach hand at each wrist. Sew a peach head and hands to one blue-check body piece in the same way. Sew the gray head and gray hands to the second blue-check body piece. Press all the seams open. Baste the ears to the gray head between the ear placement marks, folding each ear at the front edge, as shown in **Diagram 1.**

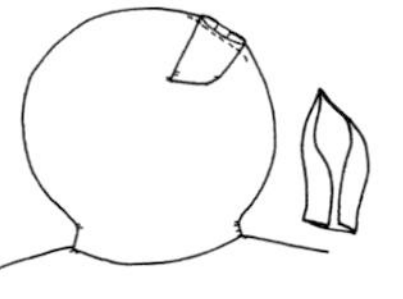

**Diagram 1**

**4** With the right sides facing, sew the red body pieces together, leaving the waist edge open. Sew the blue-check body pieces together in the same way. Clip the seams at the neck and underarm corners. Turn one of the bodies right side out. Tuck this body inside the other so that the right sides of the fabrics are facing and the seams match. Sew the waist edges together, as shown in **Diagram 2,** leaving an opening for turning. Turn right side out. Firmly stuff both bodies with the polyester fiberfill, and slip stitch the opening closed.

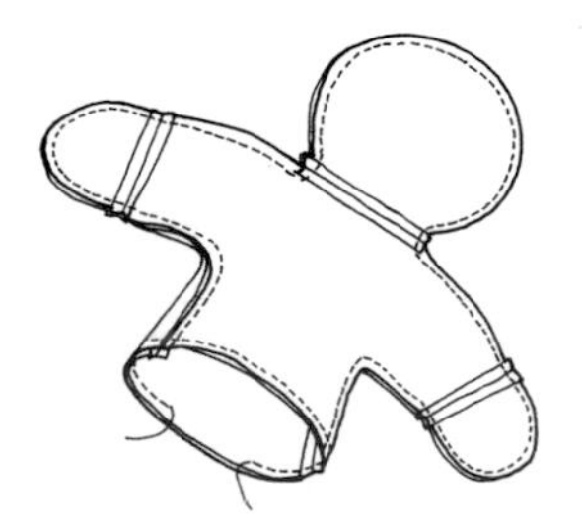

**Diagram 2**

**5** Fold the nose in half along the straight edge. Using a ¼-inch seam allowance, sew along the straight edge. Turn right side out and stuff with fiberfill. Use matching thread to sew the nose in place on the gray head, then sew the pink pom-pom to the tip of the nose.

**6** Cut a ⅜ × 2¾-inch piece of white felt, pinking one long edge of the strip for the wolf's teeth. Referring to **Diagram 3,** sew the strip to the base of the nose in a U shape. Cut a red felt tongue and tack it to the nose at the curved end of the teeth.

**Diagram 3**

**7** Use a pencil to lightly mark two ⅛-inch-diameter circles on the gray head for the wolf's eyes (see the photograph on page 25 for placement). Use three strands of the black embroidery floss to satin stitch the eyes.

**8** On the opposite side of the wolf's head, lightly mark the outlines for granny's mouth, nose, ¼-inch-diameter eyes, and eyeglasses, as shown in the photograph on page 25. Using three strands of brown embroidery floss, satin stitch the eyes. Using three strands of floss, backstitch the nose with brown, the mouth with red, and the eyeglasses with blue. Use the pink crayon or cosmetic blush to color the cheeks.

**9** Hand sew a length of eyelet along the seam edge of the gray/peach head. Then hand sew a second piece of eyelet around the entire neck.

**10** On one side of the remaining unadorned head, use a pencil to lightly mark the outlines for Red Riding Hood's mouth and ⅜-inch-diameter eyes. Using three strands of floss, satin stitch the eyes with blue and the mouth with red. Color the cheeks the same way as for granny.

**11** To make Red Riding Hood's hair, wrap the black yarn 80 times around a 13-inch piece of cardboard. Cut the yarn loops at one end of the cardboard. Open the yarn strands and lay them flat, removing the cardboard and keeping the yarn strands together. Place the strands on a piece of tracing paper, arranging them into a 4-inch-wide hank. Use a medium-length straight stitch to machine sew through the center of the yarn hank for a hair part. Sew twice along the hair part to secure the yarn strands, then peel the paper away from the yarn. Pin the hair part along the center of the head with the front of the part about 1¼ inches down from the head seam. Pin the remainder of the part along the back of the head. Hand sew the hair to the head along the part using a backstitch.

**12** Thread the large-eyed needle with a length of black yarn. Sew through the side of the head and tie the yarn ends around the hair strands to begin the braid. Braid the yarn hair below the tied yarn. Wrap a length of red yarn around the end of the braid and tie it into a bow. Trim the yarn ends even. Repeat for the braid on the other side of the head. Hand sew a length of eyelet around the neck.

**13** Cut a 12 × 24-inch piece each from the red print and blue print for the skirt. With right sides facing, sew the narrow edges of each piece together to make a tube. Press under ¼ inch along one long edge of each fabric tube. With the right sides facing and matching the seams, sew the red and blue tubes together along the other long edge. Turn right side out and press. Topstitch a length of eyelet along the red edge of the skirt hem, overlapping the eyelet ends.

**14** Pin the folded top edges of the skirt together to make the waist, and sew ½ inch from the waist edge. Sew again close to the folded edge, leaving an opening for inserting the elastic, as shown in **Diagram 4.** Use the safety pin to thread the elastic through the waist casing. Pull the elastic to fit around the doll's waist and gather the skirt. Sew the elastic ends together and trim off any excess. Stitch the casing opening closed. Place the skirt on the doll, matching the prints to the body prints.

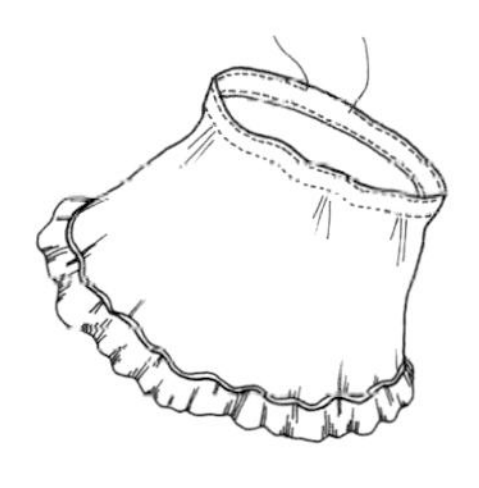

**Diagram 4**

**15** From the red felt, cut two jacket fronts, one back on the fold, and one hood on the fold. Sew the fronts and back together along the shoulder seams. On the right side of each sleeve, sew a length of rickrack ¼ inch from the sleeve edge. With right sides facing, sew the underarm and side seams together. Clip the seams at the underarm corners. Sew rickrack along the front and lower edges of the jacket.

**16** Sew the top seam of the hood. Pin the tucks in the hood where marked on the pattern, and sew the hood to the neck seam of the jacket. Cut the red ribbon in half and sew a piece to each jacket front where the hood joins the neck. Place the jacket on Red Riding Hood's body, tying the ribbons in a bow at the neck. To put the hood up, fold the braids to the back of the head before pulling the hood in place.

**17** From the blue print, cut two bonnets. With the fabric wrong sides facing, topstitch or zigzag around the markings for the two ear slits; make slits on only one side of the bonnet piece. Using scissors, cut the ear slits open. Sew the bonnet pieces together 1½ inches from the outer edge for the first elastic casing stitching line. Sew a second line of stitching ½ inch from the first, leaving a small opening for inserting the elastic, as shown in **Diagram 5.** Use the safety pin to thread an 11-inch length of elastic through the bonnet casing. Overlap and sew the elastic ends together. Complete the second line of stitching to sew the casing opening closed. Use the white bias binding to bind the outer edge of the bonnet, overlapping the binding ends. Place the bonnet on the granny/wolf head, slipping the ears through the bonnet slits.

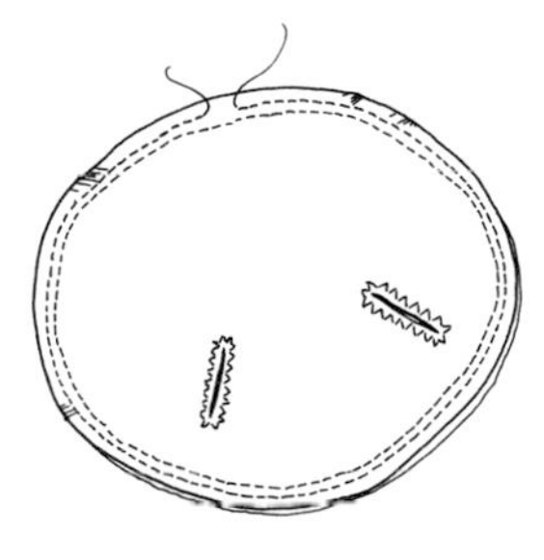

**Diagram 5**

**18** Pink the edges of the calico square and arrange in the basket. Fill the basket with fruit and vegetables. Slip it over Red Riding Hood's arm.

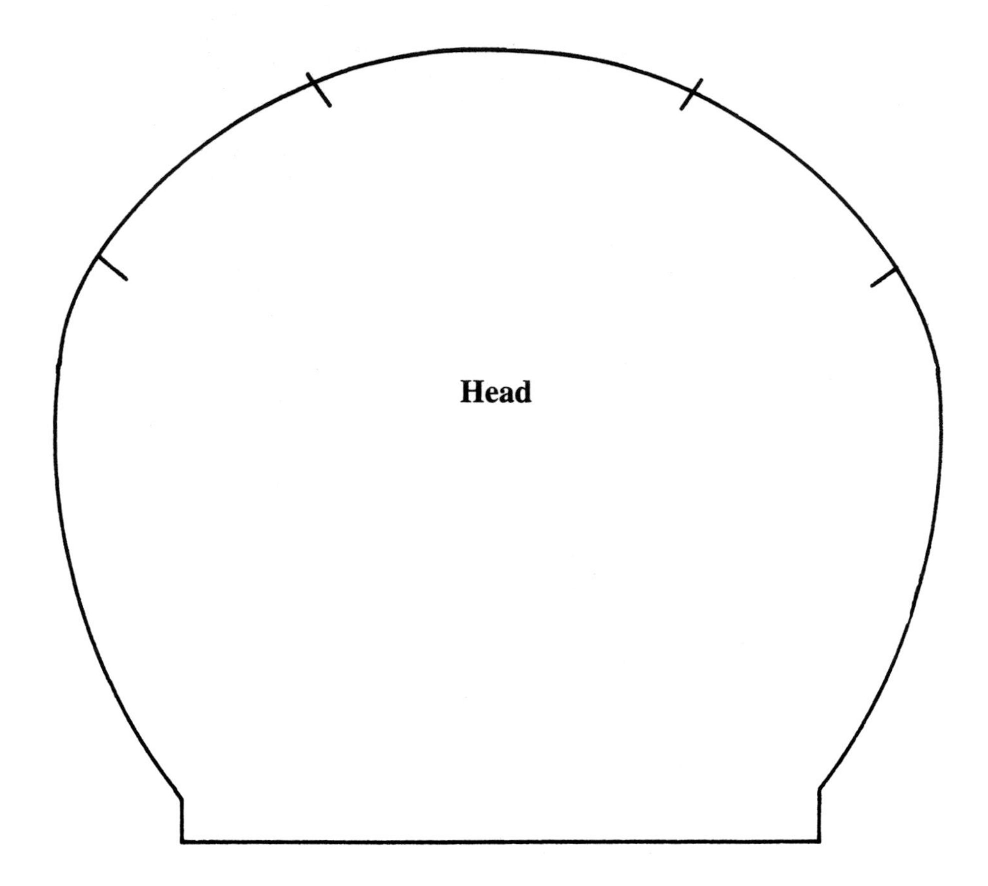
Head

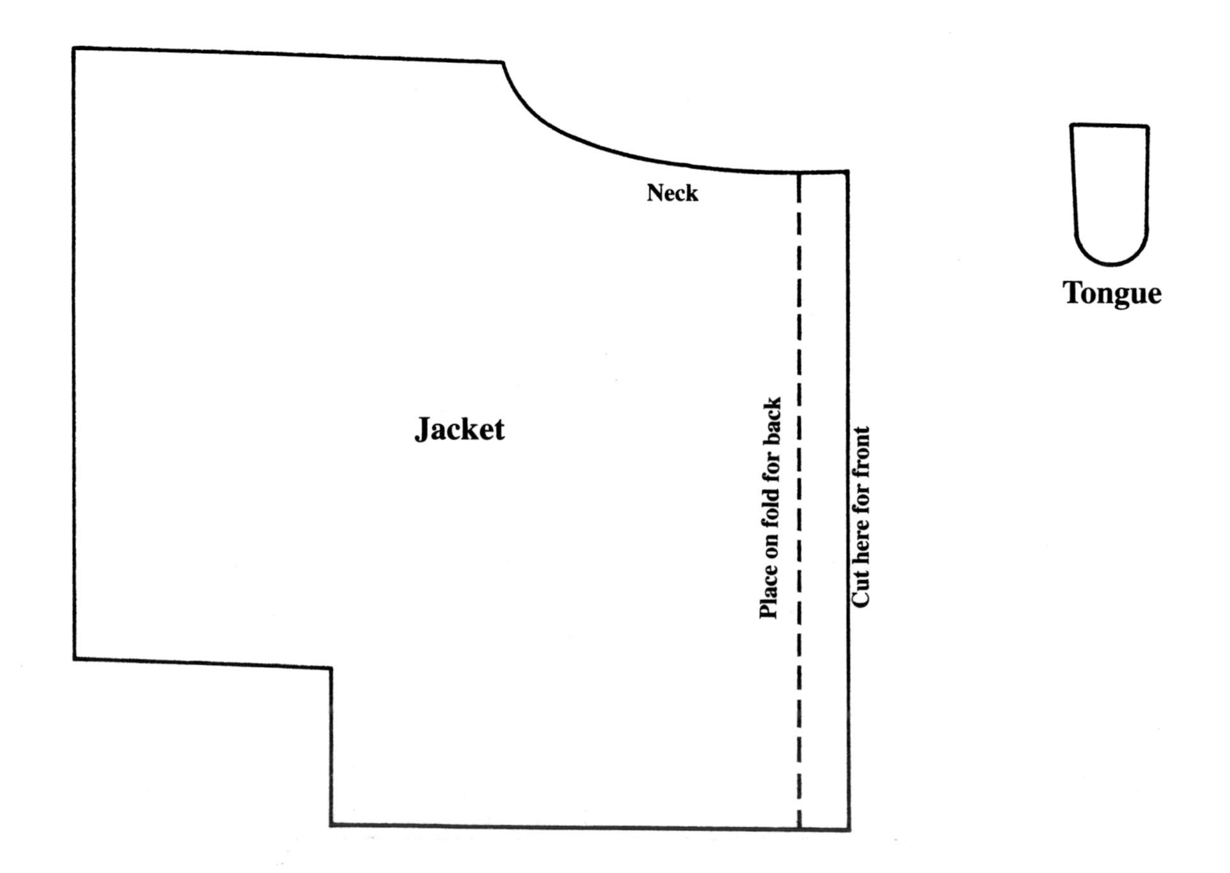
Neck
Jacket
Place on fold for back
Cut here for front
Tongue

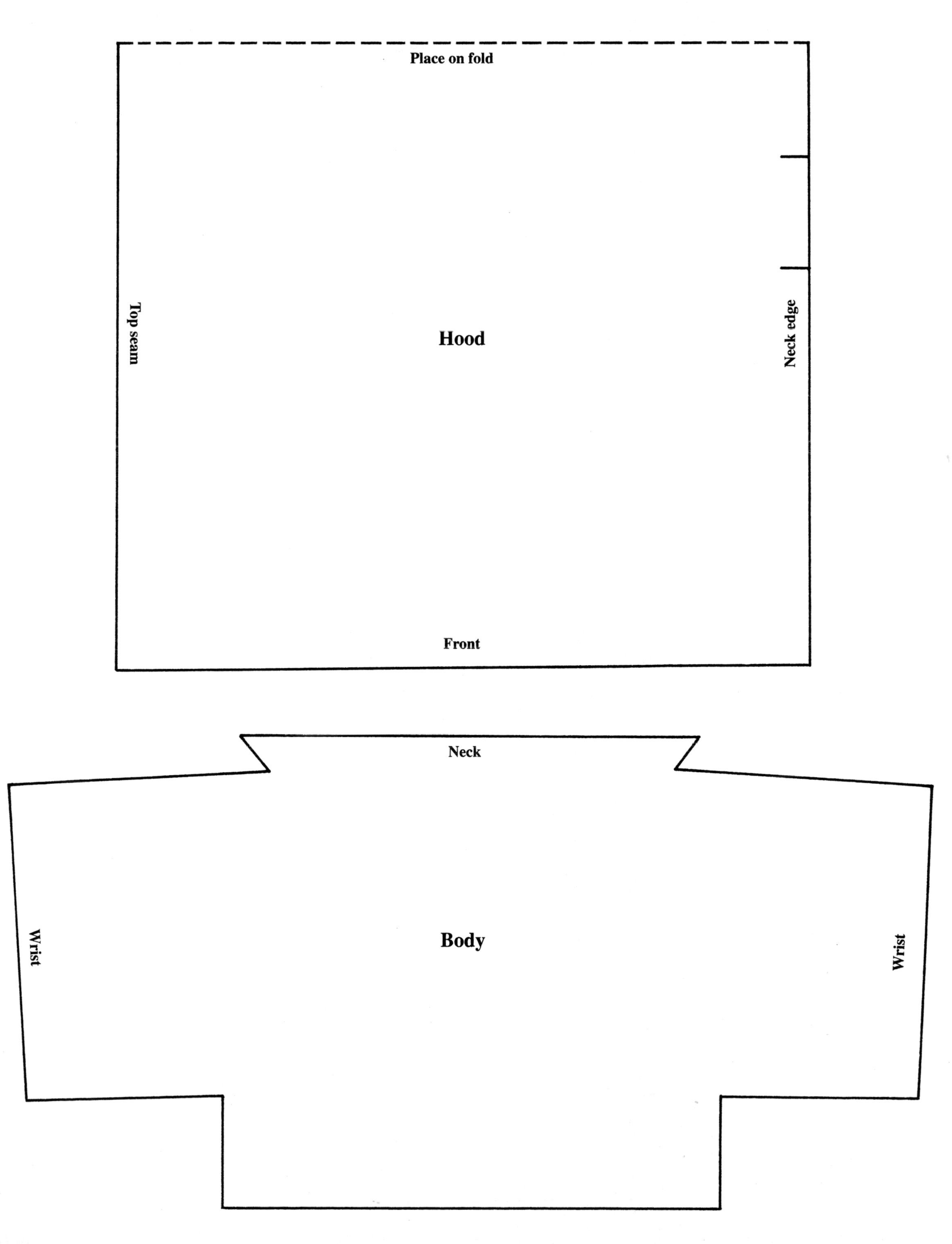
Place on fold
Top seam
Hood
Neck edge
Front
Neck
Wrist
Body
Wrist

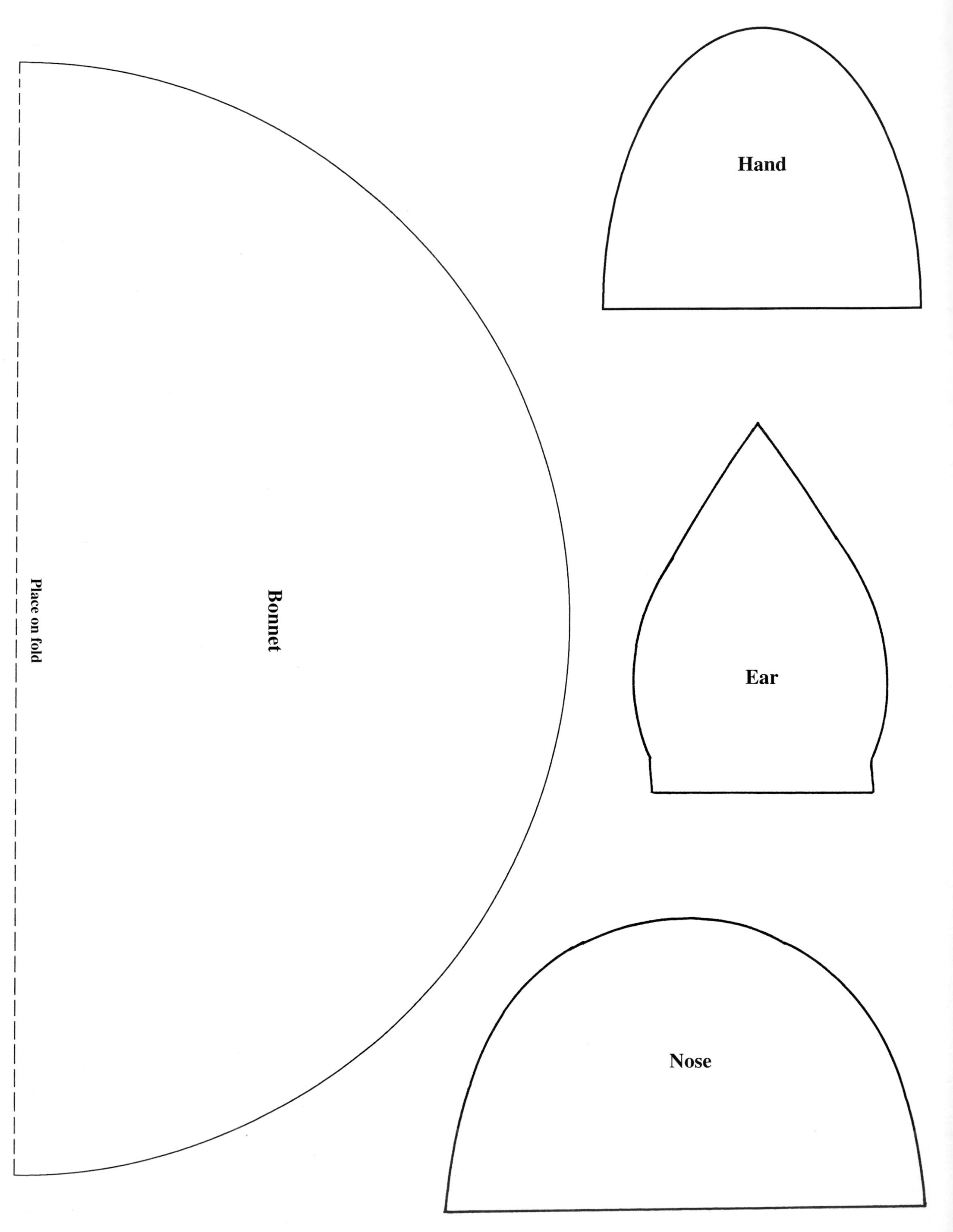
Hand
Place on fold
Bonnet
Ear
Nose

# FOLDING PLAY MAT

*You could call it Christmas Town or Our Town, but either way some lucky young city planner is going to have hours of fun "driving" through this village. And what town would be complete without a three-dimensional parking garage for small cars and trucks? The whole town folds flat for quick cleanup or easy travel. It's sure to be a hit whether you follow our directions for lettering the buildings or label them to match those on the child's hometown Main Street.*

**Size:** 28 × 34 inches when flat

## MATERIALS

- 8 × 14½-inch piece of turquoise cotton fabric
- Sewing machine
- Matching sewing thread
- Water-soluble marking pen
- Thin cardboard
- Iron
- Scissors
- 1¼ yards of unbleached canvas, 60 inches wide
- Masking tape
- Pencil
- Ruler
- Flat artist's brush
- Fabric paints in assorted colors
- Black and gray fine-point fabric markers

## DIRECTIONS

### MAKING THE GARAGE

**1** Fold under ¼ inch along the long edges of the 8 × 14½-inch turquoise piece. Topstitch close to the folded edges.

**2** On the right side of the fabric, use the marking pen to mark the placement of two center stitching lines along the lengthwise center of the piece, ½ inch apart, as shown in **Diagram 1.** These will be the lines for stitching the garage to the mat.

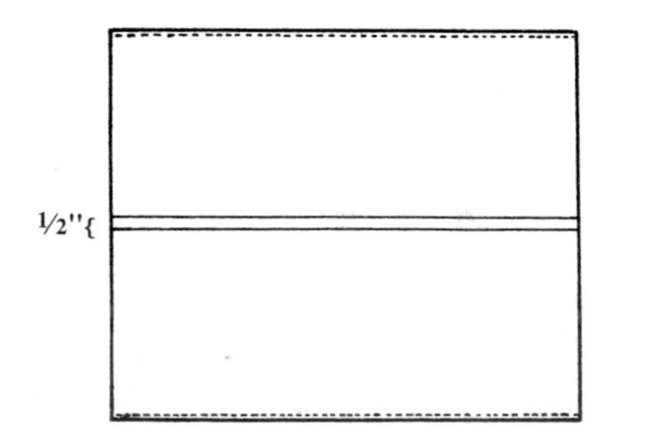


**Diagram 1**

**3** Referring to **Diagram 2,** mark the wrong side of the fabric with lines to divide the piece into segments.

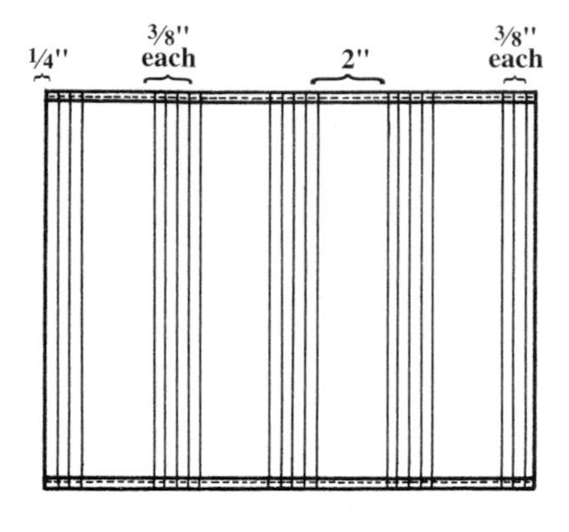


**Diagram 2**

**4** Using the thin cardboard as a straight edge, press sharp creases in the fabric along these lines, as shown in **Diagram 3.** The 2-inch segments form the garage roofs and the ⅜-inch segments form the accordion-style pleats for the garage sides. Baste the pleats in place inside the two marked center stitching lines. Press under ¼ inch on the two short edges of the garage.

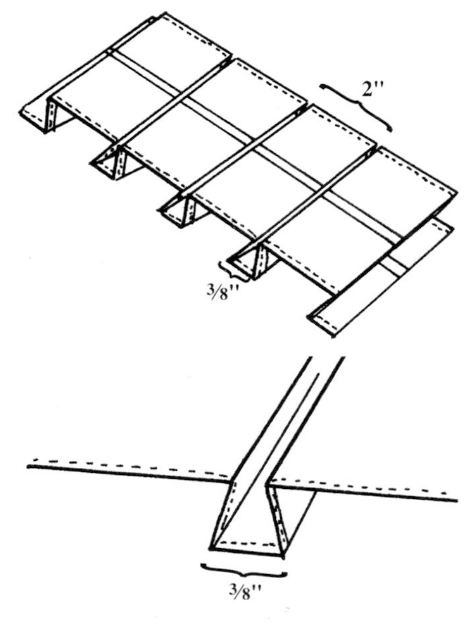


**Diagram 3**

**5** Cut a 30 × 36-inch piece of canvas. Fold it in half length wise to mark the center.

**6** Referring to **Diagram 4,** place the center of the garage on the center of the canvas 1 inch from the left edge.

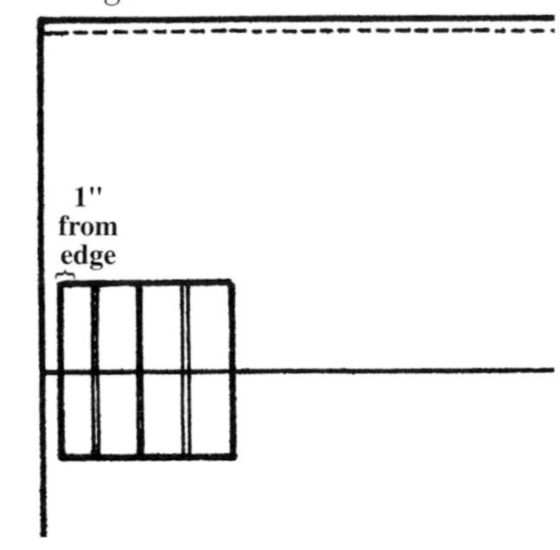


**Diagram 4**

**7** Topstitch the side edges of the garage in place, leaving the roof edges of the end garages free, as shown in **Diagram 5.** Topstitch along each of the parking space stitching lines, then along each of the center stitching lines. Remove basting stitches.

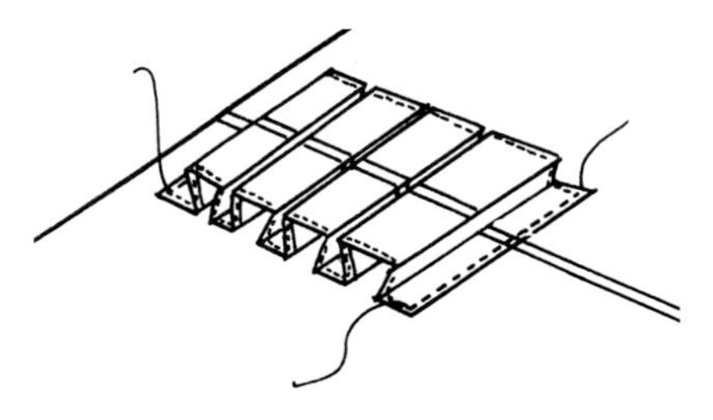

**Diagram 5**

### MAKING THE MAT

**1** Use the masking tape to mark the roadway edges on the canvas with the garage, beginning 1 inch in on all sides and referring to the **Road Diagram** on page 34 for measurements. Press the tape securely to the fabric.

**2** Referring to the **Building Diagram** on page 35, mark the buildings, doors, windows, and signs on the streets, using a pencil and a ruler for straight lines.

3 Paint the grass and buildings in colors as shown in the photograph on page 31, or as desired. Let each paint color dry thoroughly before proceeding to the next color. Next, paint the building details such as windows and doors. Use the markers for outlines and other fine-lined details, such as the signs and the center lines in the roads.

## FINISHING THE PLAY MAT

1 Trim the painted mat to 29 × 35 inches. Use this piece as a pattern to cut another piece of canvas for the back of the mat. With right sides facing, use a ½-inch seam allowance to sew these pieces together, leaving an 8-inch opening for turning. Trim the corners and turn the mat right side out. Turn in the seam allowances at the opening, then topstitch around the entire outer edge of the mat.

2 Cut two 4 × 22-inch pieces of canvas for the mat handles. Fold the long edges of each handle piece to the center and press the folded edges, as shown in **Diagram 6,** fold each piece in half lengthwise, then topstitch each long edge on each handle.

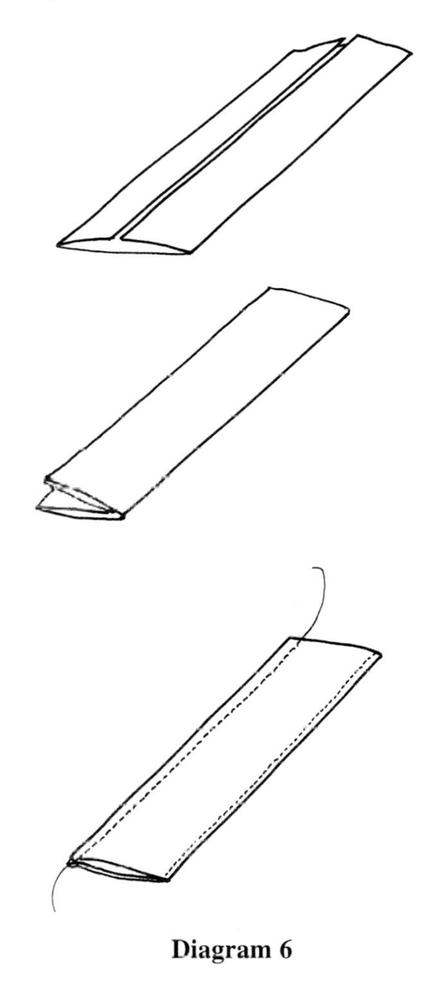

**Diagram 6**

3 Fold under ⅝ inch at each end of each handle and press. Place the handle on the long edge of the unpainted side of the mat with the ends 3 inches apart and 5 inches in from the edge, as shown in **Diagram 7.** Sew these ends in place with a ⅝-inch square of stitching, as shown in the diagram.

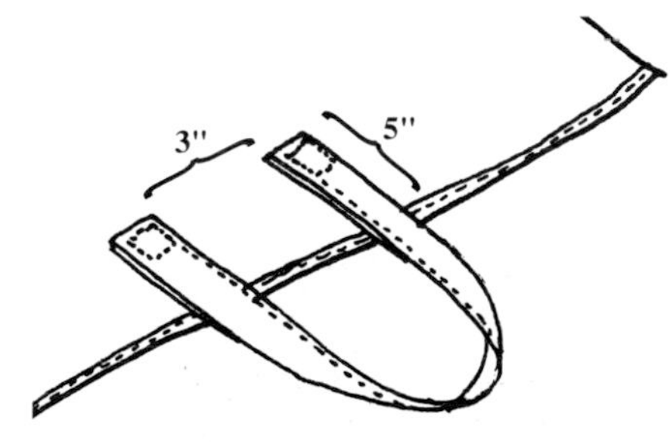


**Diagram 7**

4 Fold the mat in thirds along the length, folding the garage in first. Fold the mat in half crosswise, bringing the handles together, as shown in **Diagram 8.**

**Diagram 8**

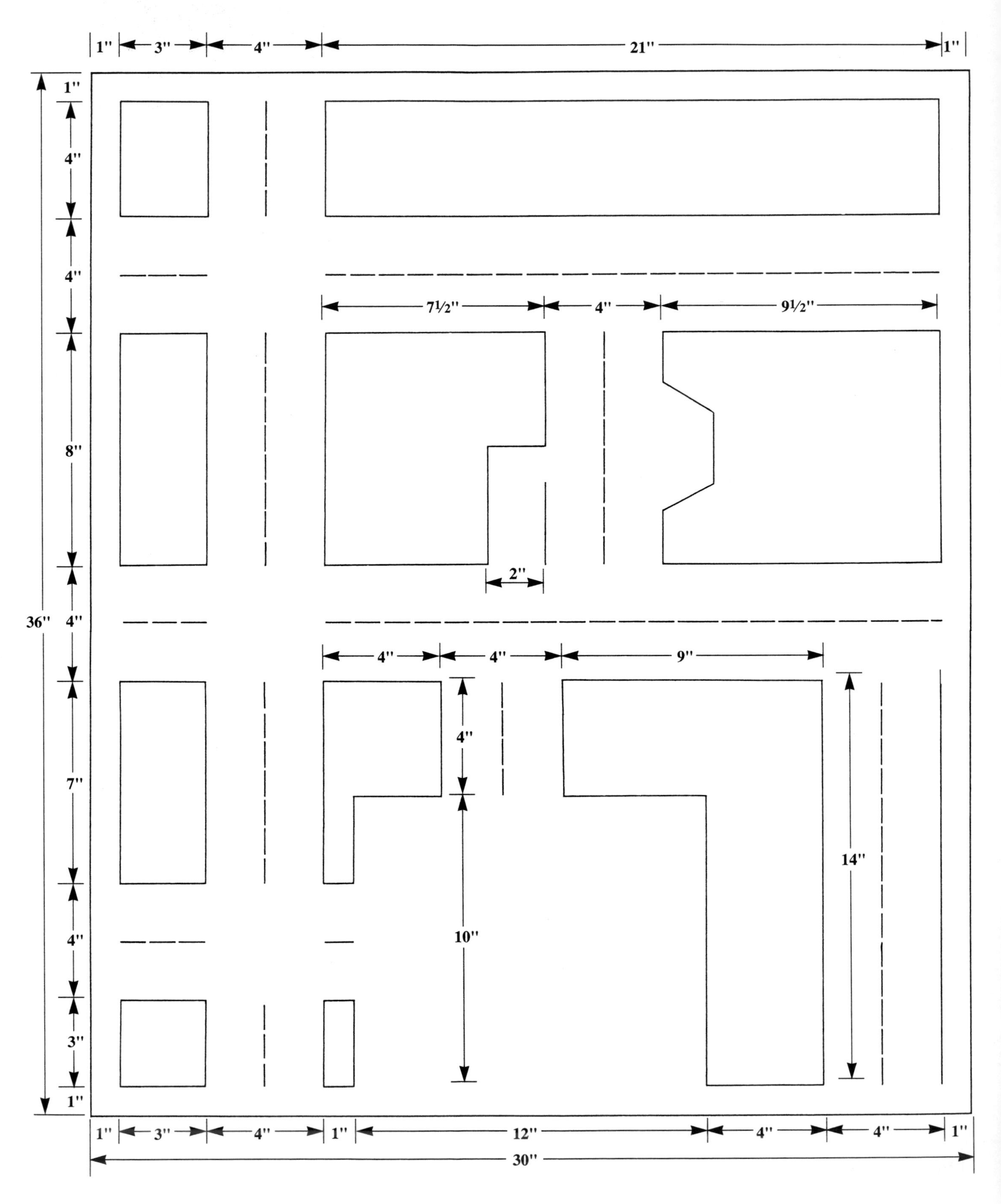


Road Diagram

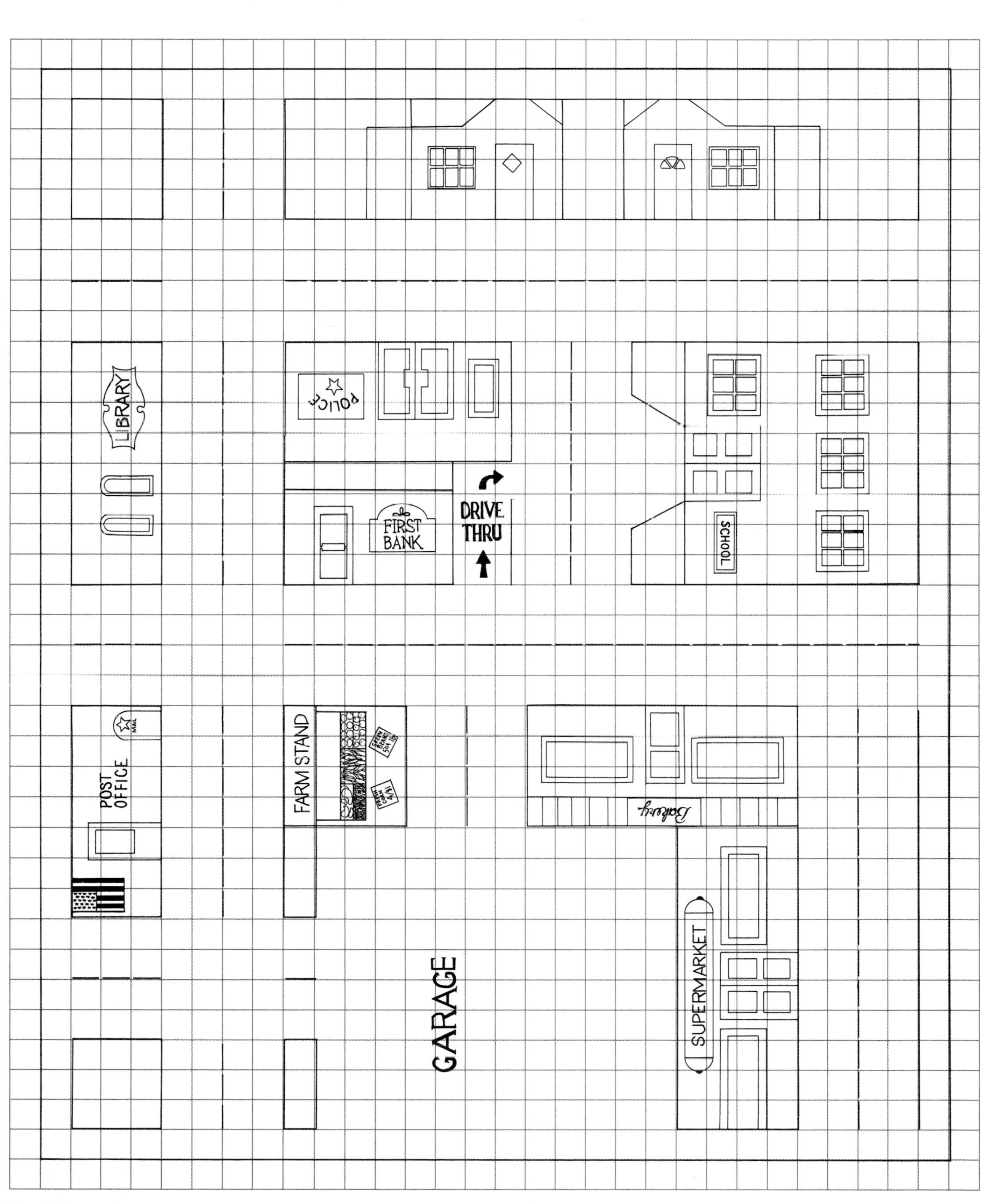


**1 square = 1 inch**

**Enlarge 448%**

**Building Diagram**

# POSY POWER SWEATER

*Stitch a blast from the past! It's "flower power" for today's teens. Just toss a bouquet of flowers onto a sweater and duplicate stitch the designs in the colors of your choice. Combine solidly stitched flowers with outlined ones. Or save time—and stitching—by working only outlined blossoms. If you want to create a sweater for a toddler, embroider only the smaller motif and scatter it around the garment.*

**Size:** As desired

## Materials

- Heavyweight cotton pullover in any solid color, with a gauge of about 5 stitches and 7 rows to 1 inch
- Six-strand embroidery floss in desired colors: 1 skein for a large flower center, 3 skeins for a large solid flower, 1 skein for a large flower outline or for a small solid or outlined flower
- Size 22 tapestry needle

## Directions

1 Working with six strands of floss in the needle, and following the chart for small or large flowers, duplicate stitch flowers randomly on the sweater.

2 Begin each flower with a solid center, then stitch the petal outlines. Leave some of these petals as outlines, but fill in others as desired; refer to the photograph on the opposite page for stitching ideas.

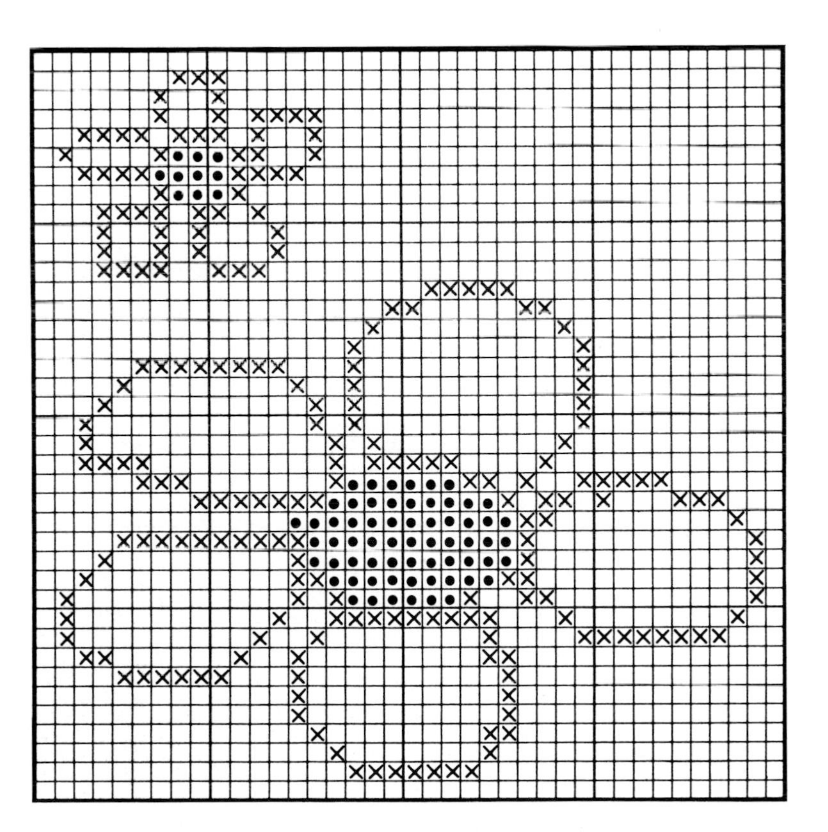

**Posy Power Sweater Chart**

## Duplicate Stitch

**Duplicate stitch is an embroidery stitch used to "duplicate" the look of plain knit stitches. Quick to learn and easy to do, duplicate stitch simply retraces the path of the original knit stitch. Keep your stitches even and take care not to pull them too tightly.**

### Here's How:

**Thread a blunt needle with embroidery floss. Bring the needle up from the wrong side to the right side of your garment in the space below the stitch you wish to duplicate. Thread it from front-to-back-to-front around the top of the stitch, then back down through the original stitch space to the wrong side. Adjust the floss to cover the base stitch. Stitches can be worked in either horizontal or vertical rows. If the design calls for you to skip over more than three stitches, end your floss length and begin again so you won't carry the floss across the wrong side of the garment.**

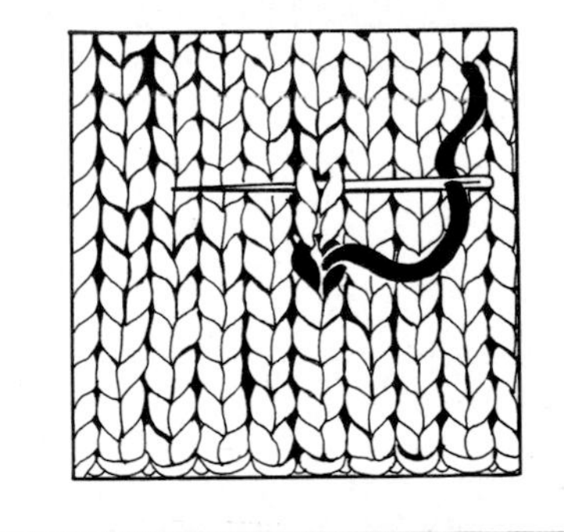

# PANSIES AND ROSEBUDS RIBBON JEWELRY

*Ladies will be delighted to receive these charming posies. Create flower-covered clips to nip in the waistlines of jackets and vests. Add a matching pair of earrings to complete the picture. Wired French ribbons make the crafting of these lovely accessories a simple matter. Choose from any number of natural floral colors.*

**Sizes:** 2¼ × 6½-inch jacket clips;
1 × 2½-inch earrings

## Basic Flower Shapes

### Materials

For all floral pieces:
- Wire-edged ribbon
- Ruler and scissors
- Air-soluble marking pen
- Low-temperature glue gun and glue sticks
- Matching sewing thread and hand-sewing needle

### Directions

**1** *To make the rosebud:* Use one color of wire ribbon. Cut a length proportionate to the size of the flower you want to make and fold the ribbon in half lengthwise. Wrap one end of the ribbon around your forefinger to create a cone, as shown in **Diagram 1.**

**Diagram 1**

Twist the ribbon a half twist, and continue to loosely wrap the end around your finger, as shown in **Diagram 2.** Wrap the entire length of ribbon around the finger, twisting the ribbon once or twice each wrap. Slip the rosebud from your finger and tuck the end of the ribbon into the bottom of the center cone to finish the bud. Slip stitch the ribbon end in place.

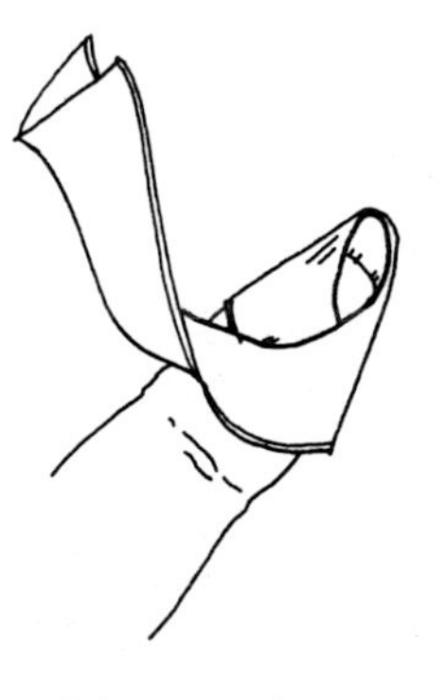

**Diagram 2**

**2** *To make the pansy:* Use two different colors of wire ribbon, one darker than the other. Cut a 6-inch length of the darker color ribbon and a 7½-inch length of the lighter color ribbon. Mark the center of the 6-inch ribbon; mark the 7½-inch ribbon every 2½ inches. Use matching sewing thread to hand sew semicircular lines of gathering stitches along the length of the ribbon between the marks, as shown in **Diagram 3.**

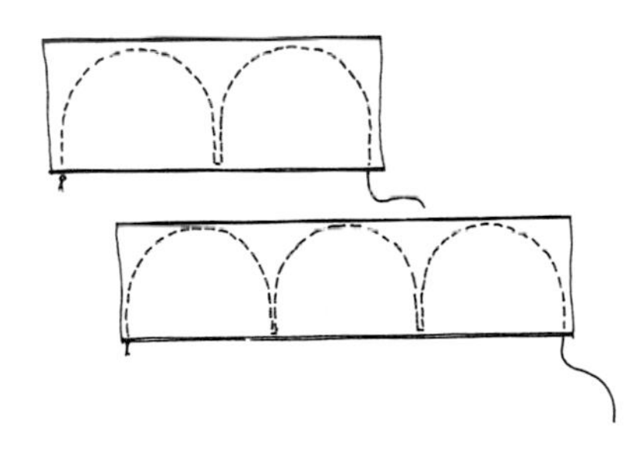

**Diagram 3**

Gently pull the thread to gather the ribbon into petal shapes. The gathers will be at the bottom of the petals, as shown in **Diagram 4.**

**Diagram 4**

Sew the two-petal piece to the bottom of the three-petal piece to form the pansy, as shown in **Diagram 5.** Glue a bead, if needed, in the center of the three-petal piece to create a flower center.

**Diagram 5**

**3** *To make the folded leaf:* Cut a 3-inch length of green ribbon. Using the marking pen, mark the middle of the piece. Fold each end of the piece over to meet the center mark of the ribbon, as shown in **Diagram 6.**

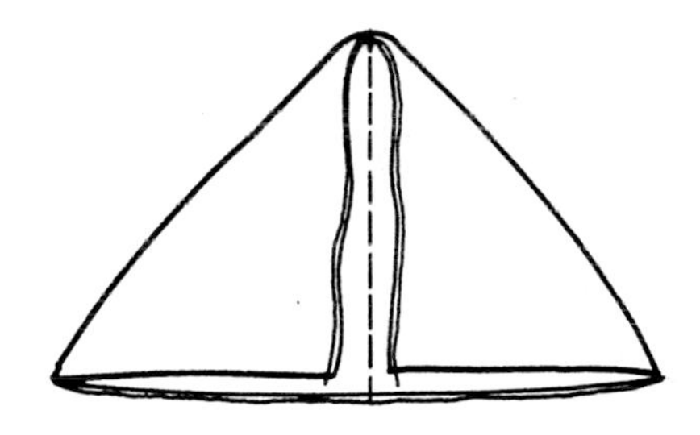

**Diagram 6**

Make a small pleat on each side of the folded leaf, as shown in **Diagram 7,** and tack it in place at the bottom with two or three stitches. Attach the leaf to a flower or other leaves.

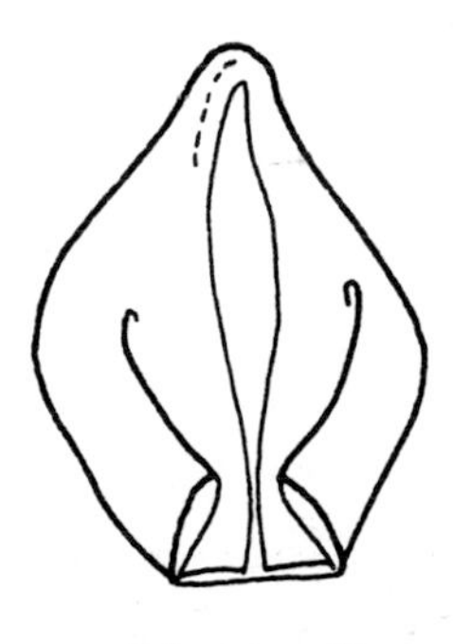

**Diagram 7**

## Pansies Jacket Clip

### Materials

- ❄ 1½-inch-wide wire-edged taffeta ribbons, such as from Offray ribbon: 18-inch length of green, 10-inch length of pink, 7½-inch length of yellow, and 6-inch length of purple*
- ❄ 6 × 8mm oval yellow bead
- ❄ 8-inch length of ⅞-inch-wide green wire-edged taffeta ribbon
- ❄ 10-inch length of 1½-inch-wide dark green grosgrain ribbon
- ❄ Pair of suspender clips

*See the "Buyer's Guide" on page 176.*

### Directions

1 Referring to the "Basic Flower Shape" directions on page 39, use the purple and yellow ribbons to make a pansy. Glue the bead in the center of the flower. Use 5-inch lengths of pink ribbon to make two rosebuds. Use 3-inch lengths of the 1½-inch-wide green taffeta ribbon to make six folded leaves, and 2-inch lengths of the ⅞-inch-wide green ribbon to make four smaller folded leaves.

2 Thread each end of the 10-inch lengths of grosgrain ribbon through a suspender clip. Overlap the ribbon ends in the center of the loop that is formed. Fold under ¼ inch on the overlapped ribbon and slip stitch the ends in place, as shown in the **Clip Diagram.**

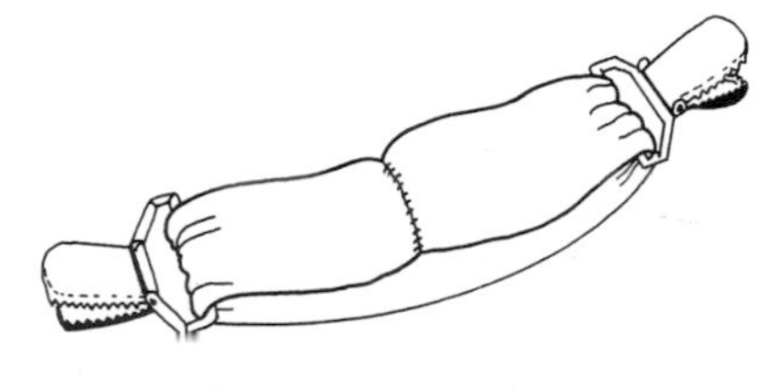

**Clip Diagram**

3 Use the glue gun to glue the flowers and leaves to the ribbon loop. Refer to the photograph on page 38 for placement. Begin with the end leaves and work toward the center. Glue the pansy on last.

## Rosebud Jacket Clip

### Materials

- ❄ 1½-inch-wide wire-edged taffeta ribbons, such as from Offray ribbon: 18-inch length of orange, 16-inch length of pink*
- ❄ 22-inch length of ⅞-inch-wide green wire-edged taffeta ribbon
- ❄ 10-inch length of 1½-inch-wide dark green grosgrain ribbon
- ❄ Pair of suspender clips
- ❄ 16-inch length of ⅜-inch-wide gold chiffon wire-edged ribbon
- ❄ 1-inch-tall cupid charm

*See the "Buyer's Guide" on page 176.*

### Directions

1 Referring to the "Basic Flower Shape" directions on page 39, use 8-inch lengths of pink ribbon for two rosebuds. Use an 8-inch length of orange for one rosebud and two 5-inch lengths for two smaller rosebuds. Use 2-inch lengths of the ⅞-inch-wide green taffeta ribbon for 11 folded leaves.

2 Thread each end of the 10-inch length of grosgrain through a suspender clip. Overlap the ends in the center of the loop that is formed. Fold under ¼ inch on the overlapped ribbon and slip stitch the ends in place. Refer to the **Clip Diagram**.

3 Use the glue gun to glue the flowers and leaves to the grosgrain ribbon loop, referring to the **Placement Diagram.** Begin with the end leaves first, working toward the center. Glue the rosebuds on next. Tie the gold chiffon ribbon into a bow and glue it below the center rosebud. Hand tack the charm below the center of the bow.

**Placement Diagram**

## Rosebud Earrings

### Materials

- ❄ ⅞-inch-wide wire-edged taffeta ribbons, such as from Offray ribbon: 12-inch length of green, 10-inch length each of orange and pink*
- ❄ Pair of ¾-inch-diameter earring backs
- ❄ Two 1-inch-tall cupid charms

*See the "Buyer's Guide" on page 176.*

### Directions

1 Referring to the "Basic Flower Shape" directions on page 39, use 5-inch lengths of ribbon for two rosebuds, one in pink and one in orange. Use 2-inch lengths of the green ribbon for six folded leaves.

2 Use the glue gun to glue the flowers and leaves to the earring back, referring to the photograph on page 38 for placement. Glue the three leaves first and the orange and pink rosebuds next. Hand tack the charm below the lower rosebud. Repeat for the other earring, facing the leaves in the opposite direction.

# VIDEO GAME RACK

*A gift that doubles as storage is certainly always welcome in a teenager's room. Craft a rack to keep video games lined up and identifiable at a glance. Wooden dowels separate each game, making retrieval a snap. By varying the distance between the dowels, you can use the same system to organize videos or tapes. By increasing the length of the base, you can organize even more games! As an added treat, stick a new video in with the gift.*

**Size:** 8½ × 15 inches

## Materials

- ❄ Ruler
- ❄ Hand saw
- ❄ 4 feet of 1-inch-wide wooden furring strip
- ❄ 6 feet of ⅜-inch wood doweling
- ❄ 16-inch length of ½-inch quarter-round molding
- ❄ Sandpaper
- ❄ Pencil
- ❄ 8½ × 15-inch piece of ¾-inch clear interior-grade plywood
- ❄ Masking tape
- ❄ Electric drill with ⅜-inch wood drill bit
- ❄ Wood stain in desired color
- ❄ Paintbrush
- ❄ Carpenter's glue
- ❄ Brads
- ❄ Polyurethane varnish

## Directions

1 Cut the furring strip into four lengths: two 8½-inch lengths and two 15½-inch lengths.

2 Cut eighteen 4-inch lengths from the ⅜-inch wood doweling. These will be used for the pegs.

3 Trim the quarter-round molding to 15½ inches.

4 Sand the cut edges of all the wood pieces smooth.

5 Use the pencil to mark the peg positions on the plywood piece. Mark two rows of nine holes each along the 15-inch length of the plywood. Referring to the **Video Game Rack Diagram,** place the first row 2 inches from the top edge and the second row 3 inches from the lower edge, with the first holes 1 inch from the left and right edges, and adjacent holes 1⅝ inches apart. Drill a ½-inch-deep hole at each peg marking.

6 Using the paintbrush, stain each wood piece. Let the stain dry thoroughly.

7 Using the carpenter's glue, glue a peg into each hole in the plywood piece.

8 Glue and nail the furring strip pieces in place on the short ends of the plywood. Then glue and nail the long furring strip pieces to the long edges of the plywood. Glue and nail the quarter-round molding in place along the back edge.

9 Varnish the surfaces of the game rack, including the pegs. Let the varnish dry thoroughly.

## *Better Woodworking Results*

❄

**When using both stain and glue in a woodworking project, always stain each component before gluing. Glue fills the pores of the wood, creating a smooth surface that will not accept stain.**

❄

**When drilling a number of ½-inch holes, make sure each hole is the same depth by wrapping a piece of masking tape around the drill bit ½ inch from the end. Stop drilling when the masking tape reaches the plywood.**

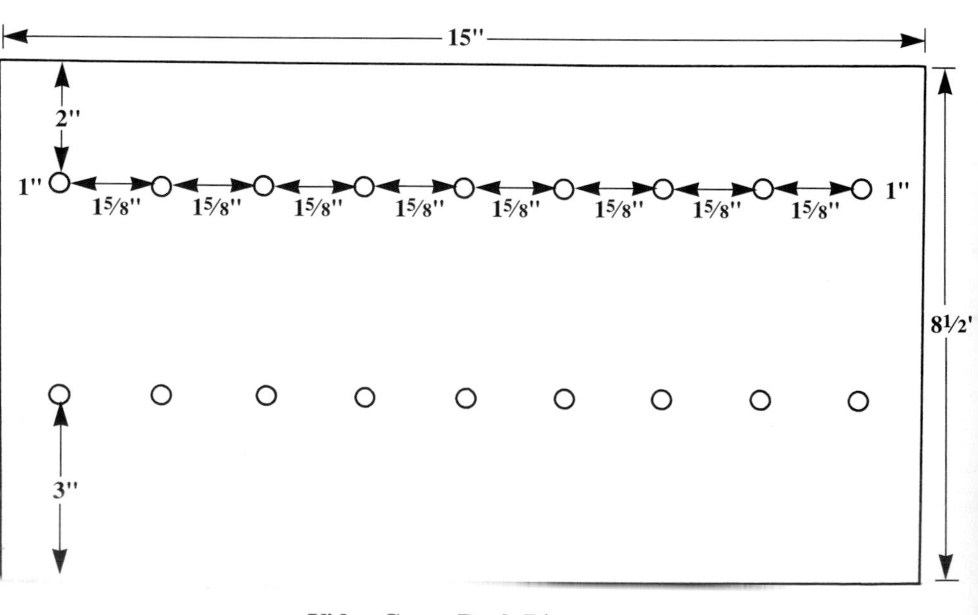


Video Game Rack Diagram

# SWITCHEMS GAME

*What a smart Santa to leave this brand new game! More challenging than tic-tac-toe and quicker to learn and play than checkers, it's fun for players of all ages. It's small enough to take along on trips and brightly colored enough not to get lost among other travel possessions. It's a snap to make from small squares of synthetic suede; use felt for a less-expensive version, if you prefer.*

**Size:** About 9 × 13 inches unrolled

## MATERIALS

- 9 × 12-inch pieces of Ultrasuede synthetic suede: 2 of orange and 1 each of turquoise and chartreuse (*Nancy's Notions* has 9 × 12-inch pieces of Ultrasuede available by mail order.)*
- Scissors or craft knife
- Ruler and pencil
- Masking tape
- 2 contrasting shades of fabric paint, such as Duncan Scribbles fashion paint in white and red*
- Paintbrush
- Fabric glue
- Sewing machine and thread to match the fabrics
- 1 yard of ⅜-inch-wide double-faced satin or grosgrain ribbon
- 12 playing pieces such as bingo markers: 4 each of 2 colors

*See the "Buyer's Guide" on page 176.

## DIRECTIONS

**1** From the two orange fabric pieces, cut one 9-inch square and one 9 × 9¼-inch piece; the extra ¼ inch on the second piece is a seam allowance for attaching the pocket. Set the 9-inch square aside.

**2** On the wrong side of the larger orange piece, with the ruler and pencil, mark a 1¼-inch border on three sides and a 1½-inch border on the fourth side (this includes the ¼-inch seam allowance), as shown in **Diagram 1** at right.

**3** Mark the center area into a grid of sixteen 1⅝-inch squares, as shown in **Diagram 2** at right.

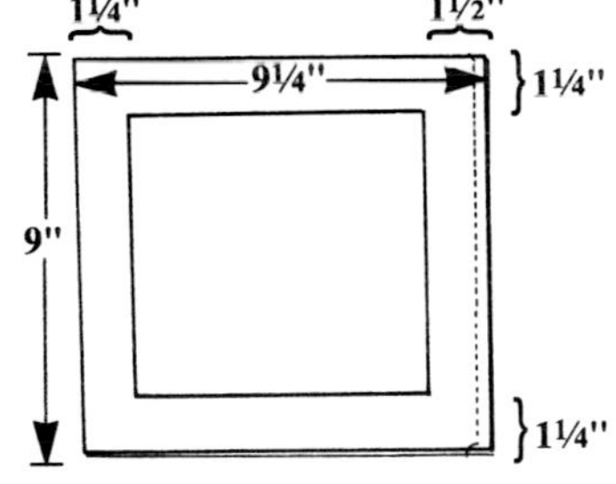

**Diagram 1**

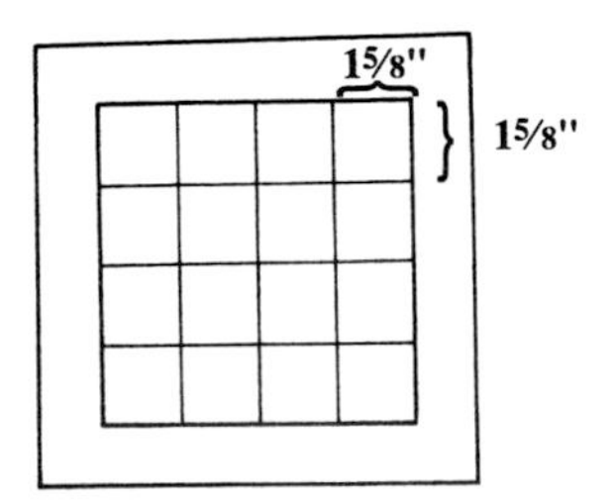


**Diagram 2**

**4** Place the masking tape along the outside edges of alternate squares to keep the lines straight

## The Game of Switchems

### OBJECT:

**The object of the game is to be the first to switch your pieces with the pieces of your opponent.**

### SETUP:

**Arrange the two four-token teams in two opposite corners, as shown in the diagram at right.**

### RULES:

**1. The younger player starts the first game. After that the winner goes first.**
**2. You may jump out from your home corner over your own piece.**
**3. Once a piece leaves its home corner, it may not return.**
**4. You must leave your home corner if your opponent is ready to enter it and has no other useful move.**

### PLAY:

**1. A piece may move into any adjacent vacant square, including diagonally.**
**2. Begin the game by moving any piece out of your home corner.**
**3. Alternate moves, following the rules, until the game's been won.**

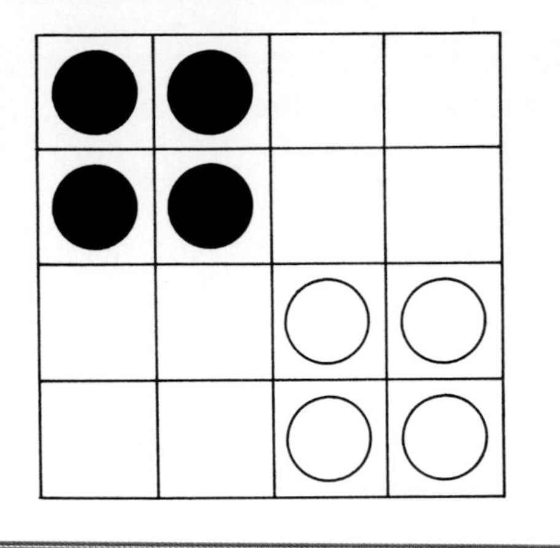

when painting. Paint squares with one paint color for the checkerboard pattern. Let the paint dry, then move the masking tape to paint the remaining squares with the other paint color.

5 Mark a 1¼-inch border on all the edges of the reserved 9-inch square and cut out the center area. Use the glue to affix this "frame" onto the larger, painted piece, making sure the frame edges meet or just cover the painted edges; remember to leave the ¼-inch seam allowance free. Use matching thread to machine topstitch the inner and outer edges of the frame, as shown in **Diagram 3.**

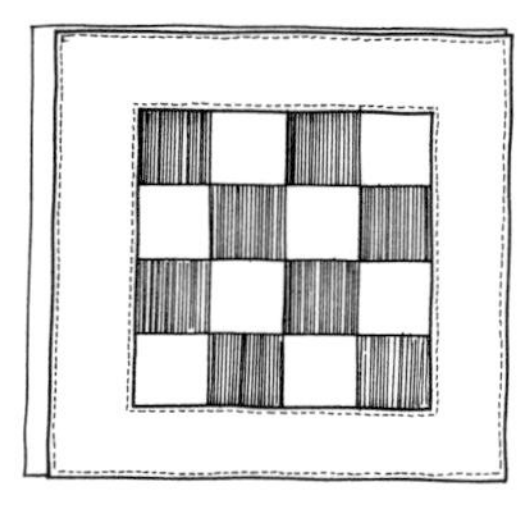

**Diagram 3**

6 From the turquoise fabric, cut a 5½ × 9-inch rectangle for the pocket back and flap. From the chartreuse fabric, cut a 3⅜ × 9-inch rectangle for the pocket front. Referring to **Diagram 4,** place the pocket front and back together with the wrong sides facing and the one long and two short edges evenly aligned. Use the glue to hold the edges together, then machine topstitch along those three edges, leaving the top edge open.

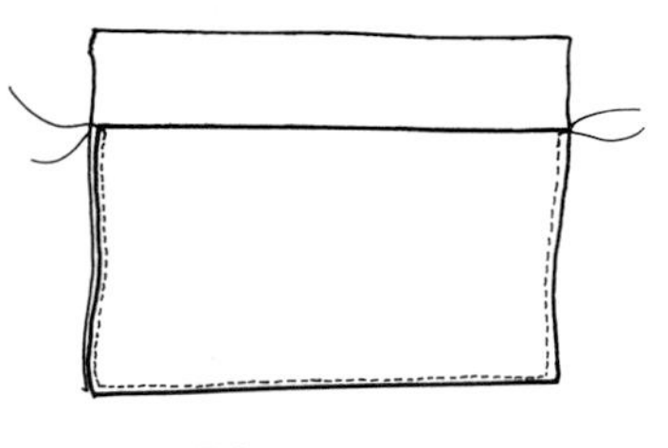

**Diagram 4**

7 Mark a line on the pocket back ¼ inch above the top of the front. Lay the game board with the checkerboard side up, and run a bead of glue along the ¼-inch seam allowance. Position the pocket, with the pocket front up, on the seam allowance so that the marked line matches the seam line, as shown in **Diagram 5.** Fold out the pocket flap so the fold of the pocket is against the edge of the game board and topstitch close to the pocket opening, sewing through the three layers.

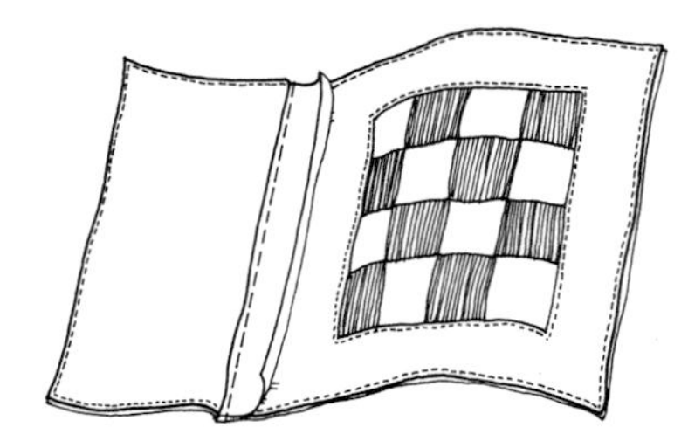

**Diagram 5**

8 From the turquoise fabric, cut four ½-inch squares. Glue one square to each corner of the game board. Referring to **Diagram 6,** tack the ribbon to the back of the game board (the outside of the roll) by placing the game board face side down and laying the ribbon along the center; securely tack the ribbon in place to the frame's inner stitching line opposite the pocket.

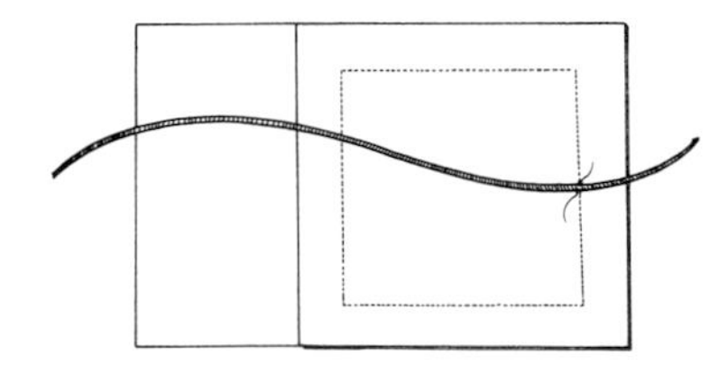

**Diagram 6**

9 Place the playing pieces in the pocket, roll up the board, and use the ribbon to tie the game closed.

# RATTLE BABY BLOCKS

*Filled with soft fiberfill, these blocks are easy for little fingers to grasp. When little hands hold and shake the blocks, the built-in rattle provides even more interest. Choose bright colors and simple shapes to appeal to baby. The small amounts of fabric required for the project make these blocks a perfect way to use up leftover scraps.*

**Size:** Each block is 5 × 5 × 5 inches

## MATERIALS

- Iron
- Six 4¾-inch squares of paper-backed fusible web for each block
- Six 5-inch squares of assorted print fabrics for each block
- Scissors and pinking shears
- Six 5½-inch squares of assorted print fabrics for each block
- Sewing machine (with decorative stitch optional)
- Matching sewing thread
- Polyester fiberfill
- Empty thread spool for each block
- 3-inch length of cardboard paper towel tube for each block

## DIRECTIONS

**1** Following the manufacturer's directions, use the iron to fuse a web square to the wrong side of each 5-inch square of print fabric.

**2** From each fused 5-inch square, use your pinking shears to cut a 2¾-inch square or a heart or star pattern on page 46. Fuse the patterns to the center of each 5½-inch square of print fabric. If desired, embellish the shape by sewing a decorative machine stitch around the edges of the shapes.

**3** Using a ¼-inch seam allowance and with right sides facing each other, sew four 5½-inch squares together to form a strip. Then, sew a 5½-inch square to the top and bottom edges of the second square of the strip, as shown in **Diagram 1.**

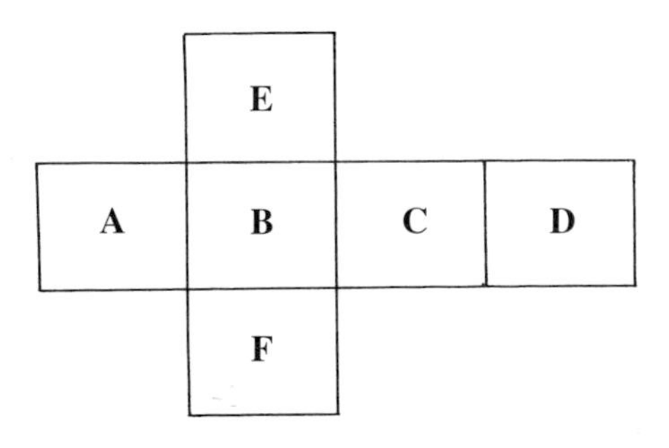


**Diagram 1**

4 Referring to the lettered blocks in **Diagram 1** on page 45 and having right sides facing, sew the top edge of A to the left edge of E, as shown in **Diagram 2.**

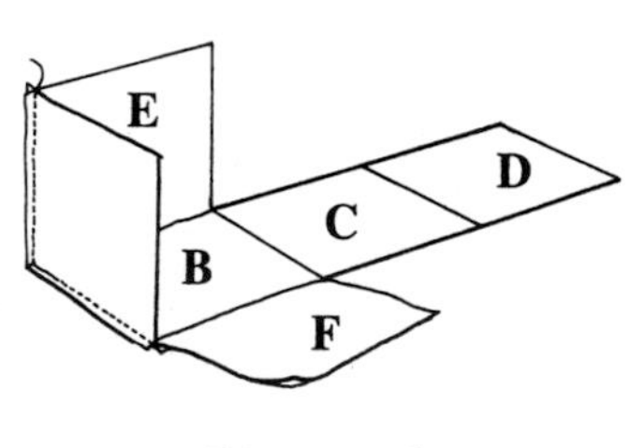


**Diagram 2**

5 Sew the right edge of E to the top edge of C and the bottom edge of C to the right edge of F, as shown in **Diagram 3.** Sew the left edge of F to the bottom edge of A. Sew around two of the three remaining open sides of D. Turn the block right side out.

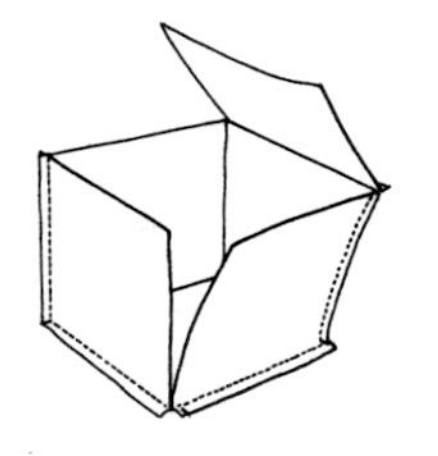

**Diagram 3**

6 Stuff the block slightly with fiberfill. Insert the spool into the center of the cardboard tube. Insert a small amount of fiberfill at each end of the tube; leave enough room in the tube for the spool to move. Insert the tube into the block. Finish stuffing the block, being sure to surround the tube. Slip stitch the opening closed.

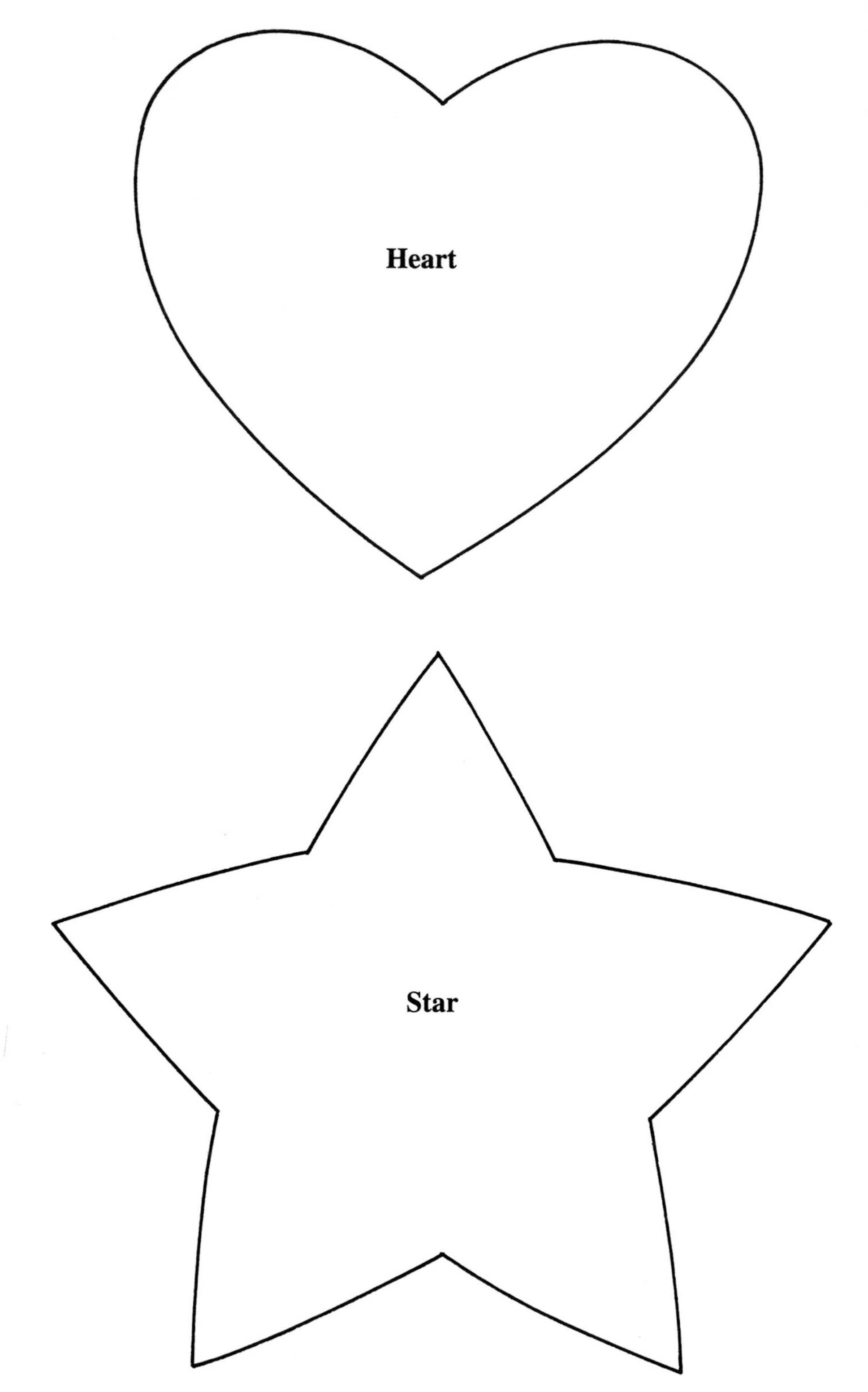

# FANCY FEET FELT BOOTIES

*Whether a gift for a wee woodsman or a budding ballerina, choose the perfect felt footgear to get him or her off and running. The Santa and elf booties will get everyone into the holiday act, while the saddle shoe and cowboy booties lend a whimsical air to pint-sized baby togs.*

**Size:** 12–18 months

### MATERIALS

For all the booties:
- ❄ Tracing paper and pencil
- ❄ Pinking shears and scissors
- ❄ Matching sewing thread
- ❄ Hand-sewing needle
- ❄ Sewing machine
- ❄ Awl

### DIRECTIONS

Trace the pattern pieces on pages 51 through 53 onto the tracing paper. Trace a full bootie pattern so it will be easier to fit the pattern on the felt pieces. Each pattern includes the ¼-inch seam allowance where needed. Cut out the pattern pieces.

## COWBOY BOOTIES

### MATERIALS

- ❄ 9 × 11½-inch pieces of felt: 3 tan and 2 turquoise
- ❄ 18-inch length of medium turquoise rickrack
- ❄ 24-inch length of gold cording

### DIRECTIONS

**1** From the tan felt, cut two soles and two booties. From the turquoise felt, cut two cowboy stars and two cowboy bootie bases, pinking the curved upper edges of the bases.

**2** Place one bootie base onto the right side of one bootie, matching the center front and lower edges. Topstitch the base in place along the pinked, curved edges, as shown in **Diagram 1.**

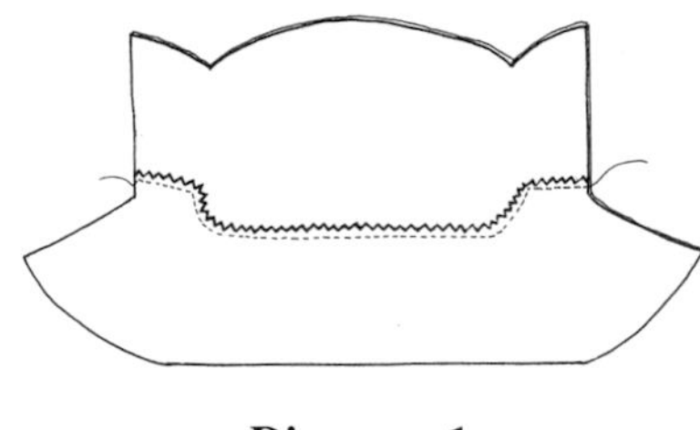

**Diagram 1**

**3** With matching thread, top stitch a turquoise star on the outside ankle of the bootie. Sew a length of rickrack about ¼ inch from the top edge of the bootie.

**4** Use the awl to punch two holes for the back ankle tie, as marked by the circle on the pattern.

**5** With the right sides together, sew the center front seam of the bootie from the toe to the front ankle. Clip the seam at the instep.

**6** With the right sides together, sew the sole to the lower edge of the bootie, as shown in **Diagram 2,** matching the toe to the center front seam and the heel to the center back of the bootie. Turn the bootie right side out.

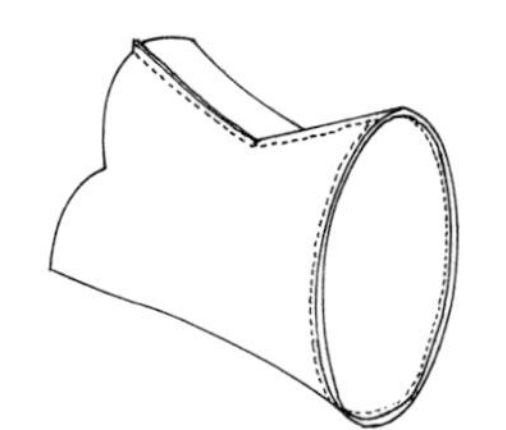

**Diagram 2**

**7** Thread a 12-inch length of gold cording through the holes at the heel. Tie the ends in a bow.

**8** Repeat Steps 2 through 7 for the other bootie, topstitching the turquoise star on the opposite side of the ankle.

## SANTA BOOTIES

### MATERIALS

- ❄ Three 9 × 11½-inch pieces of red felt
- ❄ 9-inch square of white fake fur
- ❄ Red satin ribbon: 48-inch length of ⅜-inch-wide

### DIRECTIONS

**1** From the red felt, cut two soles and two booties. From the white fake fur, cut two 2½ × 8½-inch strips.

**2** Place the right side of one long edge of a fur strip to the wrong side of the top edge of the bootie. Using a ¼-inch seam allowance, sew the two edges together. Fold the fur cuff to the right side of the bootie. With the right sides together, sew the center front seam from the toe to the front ankle, catching the ends of the fur cuff in the seam. Clip the seam at the instep.

**3** With the right sides together, sew the sole to the lower edge of the bootie, as shown in **Diagram 2** of "Cowboy Booties." Be sure to match the toe to the center front seam and the heel to the center back of the bootie. Then turn the bootie right side out.

**4** Cut the ribbon in half. Tack the center of one length to the instep area of the center front seam. Tie the ribbon ends in a bow at the back of the heel.

**5** Repeat Steps 2 through 4 for the other bootie.

## Elf Booties

### Materials

- ❄ 9 × 11½-inch pieces of felt: 3 green and 1 red
- ❄ Red satin ribbons: 48-inch length of ⅜-inch-wide and 24-inch length of ¼-inch-wide

### Directions

1 From the green felt, cut two soles and two elf booties, pinking the center front seam edges as indicated by the dotted line on the pattern. From the red felt, cut eight hearts.

2 Topstitch an upside-down felt heart to the wrong side of each upper edge point of the bootie, as shown in the **Cuff Diagram.** (The upper edge of the bootie will be turned down for the cuff so the embellishment on the wrong side will be on the right side of the bootie once it is turned.)

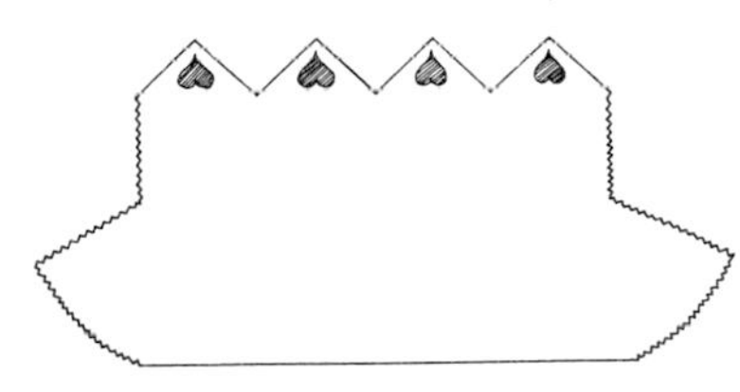

**Cuff Diagram**

3 Use the awl to punch a hole at each side of the toe for the elf bows, as marked by the small circle on the pattern.

4 With the wrong sides together, sew the center front seam of the bootie.

5 Turn the bootie wrong side out. With the right sides together, sew the sole to the lower edge of the bootie, as shown in **Diagram 2** of "Cowboy Booties" on page 48. Be sure to match the toe to the center front seam and the heel to the center back of the bootie. Turn right side out.

6 Cut the ⅜-inch-wide ribbon in half. Tack the center of one length of ribbon to the instep area of the center front seam. Tie the ribbon ends in a bow at the back of the heel. Fold the cuff down over the ribbon.

7 Cut the ¼-inch-wide ribbon in half. Thread the ribbon through the toe holes. Tie the ribbon ends in a small bow.

8 Repeat Steps 2 through 7 for the other bootie.

## Hunter's Booties

### Materials

- ❄ 9 × 11½-inch pieces of felt: 2 green and 2 tan
- ❄ Large-eyed needle
- ❄ 2 yards of yellow soutache braid

### Directions

1 From the green felt, cut two soles and two booties. From the tan felt, cut two hunter's bootie tops, pinking the top edges.

2 Place the tan bootie top onto the right side of the bootie, matching the center front edges. Topstitch the tan top in place along the upper and lower edges.

3 Use the awl to punch the three lacing holes on each center front edge and the two holes for the back ankle tie, as marked by the small circles on the pattern.

4 With the right sides together, sew the center front seam of the bootie from the toe to the front ankle. Clip the seam at the instep.

5 With the right sides together, sew the sole to the lower edge of the boot, as shown in **Diagram 2** of "Cowboy Booties" on page 48. Be sure to match the toe to the center front seam and the heel to the center back of the boot. Turn the bootie right side out.

6 Use the large-eyed needle to thread a 12-inch length of yellow braid through the two holes punched at the heel. Tie the braid ends in a bow.

7 Lace a 24-inch length of braid through the holes on either side of the center front seam, tying the braid ends in a bow at the top, as shown in the photograph on page 47.

8 Repeat Steps 2 through 7 for the other bootie.

## Ballet Slippers

### Materials

- ❄ 9 × 11½-inch pieces of felt: 2 each of white and pink
- ❄ 18-inch length of 1-inch-wide white ruffled eyelet
- ❄ 2 yards of ⅜-inch-wide pink satin ribbon

## DIRECTIONS

1 From the pink felt, cut two soles and two ballet slippers. From the white felt, cut two socks.

2 Place a slipper piece onto the right side of the sock piece, matching the center front edges. Topstitch the slipper in place along the upper and toe hole edges; then topstitch a length of eyelet, with the ruffled edge up, along the upper edge of the sock, as shown in the **Topstitching Diagram.**

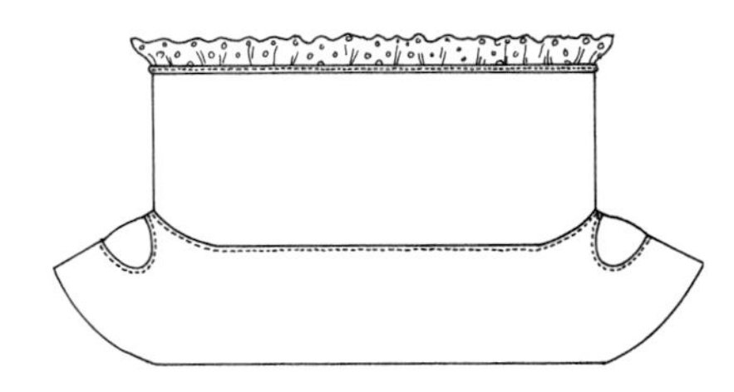

**Topstitching Diagram**

3 With the right sides together, sew the center front seam. Clip the seam at the instep.

4 With the right sides together, sew the sole to the lower edge of the bootie, matching the toe to the center front seam and the heel to the center back of the bootie. Turn right side out.

5 Cut the ribbon in half. Tack the center of one length to the slipper heel. Wrap the ribbon ends around the sock, crisscrossing it in the front. Bring the ribbon ends back to the heel and tie a bow.

6 Repeat Steps 1 through 5 for the other slipper.

# SADDLE SHOE BOOTIES

## MATERIALS

- 9 × 11½-inch pieces of felt: 3 white, 2 black, and 1 light blue
- 1½ yards of narrow red rickrack
- 24-inch length of ⅜-inch-wide red satin ribbon
- Large-eyed needle
- 1 yard of ¹⁄₁₆-inch-wide white satin ribbon

## DIRECTIONS

1 From the white felt, cut two soles and two socks. From the black felt, cut four saddle shoe saddles and two saddle shoe heels, pinking the curved edges. From the light blue felt, cut four 1½-inch squares for the argyles.

2 Place one blue square, angled as a diamond, on either edge of the white sock, about ¼ inch from the upper edge and 1½ inches from the center front. Topstitch the squares in place. Sew two 3-inch lengths of rickrack across each square, intersecting at the center. Then sew a length of rickrack along the top edge of the sock, as shown in the **Argyle Diagram.**

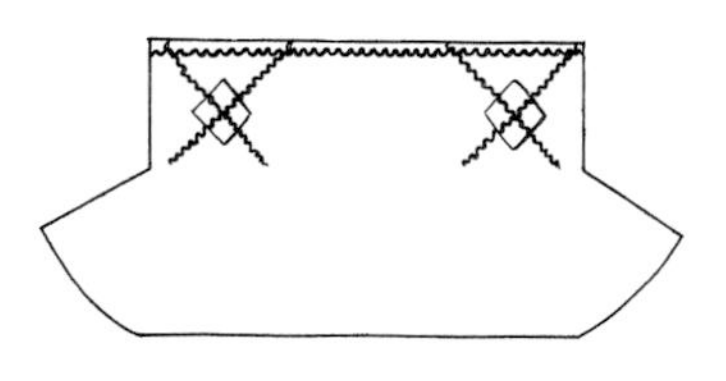

**Argyle Diagram**

3 Use black thread to sew a stitching line where marked by the horizontal dashed line on the pattern to create the illusion of the top of a shoe. Place the two black saddle pieces onto the right side of the sock piece, matching the center front edges. Place the one black heel in the center back of the sock, with the lower edges even. Topstitch the pieces in place along the pinked edges.

4 Use the awl to punch the three lacing holes on each center front edge and the two holes for the back ankle tie, as marked by the small circles on the pattern.

5 With the right sides together, sew the center front seam from the toe to the front ankle. Clip the seam at the instep.

6 With the right sides together, sew the sole to the lower edge of the bootie, matching the toe to the center front seam and the heel to the center back of the bootie. Turn right side out.

7 Cut the ⅜-inch-wide ribbon in half. Use the large-eyed needle to thread a length of ribbon through the two holes punched at the heel. Tie the ends in a bow.

8 Cut the ¹⁄₁₆-inch-wide ribbon in half. Then lace one length of the ribbon through the holes on either side of the center front seam, and tie the ribbon ends in a bow at the top, as shown in the photograph on page 47.

9 Repeat Steps 2 through 8 for the other bootie.

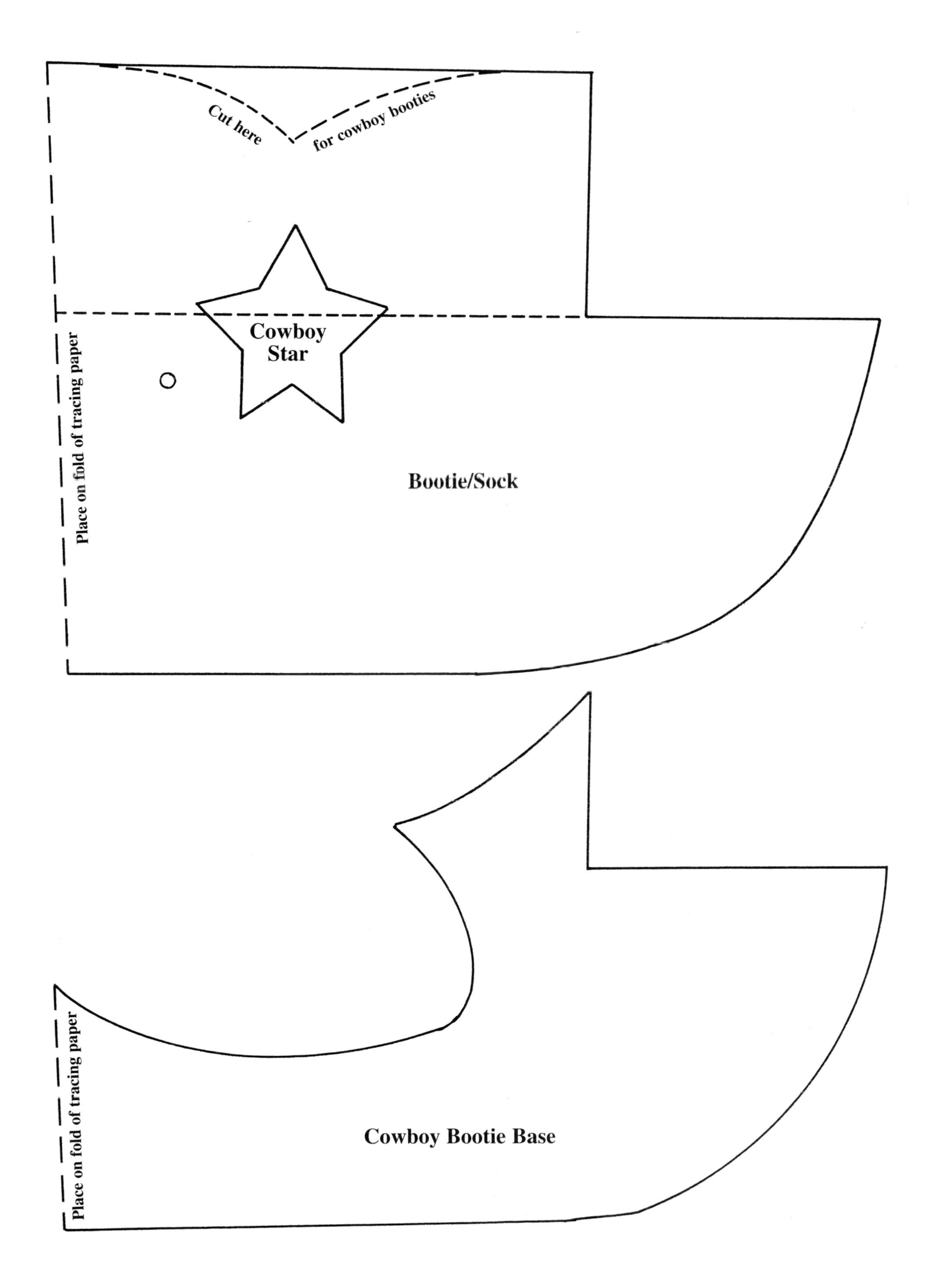
Cut here
for cowboy booties
Cowboy
Star
Place on fold of tracing paper
Bootie/Sock
Place on fold of tracing paper
Cowboy Bootie Base

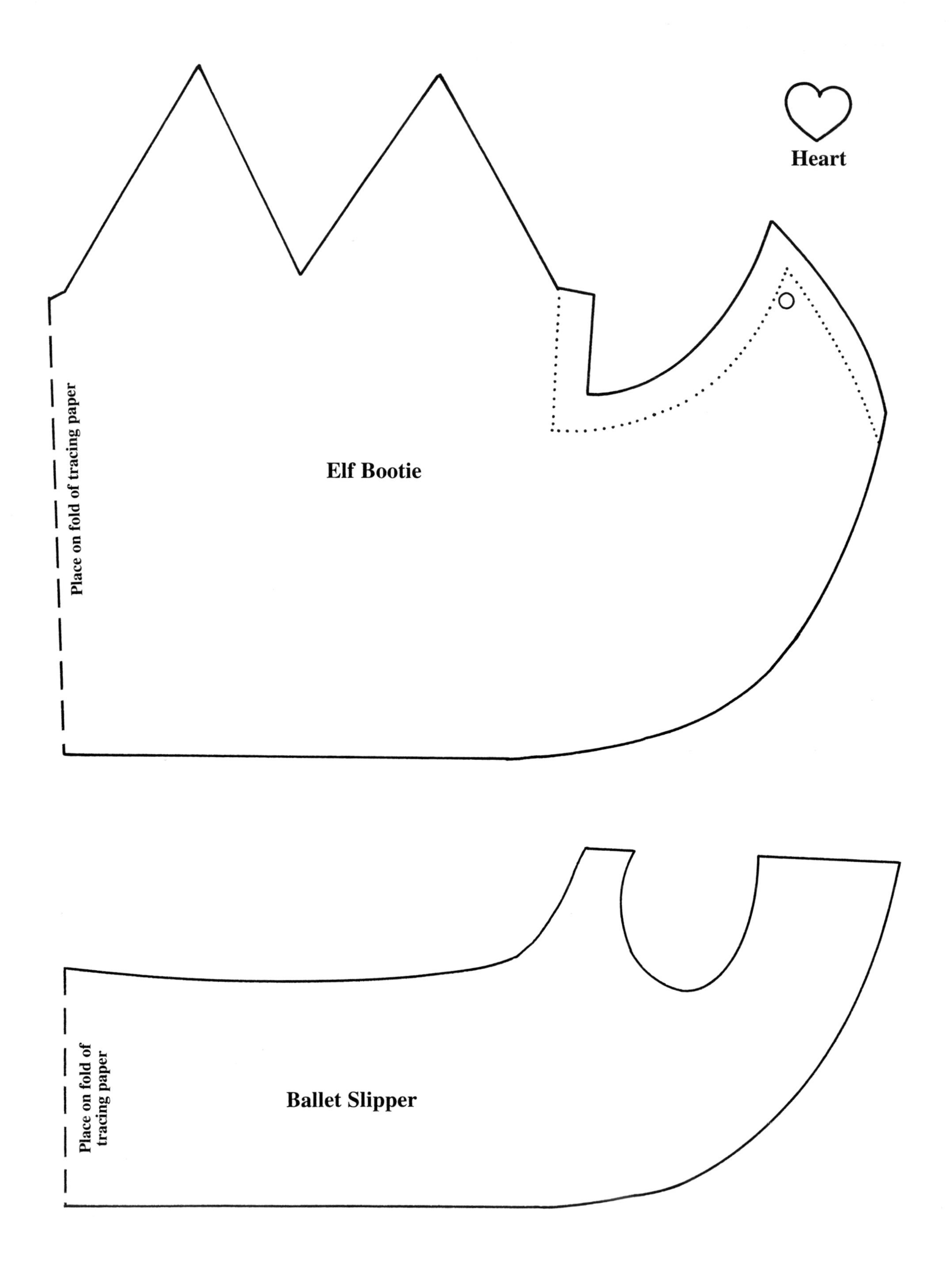
Heart
Place on fold of tracing paper
Elf Bootie
Place on fold of tracing paper
Ballet Slipper

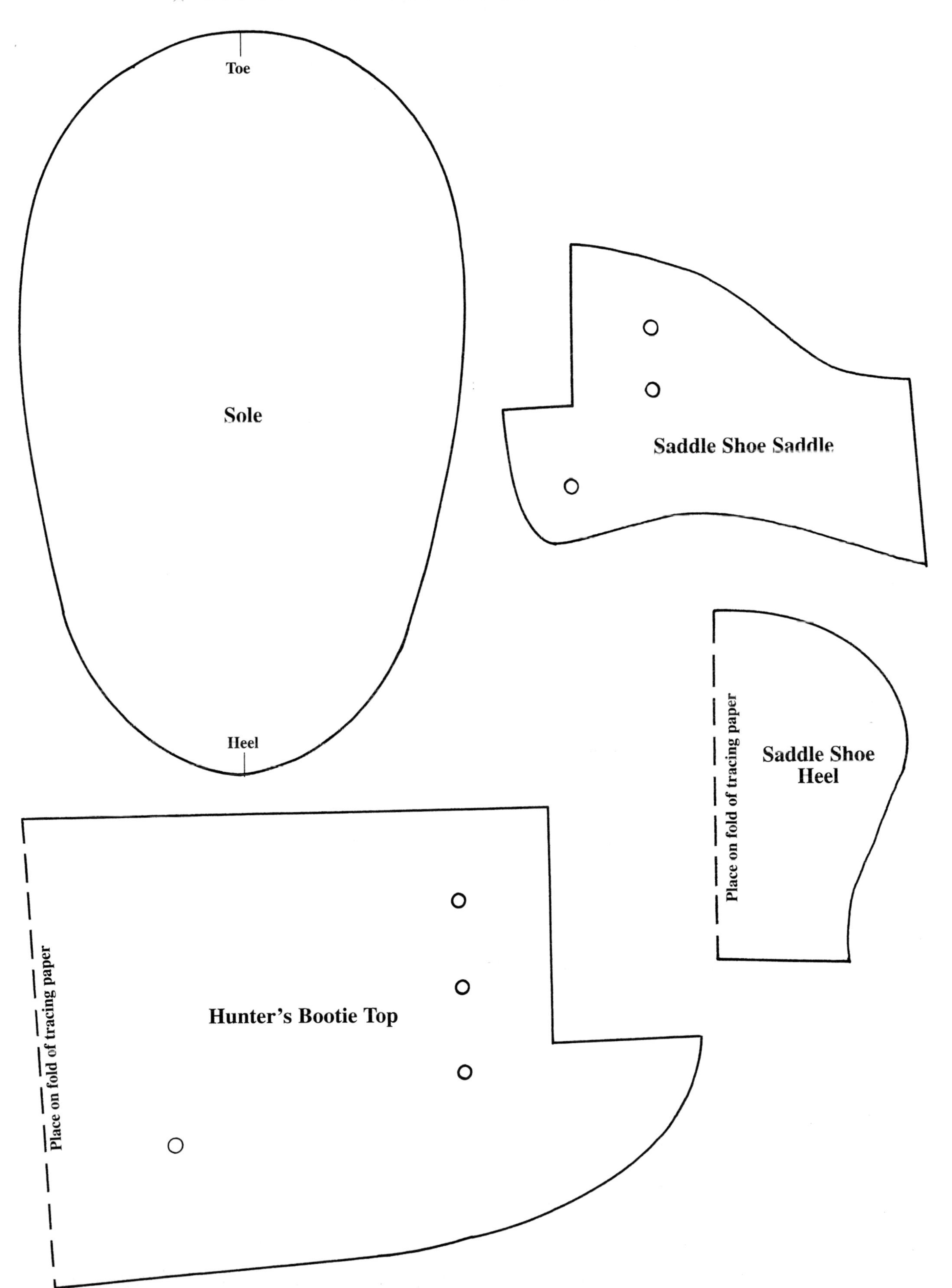
Toe
Sole
Heel
Saddle Shoe Saddle
Place on fold of tracing paper
Saddle Shoe Heel
Place on fold of tracing paper
Hunter's Bootie Top

*Chapter Two*

# *Gifts for Adults*

*Remember Mom and Dad, Grandma and Grandpa, and other special family members with handcrafted gifts made with love. For Mom, craft a jewelry piece from elegant beads or a useful trivet from her favorite color crockery. Keep Dad cozy with a warm, knitted scarf or a handsome pillow for his den. Surprise Grandma or Grandpa with personalized mementos like a family tree paper cutting or a one-of-a-kind sweatshirt.*

# OLD TIES, NEW PILLOWS

*Dad's favorite, worn ties can begin life anew as a rich silk pillow for the den or family room. Who would guess that these opulent accents were recycled from no-longer-used cravats? You might use fabric created from ties to cover the top of a footstool or hassock as well. Just be sure you cut up ties that Dad no longer wears!*

## Round Pillow

**Size:** 16-inch diameter

### Materials

- ❄ Scissors
- ❄ 11 neckties
- ❄ Sewing thread
- ❄ Air-soluble marking pen
- ❄ Ruler
- ❄ Iron
- ❄ Pencil and string
- ❄ Large sheet of paper
- ❄ ½ yard of muslin
- ❄ ½ yard of fabric for the pillow back
- ❄ Dressmaking pins
- ❄ 3 yards of decorative upholstery cording with a seam allowance
- ❄ Polyester fiberfill
- ❄ 2⅝-inch cover button
- ❄ Hand-sewing needle

### Directions

1 Slit open the ties along the back seam. Remove the interfacings, linings, and tags.

2 Beginning at the wide end of each tie, and in this order, cut 6-inch, 9-inch, 6-inch, and 9-inch pieces, as shown in **Diagram 1.** Place the 9-inch pieces in one pile and the 6-inch pieces in another pile.

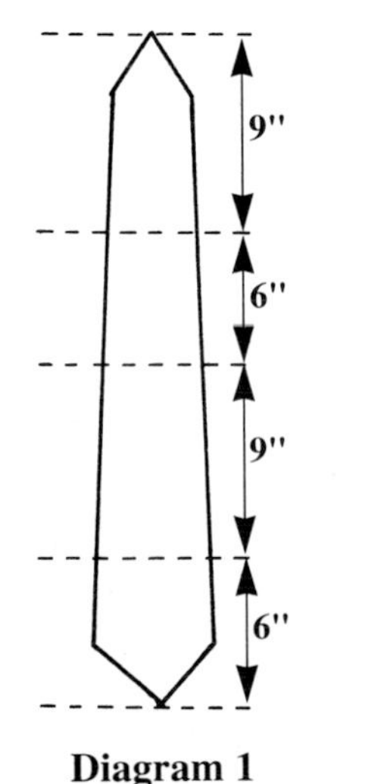

**Diagram 1**

3 Unfold the ties and press them flat. Mark the 9-inch pieces first. Mark the center of each narrow end, then mark ½ inch on either side of the center mark. At the widest end of each piece, place a mark ¼ inch outside the original fold lines of the tie. Connect the marks on each side and cut along them to trim off the excess, as shown by the dashed lines in **Diagram 2.**

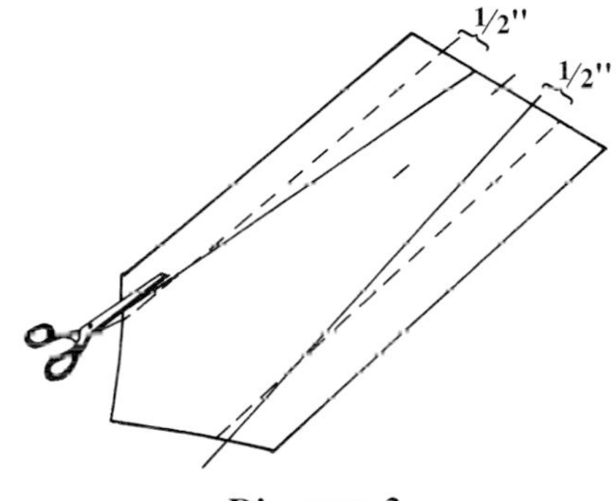

**Diagram 2**

4 With right sides facing and using a ¼-inch seam allowance, sew the 9-inch strips together along the long edges to form a circle, placing the narrow end of each strip at the same edge, as shown in **Diagram 3**; do not sew the last seam. Press the seams in the same direction.

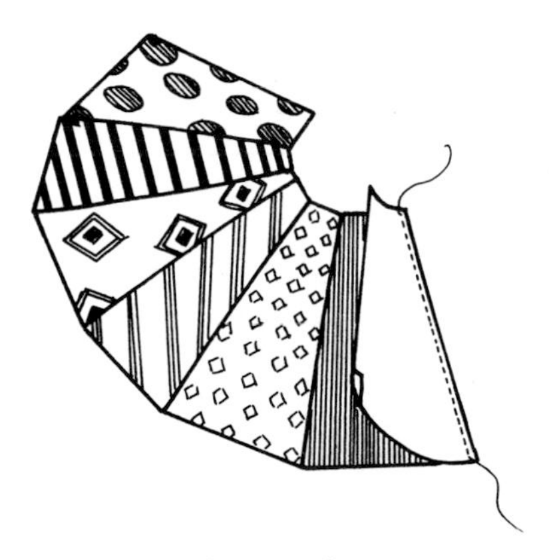
**Diagram 3**

5 Sew a line of gathering stitches ½ inch and ⅜ inch from the edge along the narrow ends of the sewn strips. Sew the last seam together to form a circle. Pull the gathers tightly and flatten the ring to shape the center of the pillow front. Tie the thread ends securely.

6 Referring to "Simple Compasses for Large Circles" on page 58 and using the pencil and string, make a compass and outline a 16½-inch-diameter circle on a large sheet of paper. Use this pattern to cut one circle each of muslin and fabric for the pillow back.

### *Tips for Ties*

❄

**If Dad doesn't have enough ties in complementary colors to create a good-looking pillow, choose a couple of his that look great together and take them with you to thrift or consignment shops. You should be able to purchase several ties for a dollar or two. You could also shop the local flea markets for bargains. Dry cleaners frequently have unclaimed ties that they are willing to sell inexpensively.**

❄

**When cutting the ties, avoid using the "knot" areas as these areas are most likely to be soiled and stretched out of shape.**

❄

**If a tie is soiled, you may wish to wash it. Hand wash it carefully in a gentle detergent or dishwashing liquid, roll it in a towel to remove any excess moisture, and dry flat. Always handle ties carefully as the fabric has been cut on the bias, and it can be stretched out of shape, especially when wet.**

7 Pin the pillow front, right side up, onto the muslin circle. Trim off the excess outer ends of the ties. Carefully baste the ties to the circle approximately ½ inch from the outside edge.

8 Using ¼-inch seam allowances, sew the 6-inch tie pieces together in a strip long enough to go around the circumference of the pillow front. When sewing the pieces together, match the color sequence of the tie patterns in the strip with those in the pillow front, and match the wide ends with the wider strips and the narrow ends with those in the narrower strips. If necessary, trim each end to the width of the corresponding strip of the pillow top, including the ¼-inch seam allowance.

9 Cut a strip of muslin 6 inches wide and long enough to fit around the circumference of the pillow front, plus 1 inch for the seam allowances. Pin the tie strip, right side up, onto the muslin strip. Trim off any excess tie ends. Baste the pieces together ½ inch from each long edge of the strip. Sew the narrow ends of the strip together to form a ring, leaving approximately a 2½-inch opening in the seam for turning the pillow. This piece is the pillow side.

10 Baste the upholstery cording along the seam line on the right side of the pillow front and back. With wrong sides facing each other, sew the edges of the pillow side to the pillow front. Sew the opposite edge of the pillow side to the pillow back, matching the order of ties on the pillow top. Turn the pillow right side out and stuff it with the polyester fiberfill to the desired firmness.

11 Cover the button with fabric and hand sew it to the center of the pillow, stitching through the entire pillow to anchor it in place.

**Tie one end of the string to the pencil. Stretching the string taut, tie a knot near the opposite end of the string so that the distance between the point of the upright pencil and the knot is exactly half the diameter (the radius) desired. Insert a pushpin into the newly tied knot, then stick the pin in the center of the paper. Holding the pencil upright and stretching the string taut, swing the pencil around to outline a circle.**

**You can also make a large compass by cutting a strip of lightweight cardboard slightly longer than half the desired diameter of the circle. Draw a line that is half the diameter of the circle (the radius) down the center of the strip. Place a pin through the cardboard at one end of the line. Punch a hole through the cardboard at the other end of the line. Use the pin end of the strip for the center of the circle and place it in the center of a piece of paper. Place the point of a pencil through the punched hole at the other end. Rotate the pencil, drawing a circle.**

## Neck Roll

**Size:** 13 inches long

### Materials

- Scissors
- 9 neckties
- Ruler
- Air-soluble marking pen
- ½ yard muslin
- Iron
- Dressmaker pins
- Sewing thread
- 1¼ yards of decorative upholstery cording with a seam allowance
- Two 7-inch-diameter matching fabric circles to line the pillow ends
- 2 yards of ⅜-inch-wide cording
- Four 3-inch long tassels to match the cording
- Fabric glue
- Polyester fiberfill

### Directions

1 Slit open the ties along the back seam. Remove the interfacings, linings, and tags.

2 Beginning at the widest point of the wider end of each tie, cut 5-inch, 15-inch, and 5-inch pieces, as shown in **Diagram 1.**

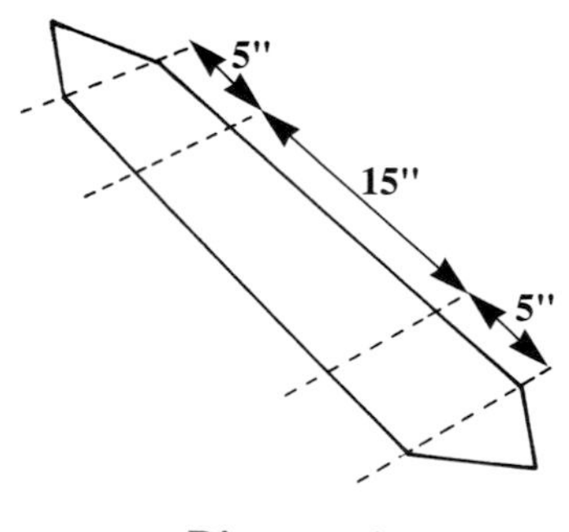


**Diagram 1**

3 Unfold the ties and press them flat. Mark the 15-inch pieces first. Mark ¼ inch outside the origi-

nal fold lines of the tie. Connect the marks on each side; cut along them to trim off the excess, referring to **Diagram 2** of the "Round Pillow" on page 57.

4 Cut a 15 × 21-inch piece of muslin. Pin one 15-inch tie strip, right side up, onto the muslin at one narrow end. Place a second tie strip face down on top of the first, but facing in the opposite direction, lining up the edges on one side. Using a ¼-inch seam allowance, sew the ties to the muslin along the long inner edge of the tie strips, as shown in **Diagram 2.**

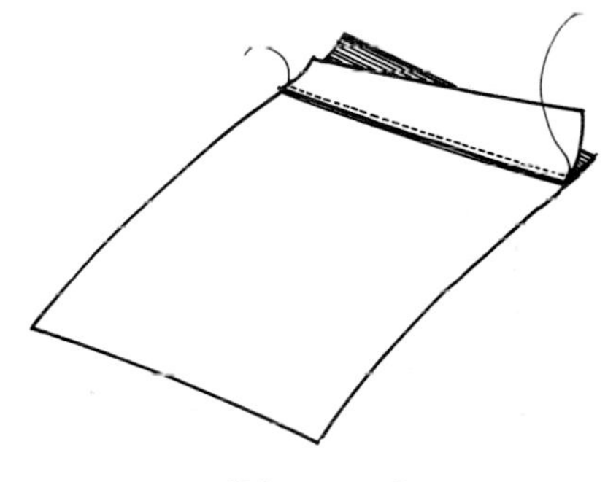

**Diagram 2**

5 Open the second tie strip right side up and press it flat. Baste the other long edge of the first tie strip to the muslin, as shown in **Diagram 3.**

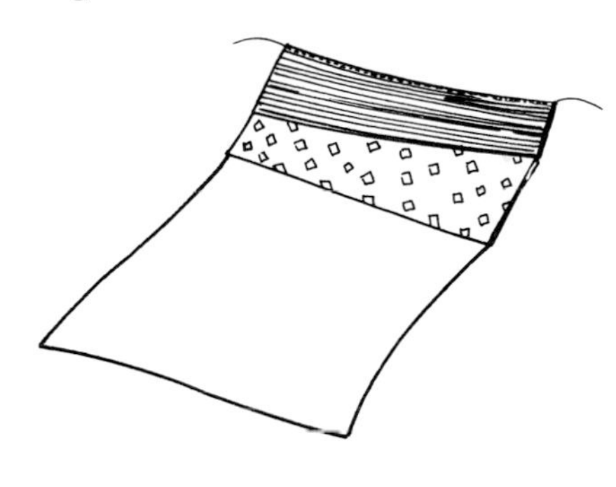

**Diagram 3**

6 Place a third tie strip, face down and reversing direction again, on top of the second strip, matching the long edges. Sew the ties to the muslin along the long inner edge of the tie strips. Open out the third strip and press it flat. Continue to sew the remaining long strips in this way until the muslin piece is covered. Trim the piece to 13½ × 19½ inches. Using a ½-inch seam allowance, baste around all edges of the joined tie fabric to secure it to the muslin. With right sides facing each other, use a ½-inch seam allowance to sew the 15-inch-long edges of the piece together to form a tube.

7 To make the pillow ends, cut two 6 × 21-inch pieces of muslin. On each piece of muslin, sew the 5-inch tie strips together in the same order as on the larger piece, trimming them to the width of the corresponding 15-inch tie piece but adding a ½-inch seam allowance before cutting. (Cut these pieces straight. Disregard the tie's original fold lines.) Pay strict attention to the order in which each strip is sewn to the muslin so that each end matches the corresponding edge of the tube. Trim the completed sewn piece to 4 × 19½ inches.

8 To form a tube, sew the narrow ends of each pillow end together, right sides facing, with a ½-inch seam allowance and leaving the last 1 inch of the outer end of the seam open for a casing opening, as shown in **Diagram 4.** Press the seam open and topstitch close to the folded edges of the casing opening.

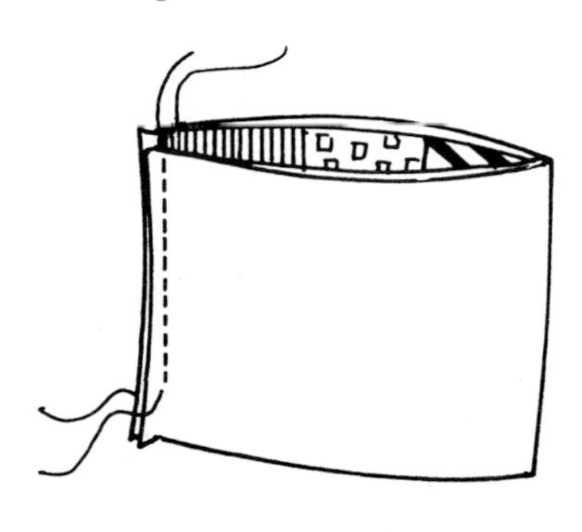

**Diagram 4**

9 Press under ¼ inch, then ½ inch along the casing edge. Topstitch the casing edge in place, as shown in **Diagram 5.**

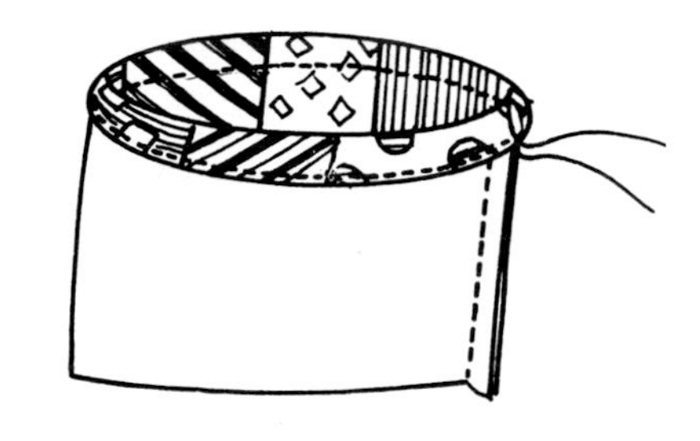

**Diagram 5**

10 Baste the upholstery cording on the right side and along the seam line on each end of the larger pillow tube. With right sides together, use a ¼-inch seam allowance to sew the pillow end tubes to the larger pillow tube. With the right side facing out, sew one of the fabric circles to the seam allowance at one end of the larger pillow tube. Turn the pillow right side out.

11 Cut the narrow twisted cording in half and thread one length through the casing on each pillow end tube. Tie a tassel 1 inch from each end of the cord. Fold up the cord end and glue it in place. Wrap matching thread around the cording to cover the glued end. Pull the twisted cord on the fabric-lined end to gather the pillow end. Tie the cord into a knotted bow. Stuff the neck roll with polyester fiberfill.

12 Hand sew the other fabric circle inside the remaining pillow end. Insert the cord and tie a tassel 1 inch from each end of the cord. Fold the cord end and glue it in place. Wrap matching thread around the cording to cover the glued end. Pull the cord to gather the second fabric end and tie it in a bow.

# DAD'S HOLIDAY MUFFLER

*"Knit one, purl two" goes the old expression. Simply reverse that to "Knit two, purl one," and you have memorized the super-simple pattern stitch for this wonderful scarf. Each and every row is the same, so it works up in a wink. Be sure to knit more than one since Dad's not the only one who would enjoy its colorful warmth in winter!*

**Size:** About 11 × 48 inches, including fringe

## MATERIALS

- Four 3-ounce/85-gram balls of Lion Brand Wool-Ease Sprinkles worsted-weight yarn*
- Pair of size 8 knitting needles
- Scissors
- 6-inch square of cardboard
- Size G or H crochet hook

*See the "Buyer's Guide" on page 170.

## DIRECTIONS

### CHECKING THE GAUGE

To make sure the finished size will be correct, take the time to check your gauge. Here we are using a gauge of 14 stitches = 2 inches. (See "Checking Gauge" on the opposite page for additional information.)

### MAKING THE HOLIDAY MUFFLER

1 Begin the muffler by casting on 72 stitches.

2 Row 1: * Knit 2 stitches, purl 1 stitch; repeat these 3 stitches from the * across all the stitches on the needle.

3 Repeat Row 1 for the pattern until the muffler is 42 inches long. Bind off in pattern.

## Knotting the Fringe

1 Use the cardboard square to measure and then cut the yarn strands for the fringe. (See "How to Make Fringe" on this page.)

2 Use four strands of yarn for each fringe. Knot a fringe in the first stitch, then in every third stitch across each narrow end of the muffler.

## Checking Gauge

❄

**Gauge is the number of stitches and rows per inch. You can change your gauge depending on the needle or hook size and the yarn you are using, as well as how tightly or loosely you knit or crochet. In order for a garment to fit properly, it is essential that your gauge matches the one given in the instructions. Even if you are knitting or crocheting an item for which fit is not an issue, gauge is still very important. The way the completed project feels—referred to as the "hand"—depends on the gauge. If your gauge is too tight, your piece will be stiff as a board. If the gauge is too loose, your piece will be limp and uneven. Even if you want to get started right away on the project you have planned, take time to check your gauge.**

❄

**To make sure the finished size of the knit piece will be correct, check the knitting for the proper gauge. You may want to knit a sample swatch, or a few inches of the item to test the gauge. Referring to the diagram below, use a ruler to measure horizontally across a row to determine the number of stitches per inch. Don't measure the first row of knitting; your tension may be tighter than normal when you first start to knit. Measure vertically along the side of the stitches to determine the number of rows per inch. Change your needle size if your gauge is incorrect: Use a larger needle if the knitting has too many stitches and rows per inch, or a smaller needle if the knitting has not enough stitches and rows per inch. Knit another swatch until you obtain the correct gauge.**

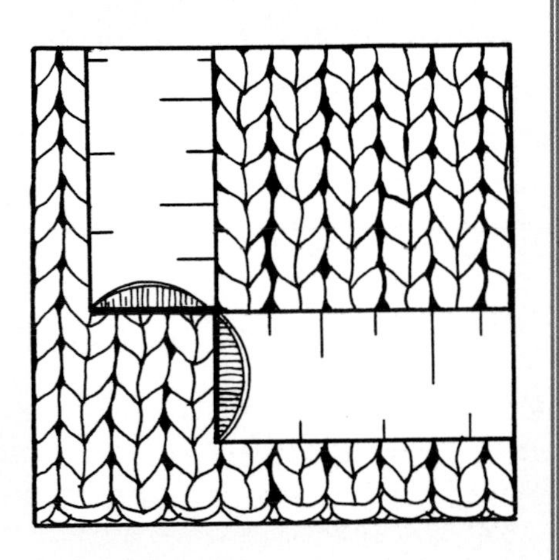

## How to Make Fringe

❄

**1. Wrap yarn around a piece of cardboard and cut the loops at one edge, as shown in Diagram 1.**

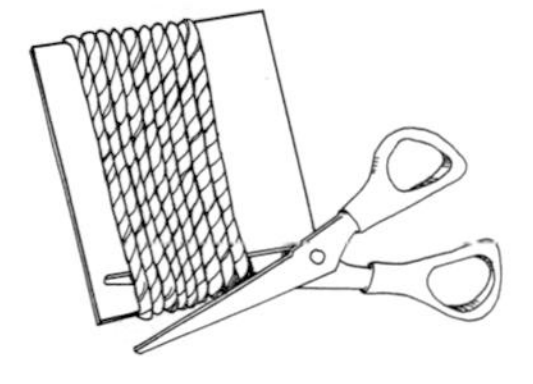

Diagram 1

**2. Fold four of the cut yarn strands in half. Insert the crochet hook into an edge stitch and pull the folded yarn ends through, as shown in Diagram 2.**

Diagram 2

**3. While the folded yarn is still on the hook, pick up the yarn ends and pull them through the loops, as shown in Diagram 3. Pull the yarn ends to tighten the knot.**

Diagram 3

**4. After all the fringe is knotted across the edge, trim the ends even, as shown in Diagram 4.**

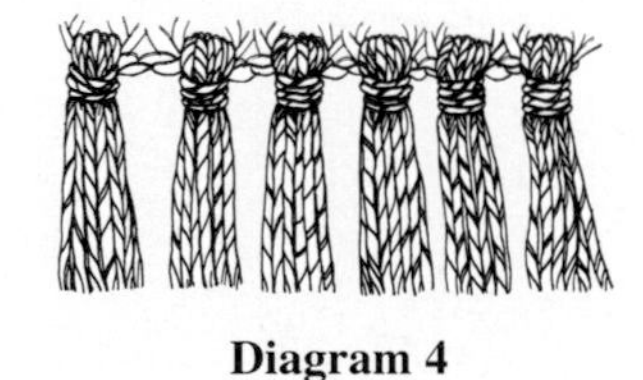

Diagram 4

# TIME FOR BEADS JEWELRY

*Use dramatic beads in rich patterns to produce timely jewelry such as this elegant wristwatch, pendant watch, and eyeglass chain. Or give new life to an old watch by adding one of these unique beaded bands.*

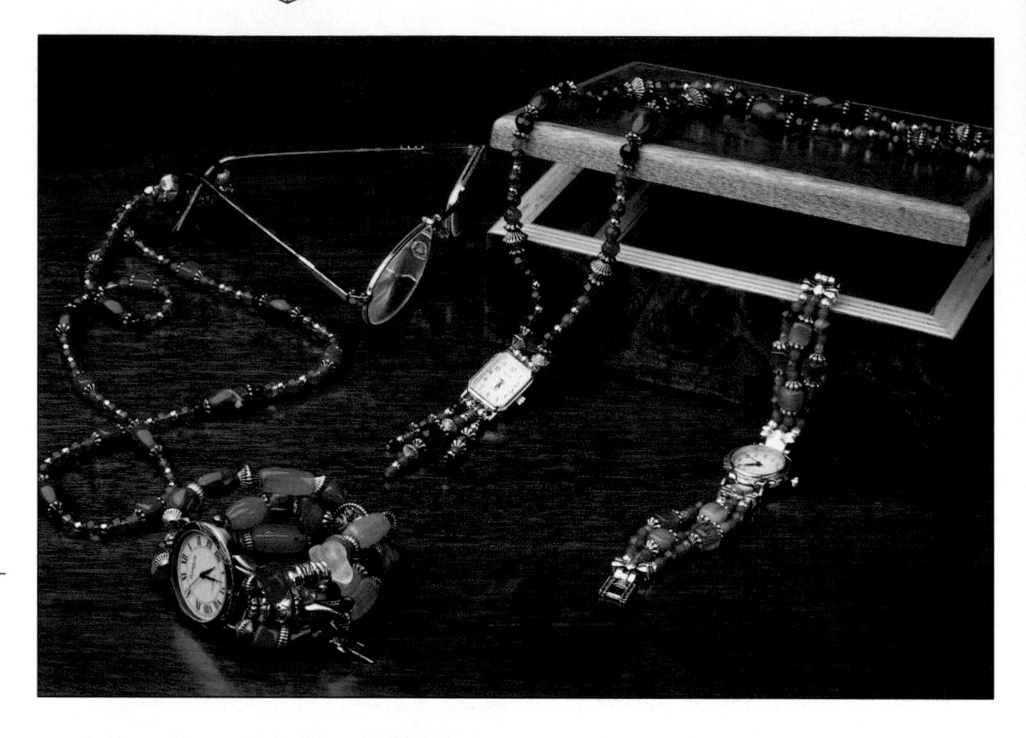

## Adjustable Beaded Watchband

**Size:** Adjustable

### Materials

- Scissors
- Ruler
- 48-inch length of 1⁄32-inch diameter elastic beading cord
- 30 spacers
- Extra large face watch with 3⁄4-inch pins
- Thick white craft glue
- 16 small beads
- 6 medium beads
- 11 large beads
- 6 jump rings
- 3 charms

All beads and jewelry findings used here are from The Beadery.* Use the **Bead Identification** chart on the opposite page to assist in bead selection.

*See the "Buyer's Guide" on page 176

### Directions

**1** Cut a 16-inch length of cord, then string on the first bead in Pattern A, as shown in **Diagram 1.**

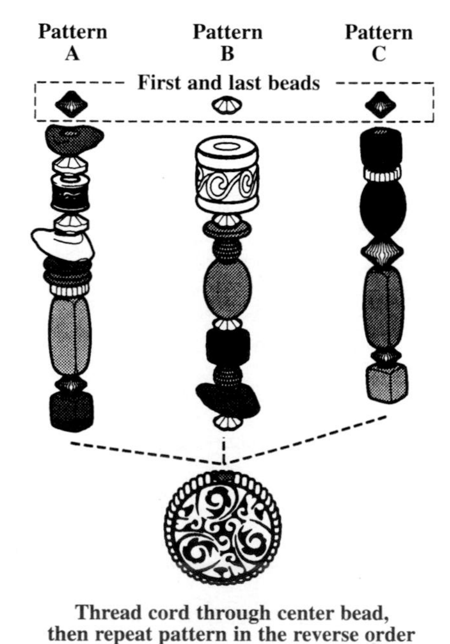


Thread cord through center bead, then repeat pattern in the reverse order

**Diagram 1**

**2** Working from front to back, thread the cord around the lower watch pin. Securely knot the cord ¼ inch after the bead, as shown in **Diagram 2.** Put a dab of glue on the knot and trim the cord end. The knot should be tucked into the adjacent bead.

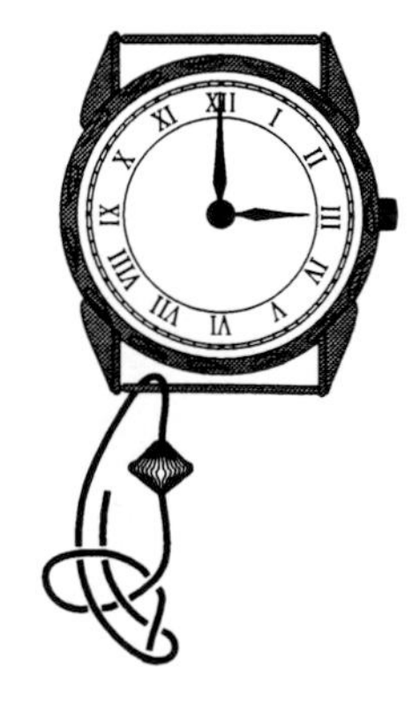

**Diagram 2**

**3** Referring to **Diagram 1,** string the rest of Pattern A and the large center bead (a filigree puff disc on the **Bead Identification** chart), then repeat Pattern A in the reverse order.

**4** Working from front to back, thread the cord around the watch pin on the opposite side of the watch face. Estimate the size of the recipient's wrist or try the watch on; add or subtract beads to adjust the length to fit. Make a knot around the last bead as in Step 1.

**5** Repeat Steps 1 through 3 twice more as follows: String Pattern B beads first and then Pattern C beads, as shown in **Diagrams 1** and **3,** threading each cord through the large single center bead before reversing the order of the beads.

**Diagram 3**

**6** Using two jump rings, attach each of the three charms randomly on the watchband.

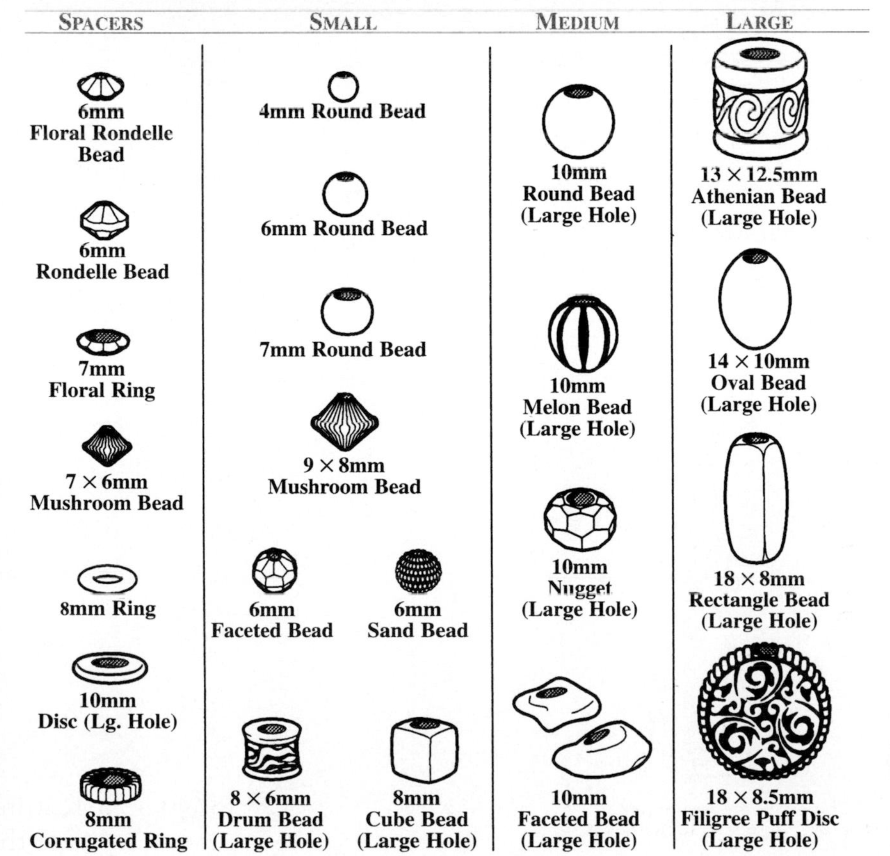


## BEADED WATCH PENDANT

**Size:** 30 inches long with a 3-inch pendant

### MATERIALS

- Small-face watch with ½-inch gold pins
- 4mm round beads: 20 Frosted Grape, 4 Opaque Black, and 39 in 24K Gold Washed (plus 5 more if decorating watch pins)
- 40-inch length of 8-pound test monofilament thread
- Scissors
- Thick white craft glue
- Beading needle
- 7 × 6mm small mushroom beads: 2 Antiqued 24K Gold Washed
- Floral rondelles: 30 Antiqued 24K Gold Washed
- 6mm round beads: 44 Teal
- 6mm faceted beads: 14 Dark Amethyst and 12 Opaque Black
- 7mm floral rings: 14 Antiqued 24K Gold Washed
- 9 × 8mm mushroom beads: 7 Antiqued 24K Gold Washed
- 14 × 10mm oval beads: 6 Teal
- 10mm faceted round bead: 1 Dark Amethyst
- Three 3-inch gold head pins
- Wire cutters
- Round-nose jeweler's pliers

All beads and jewelry findings used here are from The Beadery.* Use the **Bead Identification** chart to assist in bead selection.

**See the "Buyer's Guide" on page 176.*

### DIRECTIONS

Note: If space allows for decorating pins, remove the upper pin from the watch and string three 4mm gold beads onto the pin. Replace the pin in the watch.

**1** Wrap one end of the 40-inch length of monofilament thread around the top watch pin and tie a secure knot. Put a dab of glue on the knot to completely secure it.

**2** Thread a beading needle onto the long end of the monofilament thread. String a small mushroom bead and floral rondelle, as shown in **Diagram 1.** String the beads, as shown in the **Necklace Pattern,** six times.

**Diagram 1**

**3** Repeat the necklace pattern again, omitting the last nine beads. String a floral rondelle bead and a small mushroom bead.

**4** Referring to **Diagram 2,** thread the needle around the top watch pin. Make sure that all the beads are nestled together, then tie a secure knot. Put a dab of glue on the knot. Feed the ends back through the adjacent beads. Trim.

**Diagram 2**

**5** String **Pin Pattern A** onto a head pin. Use the wire cutters to trim the pin to ⅜ inch. Referring to **Diagram 3,** make a loop at the end of a pin, using the round-nose pliers to form the loop. Repeat this step to make a second **Pin Pattern A** and one **Pin Pattern B.**

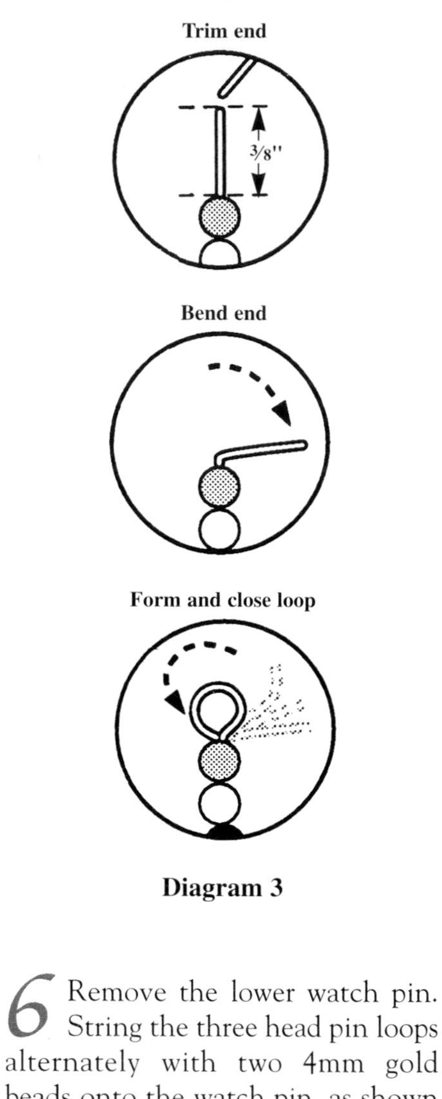


**Diagram 3**

**6** Remove the lower watch pin. String the three head pin loops alternately with two 4mm gold beads onto the watch pin, as shown in **Diagram 4.** Replace the pin in the watch.

**Diagram 4**

Teal
Gold
Dark Amethyst
Gold Floral Ring
Gold Mushroom
Frosted Grape
Gold Rondelle
Opaque Black
Teal
Opaque Black

**Necklace Pattern**

Opaque Black
Gold
Frosted Grape
Gold Rondelle
Teal

**Pin Pattern A**

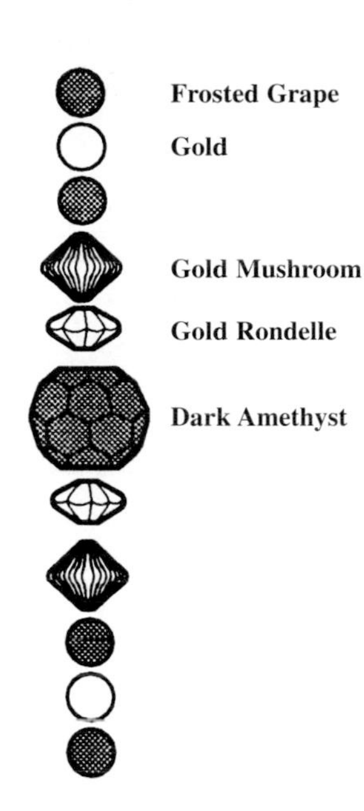


**Pin Pattern B**

# Beaded Watchband

**Size:** 7¼-inch total length

## Materials

- Silver-tone watch with connector findings with 3 holes and clasp
- Wire cutters
- Ruler
- 40-inch length of tiger tail (plastic-coated twisted wire)
- 4 crimp beads
- Jeweler's pliers or crimp bead tool
- 4mm round beads: 8 each of Antiqued Silver Washed, Oriental Jade, and Teal; 24 Frosted Grape
- 6mm round beads: 8 Teal
- 6mm floral rondelle beads: 16 Antiqued Silver Washed
- 8mm cube beads with a large hole: 4 each of African Amethyst and Oriental Jade
- Thick white craft glue

All beads and jewelry findings used here are from The Beadery.* Use the **Bead Identification** chart on page 63 to assist in bead selection.

**See the "Buyer's Guide" on page 176.*

## Directions

**1** Attach the connector findings to the watch by removing one of the pins and sliding one of the connector findings onto it. Compress the pin and replace it on the watch, making sure the connector is attached right side out. Repeat for the second connector.

**2** Use the wire cutters to cut a 20-inch length of tiger tail. This length will make a watchband with 2 inches of beads on either side of the face. If desired, this length and the number of beads strung on the wire can be adjusted. Insert one end of the wire into one of the outside holes of a connector finding and pull about 6 inches through the hole. Then string a crimp bead onto the wire. Thread the short end of the wire around and through the crimp bead a second time, as shown in **Diagram 1.** Pull the wire tight and use the pliers or crimp bead tool to securely crimp the bead onto the wire near the end. Trim the excess wire close to the bead.

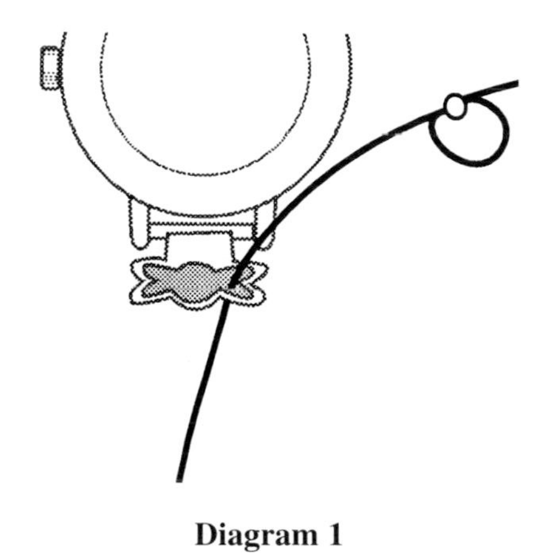

**Diagram 1**

**3** Pull the wire until the crimp bead is snugly inside the connector finding. String **Pattern A** beads, as shown on page 66. Referring to **Diagram 2,** thread the wire into an outside hole of the clasp and out through the center hole, making sure the clasp is attached right side out. String **Pattern B** beads, as shown on page 66, then insert the wire into the center hole of the connector finding and out the last hole. String **Pattern A** beads, inserting the wire into the last hole of the clasp and pulling the wire to remove all but 1⁄16 inch slack on each bead strand. String a crimp bead. Thread the wire around and through the bead a second time and crimp the bead as close to the clasp as possible. Trim the end.

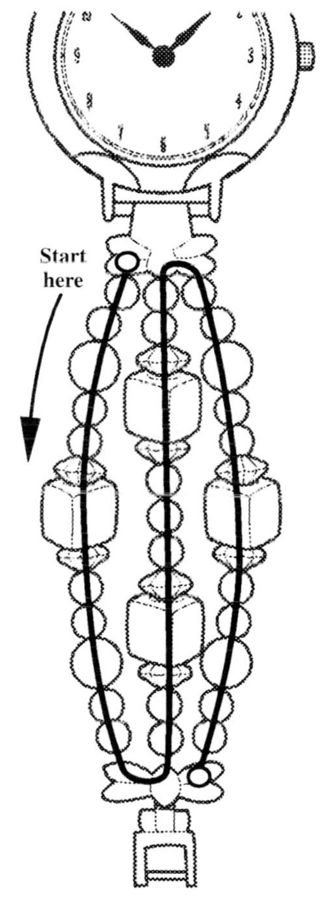


**Diagram 2**

**4** Repeat Steps 2 and 3 of the beading procedure for the other side of the watch face.

**5** Make sure the trimmed wire ends are tucked inside the connectors then fill the backs of the connectors and clasps with glue.

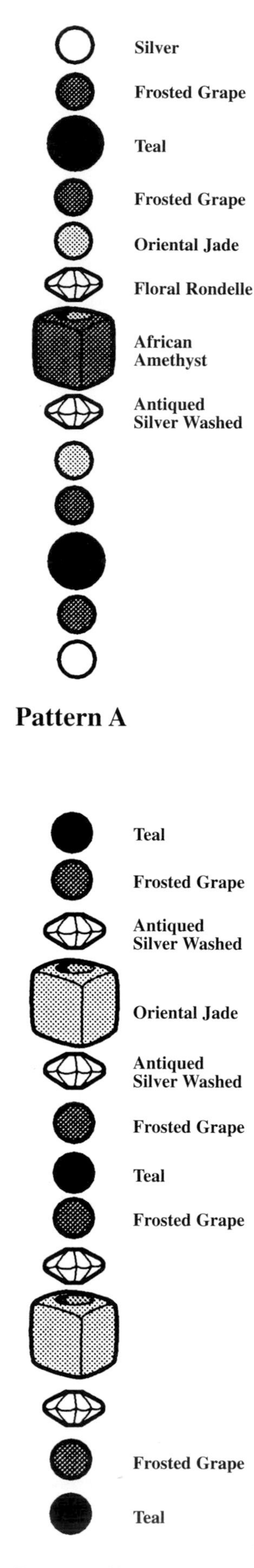


**Pattern A**

**Pattern B**

# Beaded Eyeglass Holder

**Size:** 29 inches long

## Materials

- 40-inch length of gold tiger tail (plastic-coated twisted wire)
- Jeweler's pliers and wire cutters
- 2 double-bead gold-tone tips
- 2 gold-tone eyeglass holders
- 6mm round beads: 48 African Amethyst
- 4mm round beads: 16 Frosted Grape, 14 Opaque Black, and 32 in 24K Gold Washed
- 6mm floral rondelle beads: 30 Antique 24K Gold Washed
- 8mm cube beads with a large hole: 8 Oriental Jade
- 14 × 10mm oval beads with a large hole: 7 Teal
- Straight pin or needle

All beads and jewelry findings used here are from The Beadery.* Use the **Bead Identification** chart on page 63 to assist in bead selection.

**See the "Buyer's Guide" on page 176.*

## Directions

**1** Tie a double overhand knot near one end of the tiger tail. Trim the excess wire close to the knot. Thread the long end of the wire through the hole in a bead tip so the knot rests in the cup, as shown in **Diagram 1.**

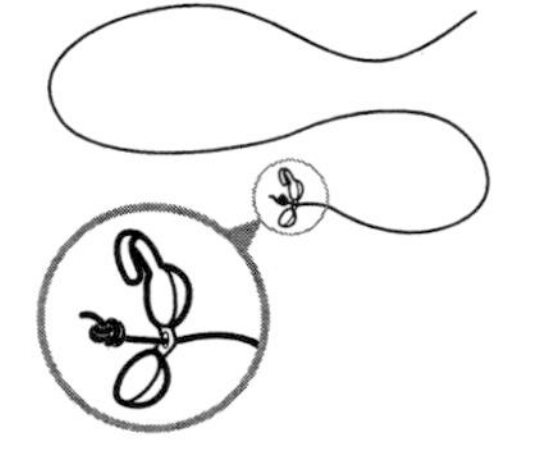

**Diagram 1**

**2** Close the bead tip cup, hiding the knot. Close the loop of the bead tip around the loop in an eyeglass holder, as shown in **Diagram 2.**

**Diagram 2**

**3** String **Pattern A** beads, as shown below, onto the wire seven times. Then string **Pattern A** beads onto the wire once more, omitting the last five beads.

**4** String on a bead tip, as shown in **Diagram 3.** Remove all but ⅛ inch of slack from the beaded wire. Tie an overhand knot in the wire, sliding the knot into the cup of the bead tip and using the tip of a pin or needle to work the knot along the wire. Trim off the excess wire.

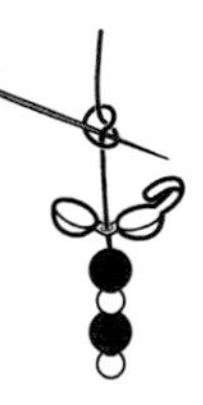

**Diagram 3**

**5** Repeat Step 2 to finish the eyeglass holder strand.

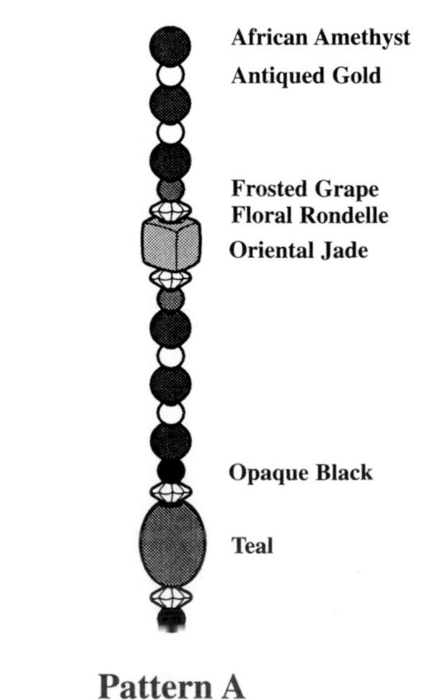


**Pattern A**

# FAMILY TREE SCHERENSCHNITTE

*German artisans call it* Scherenschnitte; *we call it fabulous! What grandparent wouldn't be thrilled to have a cut-paper wall piece to commemorate that new family member. We chose a cream parchment for the design to lend an heirloom look to the project. If you don't think your lettering is of professional caliber, simply trace the letters from our calligraphy alphabet.*

**Size:** 9¼ × 12½ inches

## MATERIALS

- ❄ Tracing paper
- ❄ #2H pencil
- ❄ 11 × 14-inch piece of parchment paper
- ❄ Graphite or transfer paper
- ❄ Stapler or paper clips
- ❄ Sharp embroidery or Scherenschnitte scissors, such as Mundial straight and curved blade embroidery scissors or Mundial 3½-inch Scherenschnitte scissors*
- ❄ Fine-blade craft knife
- ❄ Cutting board or heavy cardboard
- ❄ 2 sheets of lightweight paper
- ❄ Iron
- ❄ Repositionable spray adhesive
- ❄ 11 × 14-inch piece of colored paper
- ❄ Fine-line pen

**See the "Buyer's Guide" on page 176.*

## DIRECTIONS

**1** Enlarge the **Family Tree Half-Pattern** on the opposite page. Use the tracing paper and pencil to trace it, including the fold line.

**2** Carefully fold the piece of parchment paper in half lengthwise, matching the paper corners and taking care to make a crisp crease.

**3** Place the graphite or transfer paper, carbon side down, on the folded parchment. Layer the **Family Tree Half-Pattern** on top of the graphite paper, carefully matching the fold line of the design with the folded edge of the parchment paper. Staple or clip the pieces together, placing any staples in areas of the paper that will be cut away. Use the sharp pencil to trace along the pattern outlines to transfer the pattern to the parchment paper. Remove the staples or clips, the pattern, and the graphite paper.

**4** Staple or clip the folded parchment edges together outside the edges of the design.

**5** Always work with a sharp pair of scissors and a sharp blade in the craft knife. Beginning in the center of the design, cut along the design outlines, cutting through both layers of the parchment. Work on the cutting board with the craft knife to make the small inside cuts first. Use the scissors to work large outer areas. Leave the paper edge on the outside of the design for as long as possible so you have paper to grasp when cutting with the scissors. Take the time to plan the sequence of your cutting before you actually cut an area to avoid any mistakes. Do not cut past the pattern lines of the corners or the pattern joints may be weakened.

**6** After the design has been completely cut, unfold the parchment. Place the parchment between two sheets of lightweight paper and use a warm, dry iron to gently press out the crease.

**7** Spray adhesive over the wrong side of the cut design. Carefully center the design on the colored paper and finger press it in place, repositioning areas of the design if needed, until the design is flat and completely adhered.

**8** Trace the tree's apples onto tracing paper. Use the **Family Tree Alphabet** on this page to trace the family names within the apple outlines or hand letter the names in your own style. Place the carbon paper, carbon side down, on the cut tree design. Position the tracing with the family names on top of the carbon paper and trace with the pencil to transfer the lettered names to the tree. Neatly pen over the tracing lines of the names with the fine-line pen.

**9** Mount the Scherenschnitte design and frame as desired.

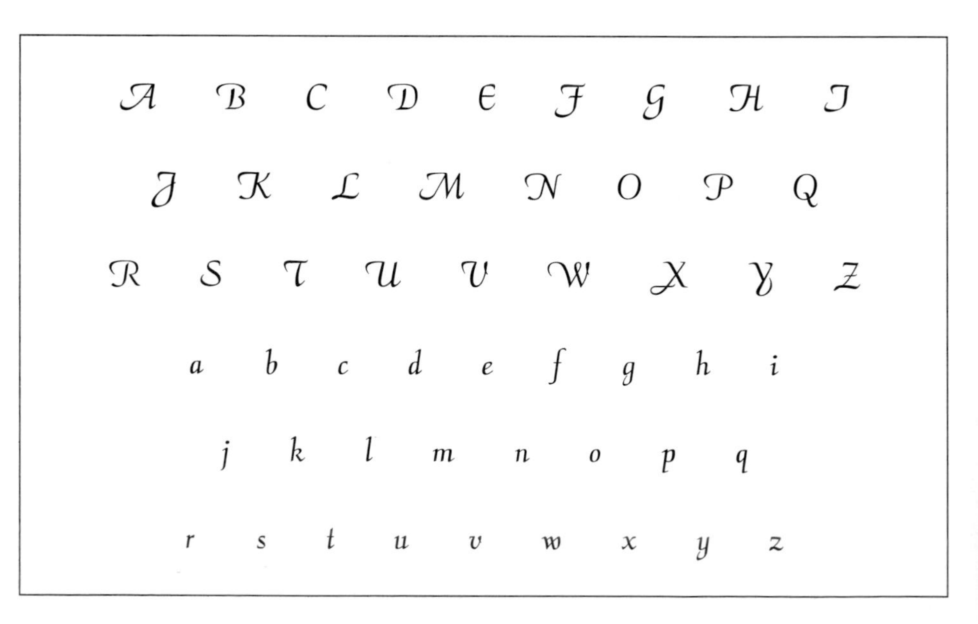


**Family Tree Alphabet**

**1 square = 1 inch**

**Enlarge 148%**

**Family Tree Half-Pattern**

# BROKEN CROCKERY TRIVET

*Transform broken bits of china and crockery into a charming trivet that is bound to delight your mom. Purchase inexpensive or dime-store china pieces in colors to match her kitchen decor. Be sure to collect and smash a few more pieces than you think you will need since it will take a large variety of sizes and shapes to fill the trivet space.*

**Size:** 7½ inches square

## MATERIALS

- ❄ Assorted crockery pieces
- ❄ Heavy plastic bag
- ❄ Small hammer
- ❄ Heavy rubber gloves and eye protection
- ❄ 7½-inch square of cardboard or heavy paper
- ❄ Spatula or putty knife
- ❄ Ceramic-tile adhesive
- ❄ 7½-inch square of ¾-inch plywood
- ❄ Craft saw
- ❄ 36-inch length of ¼ × 1⅛-inch wood trim
- ❄ Sandpaper
- ❄ Acrylic paint to match the crockery pieces
- ❄ Four 1½-inch wooden knobs
- ❄ Carpenter's glue
- ❄ Brads
- ❄ Tile grout
- ❄ Sponge
- ❄ Hot glue gun and glue sticks

## DIRECTIONS

1 Place the crockery pieces in the plastic bag and gently break them into smaller pieces with the hammer.

2 Wearing the gloves and eye protection, sort through the broken crockery pieces to select the desirable ones. Arrange these pieces in a mosaic pattern on the card-

board or the paper, moving them around until you have created the desired pattern. Be sure to leave enough gaps between the pieces for the grout.

3 Using the spatula or putty knife, apply a ¼-inch-thick layer of adhesive to the top of the plywood. One at a time, transfer the crockery pieces to the adhesive-coated surface, keeping the mosaic pattern as originally arranged. Press the pieces into the adhesive, keeping the top surfaces of the pieces as level as possible so that the trivet's surface will be as smooth as possible. Do not allow any of the pieces to extend beyond the plywood edges or the wood trim will not fit accurately. Allow the adhesive to dry overnight.

4 Using the craft saw, cut four 7¾-inch lengths of trim for the frame. Sand the ends of the lengths smooth. Apply three coats of paint to all the surfaces of each piece of trim, letting the paint dry thoroughly between each coat. Paint the wooden knobs in the same way.

5 Use the carpenter's glue and brads to attach the trim as a frame around the edges of the plywood square, as shown in the **Frame Diagram** at right. Attach the trim to the sides of the trivet so the upper edges of the trim are level with the surfaces of the crockery pieces.

6 Pour the grout over the trivet, filling in between the crockery pieces until the grout is level with the top of the trim edge. Let the grout dry for 15 minutes. Wipe off the excess with a damp sponge, leaving the surface of each crockery piece exposed. Use the sponge to remove any grout from the painted frame. Let the grout dry overnight.

7 Use the glue gun to attach a knob under each corner of the trivet for the legs.

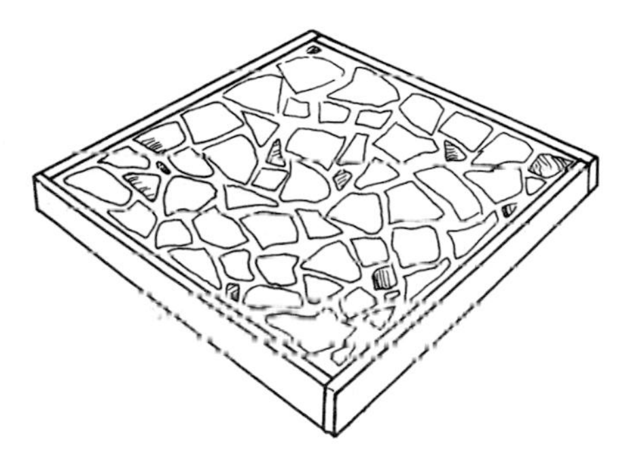

**Frame Diagram**

# BRAGGING RIGHTS SHIRTS

*What is a grandparent's favorite pastime? Talking about the grandchildren, of course! Wearing one of these conversation-opening shirts will give any proud Grandma or Grandpa the chance to brag. Do remember that if you use a colored shirt, the "white" areas of the photo will be the color of the shirt.*

## "Ask Me" Sweatshirt

**Size:** As desired

### Materials

- ❄ T-shirt or sweatshirt
- ❄ Selected photographs
- ❄ Black dimensional fabric writer
- ❄ Shirt-painting board
- ❄ Fine-pointed brush (optional)
- ❄ Clothes dryer

### Directions

1 Apply the photographs using either method in "Transferring Photos to Fabric" on this page.

2 Insert the shirt-painting board. Add the photograph "corner" effect with the fabric writer.

3 Using the fabric writer, paint the phrase "Ask me about my Grand Kids!" onto the shirt. Add different widths to the letters with a fine-pointed brush. Heat set the paint by turning the shirt wrong side out and drying it for ten minutes on a medium-heat setting in a dryer.

## "Hand Prints" Sweatshirt

**Size:** As desired

### Materials

- ❄ T-shirt or sweatshirt
- ❄ Selected photographs
- ❄ Pencil, tracing paper, and scissors
- ❄ Shirt-painting board
- ❄ Brightly colored fabric paints
- ❄ Saucers or palettes
- ❄ Paintbrushes
- ❄ Clothes dryer

### Directions

1 Apply the photographs using either of the methods described in "Transferring Photos to Fabric" on this page.

2 Using a pencil, trace around each of the children's hands. Cut out the tracings and arrange them on the shirt until you are pleased with the arrangement you have created.

3 Insert the shirt-painting board between the front and back of the sweatshirt.

4 Squirt each color of the fabric paint that you will be using to decorate onto a separate saucer or palette. With a brush, spread it into a fairly even layer; if the paint is uneven, you may have paint blobs on the shirt.

5 Working with one child at a time, lift one pattern piece of that child's hand from the shirt. Place the corresponding child's hand straight down into the paint, then lift it straight up. Press the hand straight down onto the shirt in the selected spot, pressing down fairly hard. Lift the hand straight up off the shirt.

6 Repeat for each child and the corresponding hand pattern, using the desired colors. Let the paint dry thoroughly.

7 Heat set the paint by turning the shirt wrong side out and drying for ten minutes on a medium-heat setting in a dryer.

## *Transferring Photos to Fabric*

❄

**The shirts shown in the photograph on the opposite page were done with the help of a copy shop that makes heat transfers from supplied art and applies them to shirts following your instructions. You will want to group several photographs on a single piece of paper and have them made into one transfer. This not only cuts costs but avoids accidents. Then cut the transfers apart and arrange them to your liking on your T-shirt or sweatshirt. Take everything back to the copy shop to get the arrangement fused to your shirt.**

❄

**You may also wish to use a photo-transfer medium to transfer photos to fabric. This product is similar to glue and works with photocopies. Follow the manufacturer's directions carefully when working with the product. Typically, you apply the medium to the front of the photocopy, then lay it face down on the shirt and smooth it in place, immediately clearing off any excess that oozes out. After it has dried, saturate the back of the photocopy with water and rub away the paper, leaving only the image behind. The wetting and rubbing should be repeated several times to remove the last vestiges of paper.**

# STRICTLY FOR THE BOOKS BOOKMARKS

*These luxurious bookmarks help to use up every scrap of expensive synthetic suede. The checkered bookmark uses neutral tones for a masculine look for Grandpa, but would be just as appealing in bright colors for a patchwork-quilt look for Grandma. The Navaho bookmark features the colors of the Southwest.*

## CHECKERED BOOKMARK

**Size:** 1½ × 7½ inches

### MATERIALS

- Pencil
- Ruler
- Ultrasuede synthetic suede: one 1½ × 7½-inch piece of black; one 2-inch square each of cream, taupe, and coffee*
- Scissors
- Fabric glue

**See the "Buyer's Guide" on page 176.*

### DIRECTIONS

**1** Use the pencil and ruler to mark 1½-inch-long lines at one end of the black piece of Ultrasuede, spacing the lines ⅛ inch apart; make all marks on the wrong side of the Ultrasuede pieces. Cut along the marked lines for the fringe.

**2** Use the pencil and ruler to mark a grid of ⅜-inch squares on each of the remaining Ultrasuede pieces. Cut 10 squares each from the cream and coffee pieces and 12 squares from the taupe piece.

**3** Glue the ⅜-inch squares on the front of the bookmark in a diagonal check pattern, as shown in the **Placement Diagram,** beginning with the upper cream squares.

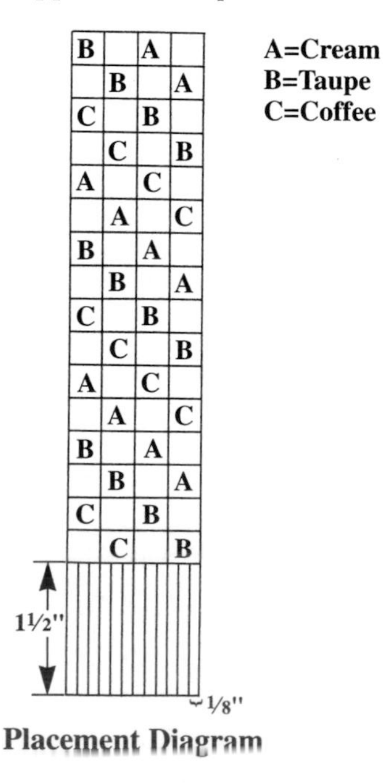


**Placement Diagram**

# Navajo Bookmark

**Size:** 2½ × 9¼ inches

## Materials

- ❄ Pencil
- ❄ Dressmaker's tracing paper
- ❄ Ultrasuede synthetic suede: one 10 × 6-inch piece of cream, one 2½ × 9-inch piece of coffee, one 2½ × 8-inch piece of taupe, and one 1 × 7-inch piece of turquoise*
- ❄ Tracing wheel
- ❄ Scissors and pinking shears
- ❄ Water-soluble marking pen
- ❄ Ruler
- ❄ Fabric glue

*See the "Buyer's Guide" on page 176.

## Directions

**1** Trace the **Navajo Bookmark Patterns** on this page onto the tracing paper, outlining the shape for each color area as a separate pattern. You will have one each of the A, B, and C patterns, and three each of the D, E, and F patterns.

**2** Mark the pattern shapes on the wrong sides of the Ultrasuede pieces as follows: Begin by placing the dressmaker's tracing paper on the wrong side of the fabric, marking side down. Position the pattern shape on top of the dressmaker's tracing paper. Roll the tracing wheel along the outlines of the pattern to mark the shape onto the fabric.

**3** Cut out all the pieces, using the pinking shears to cut out the A piece and the three D pieces to create a decorative edge.

**4** Use the marking pen and ruler to mark 1½-inch-long lines at the bottom end of the A piece, spacing the lines ⅛ inch apart. Mark on the wrong side of the fabric. Cut along the marked lines for the fringe.

**5** Glue the fabric pieces together, layering them as follows: Begin with the B piece centered on the fringed A piece. Referring to the **Navajo Bookmark Patterns** for placement, continue to glue each fabric piece in alphabetical order onto the bookmark, ending with the D diamonds, the E diamonds, and the F squares set on point.

## Synthetic Suede Savvy

❄

**If you don't have synthetic suede leftovers available from your other projects, look for bags of scraps in fabric stores that carry high-fashion fabrics.**

❄

**Synthetic suede is also sold by the "square." See the "Buyer's Guide" on page 176 for a mail-order source.**

❄

**The glue you choose for your bookmarks is very important. Be sure to use fabric glue as recommended because most craft glues will cause the synthetic suede to stiffen.**

**To remove wrinkles and creases from synthetic suede, press the wrong side of the fabric using a press cloth and an iron on the synthetic setting.**

**Navajo Bookmark Patterns**

*Chapter Three*

# Supersaver Gifts

*Everyone's Christmas list includes people to remember with "just a little something." Here are penny-wise gifts that cost just a few dollars to craft, time-wise gifts that can be finished in an hour or less, and eco-wise gifts that are kind to the environment. You'll also find that many of these gifts can be easily made in multiples for your favorite fund-raising event or charity. And most are simple enough for children to make.*

# DRESS-FORM CHATELAINE

*Any seamstress or quilt enthusiast on your gift list will be delighted to put this mini-mannequin to work. Designed to keep sewing aids at hand, this replica of a dressmaker's form holds pins, scissors, and a tape measure. The recipient can set it on the arm of her chair or close to her sewing machine to keep those easily misplaced small tools nearby.*

**Size:** About 6 inches tall

## Materials

- ❄ Pencil
- ❄ Tracing paper
- ❄ Scissors
- ❄ 8 × 10-inch piece of print fabric
- ❄ Sewing machine
- ❄ Thread
- ❄ Polyester fiberfill
- ❄ Piece of cardboard
- ❄ Hand-sewing needle
- ❄ Thick white craft glue
- ❄ ⅛ yard of white crinkled ribbon
- ❄ Long straight pin
- ❄ Assorted color and size beads to make the finial, such as a small round bead, a small flat bead, an oval bead, a medium flat bead, and a large flat bead
- ❄ Miniature tape measure or printed tape measure shoelace
- ❄ Small sewing scissors

## Directions

1 Trace the dress-form patterns onto the tracing paper. Cut out the pattern pieces. From the print fabric, cut out the front and back dress-forms. Mark the base pattern on the wrong side of the fabric. Add a ½-inch seam allowance to the outer edge and cut out the base piece.

2 Sew the darts in the front and back dress-form pieces. Using a ¼-inch seam allowance, sew the front and back pieces together, leaving the bottom edge of the form open and easing in any fullness along the bust dart. Turn right side out and stuff firmly with the fiberfill. Turn under ½ inch along the open bottom edge.

3 Cut a base piece from the cardboard. Baste around the fabric base piece, ½ inch from the edge. Place the cardboard piece, centered, on the wrong side of the fabric base piece. Pull the basting thread to gather the fabric edges around the cardboard base.

4 Slip stitch the fabric base to the bottom opening of the dress-form, adding more stuffing if needed.

5 Glue the white ribbon around the neck of the dress-form. On the long straight pin, place a small round bead, a small flat bead, an oval bead, a medium flat bead, then a large flat bead, as shown in the photograph on the opposite page. Push the beaded pin into the top of the dress-form, gluing it in place. Tack the tape measure or shoelace around the waist of the dress-form. Thread the other end of the tape measure through one handle of the small scissors, fold the tape measure over, and tack in place.

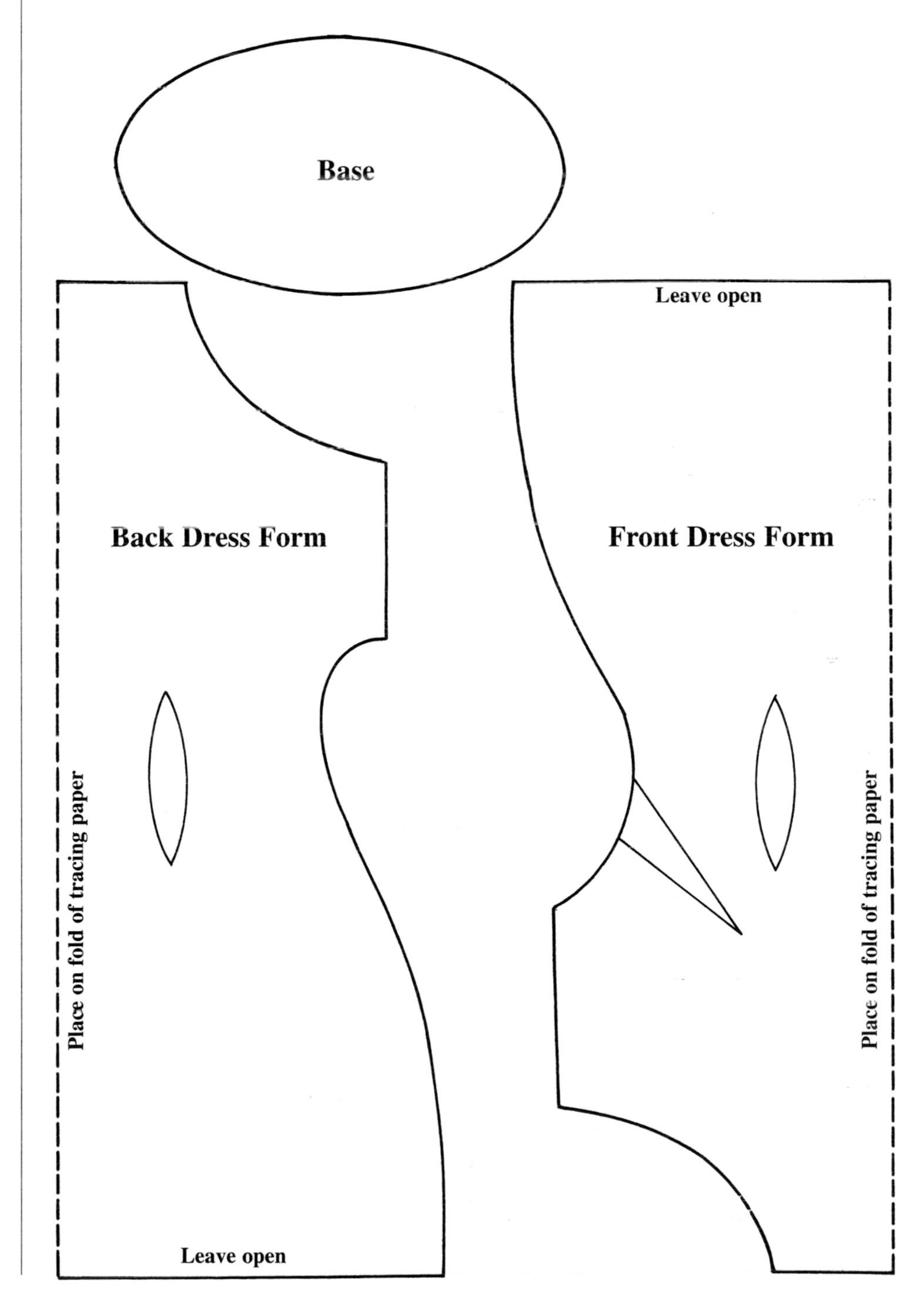

# TWINKLING TOES SOCKS

*Simple cotton socks are the palette for these creative concoctions. Use tiny bits and pieces of trim left from bigger projects and add bright new ribbons, laces, buttons, and charms to duplicate the snappy socks shown here. Or just use these as inspiration for your own creations. Since socks stretch, you need only a general idea of size to assure a perfect gift.*

## RED SOCKS

**Size:** As desired

### MATERIALS

- ❄ Scissors
- ❄ 16-inch length of ⅞-inch-wide black-and-white grosgrain ribbon
- ❄ Gold embroidery floss
- ❄ Large-eyed embroidery needle
- ❄ Pair of red socks
- ❄ Four ½-inch, red, star-shaped two-hole buttons

### DIRECTIONS

1 Cut the ribbon into four 4-inch lengths. Fold each into a loop, overlapping the ends ¼ inch. Pinch each together in the center to form a bow. Using six strands of floss, tack the loops in place.

2 Referring to the photograph on the opposite page, sew two bows to the outside of each sock cuff. Use the embroidery floss to sew a button in the center of each bow.

## GOLD SOCKS

**Size:** As desired

### MATERIALS

- ❄ Air-soluble marking pen
- ❄ Pair of gold socks
- ❄ Gold embroidery floss
- ❄ Large-eyed embroidery needle
- ❄ 32 assorted metallic gold charms

### DIRECTIONS

1 Use the pen to mark 16 evenly spaced dots around the cuff edge.

2 Use the embroidery floss to sew a charm at each mark. Refer to the photograph on the opposite page.

## PURPLE SOCKS

**Size:** As desired

### MATERIALS

- ❄ Scissors
- ❄ 1 yard of ¾-inch-wide ruffled multicolored lace
- ❄ Purple and red sewing thread
- ❄ Hand-sewing needle
- ❄ Pair of purple socks
- ❄ Pink embroidery floss
- ❄ Large-eyed embroidery needle
- ❄ Heart-shaped buttons: six ⅜-inch light purple and four ¾-inch dark purple with two holes, and eight ¼-inch red shank

### DIRECTIONS

1 Cut the lace in half. Using purple thread, sew a row of lace around the edge of each sock cuff, stretching the cuff as you sew and overlapping the raw ends. Sew a second row of lace above the first row.

2 Use the embroidery floss to sew three light purple and two dark purple buttons to the outside of each sock cuff. Referring to the photograph on the opposite page, use the red sewing thread to sew four red buttons to each cuff.

## CREAM SOCKS

**Size:** As desired

### MATERIALS

- ❄ Scissors
- ❄ Sewing machine
- ❄ Cream sewing thread
- ❄ 20-inch length of ½-inch-wide white lace
- ❄ Pair of cream socks
- ❄ Shank buttons: twelve ¼- to ⅜-inch half-round pearl, and six assorted size pearl and gold

### DIRECTIONS

1 Use a small machine zigzag stitch to sew 10 inches of lace to the lower edge of each sock cuff, stretching the cuff as you sew.

2 Sew six pearl buttons and three of the assorted buttons randomly to the outside of each cuff, as shown in the photograph on the opposite page.

## BLUE SOCKS

**Size:** As desired

### MATERIALS

- ❄ Scissors
- ❄ 22-inch length of red grosgrain ribbon with white dots
- ❄ Sewing thread
- ❄ Hand-sewing needle
- ❄ Pair of blue socks
- ❄ Gold, star-shaped shank buttons: two ⅝-inch and two $^{11}/_{16}$-inch

### DIRECTIONS

1 Cut the grosgrain ribbon into four 5½-inch lengths.

2 Run a gathering thread along one long edge of each ribbon length, pulling the thread to gather the ribbon into a rosette and overlapping the ends. Turn under about ⅛ inch on the top ribbon end. Knot the thread to secure the gathers.

3 Sew two ribbon rosettes to the outside of each sock cuff, as shown in the photograph on the opposite page. Sew a button in the center of each rosette, using one large button and one small button on each cuff.

# FAIRYLAND FINGER PUPPETS

*Give the gift of imagination. This cast of characters is definitely in need of a playwright to bring them to life. Children will have hours of fun spinning yarns and acting out dramatic plays with these simple heroes or heroines. The puppets are cut from craft foam and are so easy you may be inspired to branch out with some variations all your own.*

**Size:** Each about 4 inches tall

## MATERIALS

- Pencil
- Tracing paper
- Scissors and pinking shears
- Fine-point, permanent marking pen
- 1 sheet each of craft foam, such as from Westrim Crafts, in light and dark pink, bright and lime green, white, black, gray, red, and yellow*
- Craft knife
- Thick white craft glue
- Toothpicks
- Paper punch in ¼-inch and ⅛-inch sizes
- Pointed artist's brush
- Acrylic paints in white, black, red, and light pink
- 2 yards of yellow yarn

**See the "Buyer's Guide" on page 176.*

## DIRECTIONS

### BASIC DIRECTIONS FOR ALL THE PUPPETS

**1** Use the tracing paper to trace each piece of the finger puppet patterns, including a puppet base, on the opposite page and page 84. Make a pattern piece for each colored section of the puppet, extending the piece if needed where a shape might overlap. A separate pattern is provided for the fairy's dress. The dashed lines on the patterns indicate where pieces overlap. The smaller circles, such as the eyes and cheeks, will be cut out with the paper punches, so a pattern piece is not necessary. Other pattern details will be painted. No pattern is needed for the fairy's hair; it will be braided from yarn. Cut out the individual pattern pieces.

**2** Use the fine-point permanent marking pen to outline each pattern piece on the wrong side of the craft foam. Refer to the photograph on this page or the specific assembly instructions for the color of each piece.

**3** Cut out each foam piece using the scissors for smooth edges, and the pinking shears for zigzag edges, such as the fairy and frog crowns and the fairy apron. Use the craft knife to cut the finger slit in the puppet base.

4 Apply a thin coat of the craft glue to the wrong side of each foam shape and glue it to the puppet base. Begin with the largest shapes, adding the smaller details on top. Do not glue any part of the shapes below the finger slit. Use toothpicks to get the glue into the corners and onto any other tiny spaces, such as the eyes.

## Individual Directions for Each Puppet

1 *To make the frog:* Glue the white tummy in place on the bright green base. Glue the green arms on either side of the tummy. Then glue the yellow crown at the center top of the base, and glue the white eyes onto either side of the crown. Punch out ¼-inch pupils from the black foam and glue them onto the center of the white eyes. Paint the frog's smile with black acrylic paint.

2 *To make the mouse:* Glue the large gray ears to the top of the gray base. Glue the smaller, light pink ears centered on the lower edge of the gray ears. Then glue the white tummy and the gray tail in place, just above the finger slit. Punch out a ¼-inch nose from the light pink foam and glue it, along with the four white whiskers, above the tummy of the mouse. Paint the eyes with black acrylic paint.

3 *To make the flower:* Glue two bright green leaves on the lime green base, just above the finger slit. Glue the white flower petals at the top of the base. Glue the yellow flower center in the middle of the white petals. Punch out two ¼-inch, light pink cheeks and glue them on the yellow face. Paint the eyes with black acrylic paint and the smiling mouth with pink acrylic paint.

4 *To make the ladybug:* Glue the large red wings in place on the red base, leaving the wings free below the finger slit. Glue the black wing dots onto the wings. Glue the black face and antennae above the wings. Glue the small white wings on either side of the large red wings. Punch out two ¼-inch, light pink cheeks and glue them on the face. Paint the eyes and smile with white acrylic paint.

5 *To make the fairy:* Glue the dark pink dress to the light pink base, leaving the dress free below the finger slit. Punch out ⅛-inch holes along the bottom edge of the white apron, then glue the apron on the dress. Glue the white wings on either side of the dress. Glue the light pink face above the dress neck. Glue the lime green antennae above the head. Punch out two ¼-inch, dark pink cheeks and glue them on the face. Cut six 12-inch lengths of yarn for the hair. Knot the strands together about ½ inch from one end. Divide the strands into three groups of two strands each. Braid these strands for 3 inches, and knot them together again at the other end. Trim the ends even and glue the center of the braid around the top and sides of the face. Glue the yellow crown on top of the hair braid. Paint the eyes with black acrylic paint and the smile with red acrylic paint.

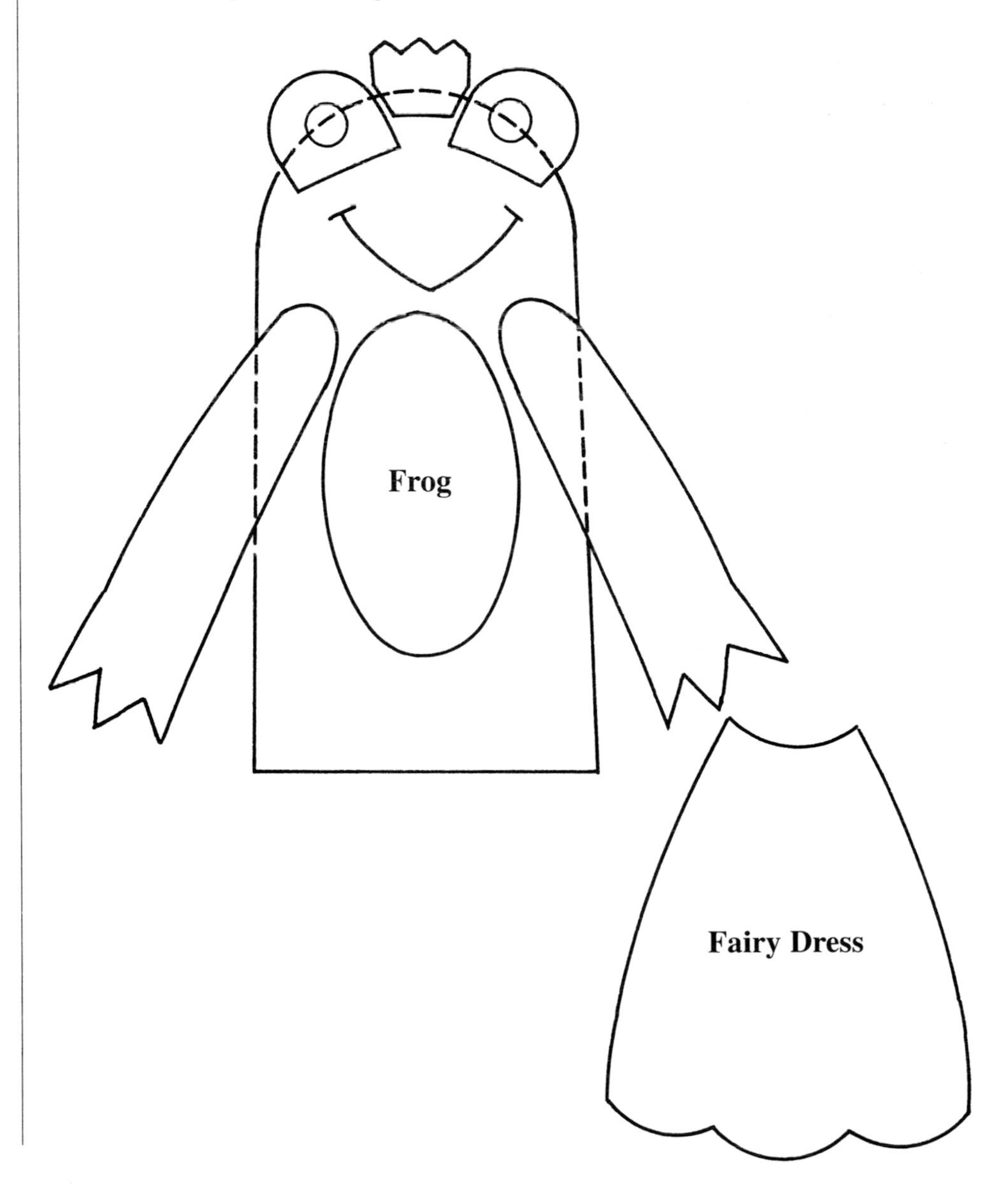

Puppet Base
Fairy
Flower

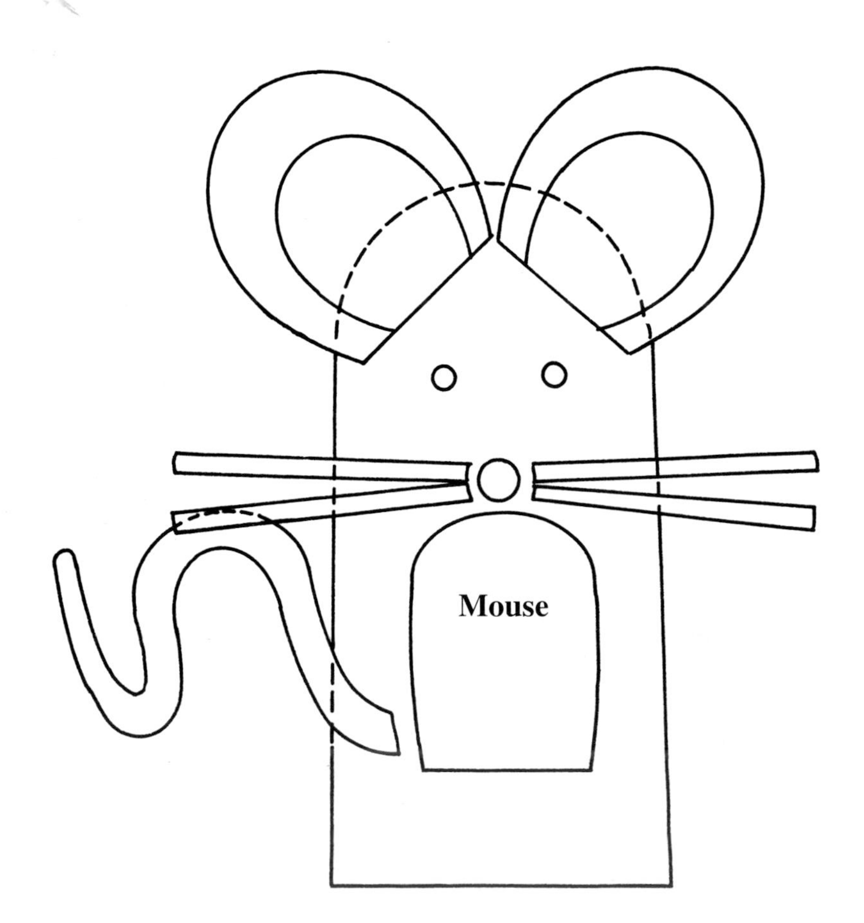
Mouse

Ladybug

# KITCHEN CUTTING WREATH

*Whether grown in your own garden or purchased in your local farmer's market, herbs are widely available to suit every taste. Broad-leaved basil in green or purple, silvery sage, tangy tarragon, rosemary, and rue can all be blended together in a gourmet treat of a wreath to season cooking all year long. The greater the variety of leaf types and shades of green, the more interesting the wreath to the recipient.*

**Size:** As desired

## Materials

- Small rubber bands
- Several large bunches of desired fresh herbs without roots
- Wire hanger or wreath form
- Wire cutters
- Thin floral wire

## Directions

1 Using the rubber bands, gather the herbs into small bunches about 5 inches long and about ¾ inch thick at the base of the stems.

2 If you use a wire hanger, pull it into a circular shape and cut off the hook. Using the floral wire, attach the herb bunches to the hanger or wreath form, and overlap the ends of the bunches to cover the wire and the rubber bands. Alternate the different types and colors of herbs to create a pleasing wreath arrangement.

3 If you plan to give away the dried wreath, turn the wreath a quarter turn every few days until the herbs are dried. If you intend to give away a fresh wreath, craft the wreath no more than two days in advance and mist it with water about every four hours.

# CHEERY CHERRIES CROSS-STITCH TOWEL

*Fresh and crisp, the blue-and-white background sets off luscious red fruit, giving this cross-stitched towel a summertime look. You might want to adapt the simple motif to decorate other kitchen gifts, including pot holders, oven mitts, and aprons.*

**Size:** 3 × 13½-inch cross-stitch area

## Materials

- Contrast basting thread and hand-sewing needle
- Towel with a 14-count stitching area of 42 × 190 stitches, such as CharlesCraft KitchenMates terry towel*
- 1 skein of embroidery floss for each color in the **Color Key**
- Size 22 or 24 tapestry needle
- Embroidery scissors

**See the "Buyer's Guide" on page 176.*

## Directions

1 Use the basting thread to hand sew a line of running stitches to mark the horizontal center of the cross-stitch area of the towel. Use this line for reference when positioning the embroidery.

2 Follow the **Cheery Cherries Cross-Stitch Towel Chart** on the opposite page to cross-stitch the design on the towel. Using the tapestry needle and referring to the **Cross-Stitch Diagram** on the opposite page, use two strands of the six-strand floss to work the cross-stitches and backstitches. Work the cross-stitches first, working the rows of medium royal blue cross-stitches in vertical columns for the neatest effect. Take care to cross all the cross-stitches in the same direction. Once the cross-stitching is completed, use two strands of medium Christmas red for the backstitches.

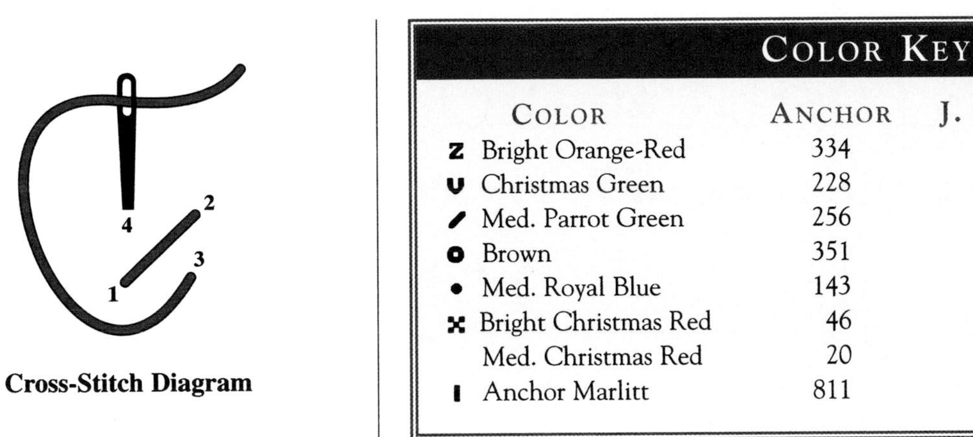


**Cross-Stitch Diagram**

## COLOR KEY

| | COLOR | ANCHOR | J. & P. COATS | DMC |
|---|---|---|---|---|
| Z | Bright Orange-Red | 334 | 2334 | 606 |
| U | Christmas Green | 228 | 6227 | 700 |
| / | Med. Parrot Green | 256 | 6256 | 906 |
| O | Brown | 351 | 5349 | 400 |
| • | Med. Royal Blue | 143 | 7020 | 800 |
| X | Bright Christmas Red | 46 | 3046 | 666 |
| | Med. Christmas Red | 20 | 3072 | 816 |
| I | Anchor Marlitt | 811 | — | — |

Repeat this section two more times

NOTE: Work the chart from left to right. Repeat the section within the marked arrows two more times. Then work the side border in reverse to complete.

**Cheery Cherries Cross-Stitch Towel Chart**

# DECORATOR PICTURE FRAMES

*Frames make thoughtful gifts, especially when they create a personal environment chosen with a particular photo in mind. Purchase inexpensive wooden frames or recycle ones on hand to create fresh and unusual surroundings for that special image.*

## Fabric Frame

**Size:** Fits an 8 × 10-inch photograph

### Materials

- ❄ Frame to fit an 8 × 10-inch photograph, with 1-inch-wide molding
- ❄ ¼-inch-wide paintbrush
- ❄ Acrylic sealer, such as Plaid Enterprises Royal Coat*
- ❄ 12 × 14-inch piece of fabric
- ❄ Craft knife
- ❄ Scissors
- ❄ Thick white craft glue
- ❄ 1¼ yards of 4mm pearls by the yard
- ❄ 12 large ribbon roses

*See the "Buyer's Guide" on page 176.

### Directions

1 If the frame has a glass insert, remove it before proceeding. Use the paintbrush to apply a thick coat of the sealer to the frame.

2 Before the sealer dries completely, center the fabric piece, with the right side up, on the frame and gently press the fabric into the sealer to hold it in place. Apply a coat of sealer to the surface of the fabric, then use the paintbrush to press the fabric into the molding. Referring to **Diagram 1**, cut an X in the center of the fabric piece with the craft knife, cutting exactly to the inner corners of the frame.

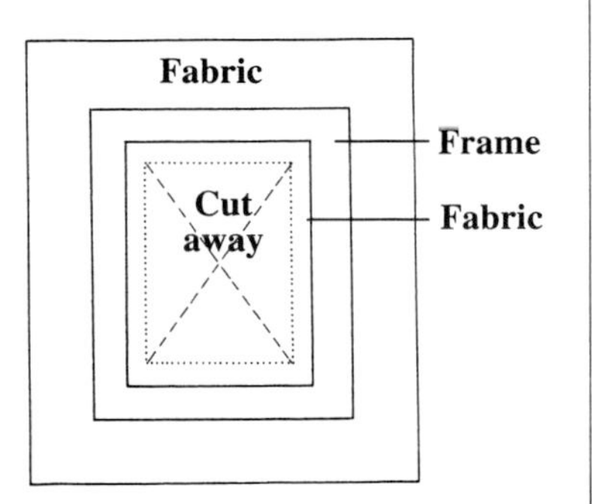


**Diagram 1**

3 Using the dotted line shown on **Diagram 1** as your guide, trim away the excess center of the fabric with the scissors. Press the remaining fabric around the inner and outer edges of the frame, folding the fabric in at the outer corners for a smooth finish, as shown in **Diagram 2.** Allow the acrylic sealer to dry thoroughly.

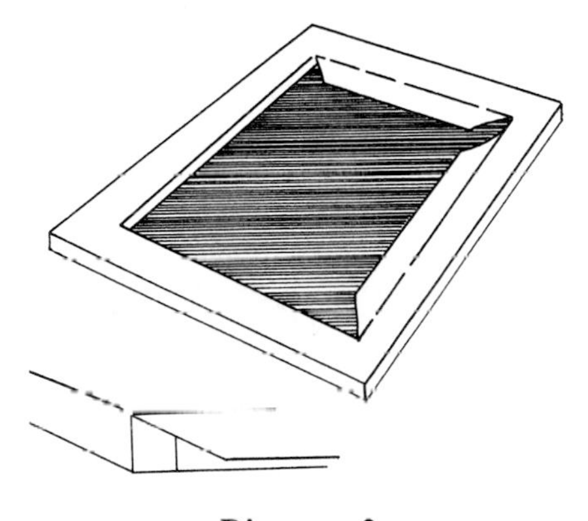

**Diagram 2**

4 Glue the unbroken strand of pearls along the center of the molding. Glue three ribbon roses in each corner.

## Silk Flower Frame

**Size:** Fits an 8 × 10-inch photograph

### Materials

- ❄ Frame to fit an 8 × 10-inch photograph, with 1½-inch-wide molding
- ❄ Sandpaper
- ❄ Paintbrush
- ❄ Vanilla-colored acrylic paint
- ❄ Silk flower stems: 1 with 3 large blossoms and leaves, and 1 with small blossoms and leaves
- ❄ Hot glue gun and glue sticks
- ❄ Six 4mm gold-tone round beads, such as The Beadery round beads*

*See the "Buyer's Guide" on page 176.

### Directions

1 If the frame has a glass insert, remove it before proceeding.

2 Sand the frame, if necessary, so the paint will adhere better. Paint the frame, using as many coats as needed to cover the existing finish and letting the paint dry thoroughly between coats.

3 Separate both the flowers and leaves from the floral stems. Glue two or three large leaves, slightly overlapping the ends, to either side of the center along the top and bottom edges of the frame. Glue two large blossoms to the center of the top edge. Glue one blossom to the center of the bottom edge. Then glue two smaller leaves beside each blossom.

4 Remove the centers from the smaller blossoms and glue a round bead in the center of each blossom. Glue a single blossom on either side of the top blossoms. Glue two single blossoms on either side of the bottom blossom.

# Twig Frame

**Size:** Fits an 5 × 7-inch photograph

## Materials

- ❄ Frame to fit a 5 × 7-inch photograph, with 1½-inch-wide molding
- ❄ Sandpaper
- ❄ Paintbrush
- ❄ Acrylic paint in a color to match the twigs
- ❄ Hot glue gun and glue sticks
- ❄ Assorted twigs (as straight as possible)
- ❄ Clear matte acrylic sealer

## Directions

1 If the frame has a glass insert, remove it before proceeding.

2 Lightly sand the frame, if necessary, so the paint will adhere better. Paint the frame with a coat of the twig-colored paint. Let the paint dry thoroughly.

3 Glue the twigs to the frame, beginning at the outer side edges. Alternate from the sides to the top and bottom, working toward the inner edges of the molding to completely cover the frame. Break or cut the twigs to get lengths as straight as possible. Use two or three pieces along one side of the molding. Use smaller twigs to fill in any remaining openings.

4 Following the manufacturer's directions, apply a coat of the matte sealer over the frame.

# "BROWN BAG IT" PAPER JEWELRY

*Examine this wonderful gift jewelry and consider its humble beginnings—brown paper bags and torn scraps of magazine photos! The simple shapes are easy to duplicate, and we bet it will be one of your easiest craft projects this holiday season. We added metallic beads on each piece for a glittering contrast.*

## MATERIALS

For all the bracelets:
- ❄ Ruler
- ❄ Scissors
- ❄ Disposable gloves
- ❄ Foam brush
- ❄ Plaid Enterprise's Mod Podge glue-type finishing sealer*
- ❄ Large sewing needle
- ❄ Needle-nose and flat-nose pliers
- ❄ Wire cutters

*See the "Buyer's Guide" on page 176.

# PLEATED-PAPER BRACELET

**Size:** As desired

## MATERIALS

- ❄ Brown Kraft paper or grocery bag
- ❄ Round toothpicks
- ❄ ½ yard of tiger tail plastic-coated twisted wire
- ❄ 2 crimp beads
- ❄ 1 barrel clasp
- ❄ Twenty-two 8mm faceted beads, such as The Beadery No. 700*
- ❄ Ten 8mm corrugated disc beads, such as The Beadery No. 856*

*See the "Buyer's Guide" on page 176.

## DIRECTIONS

1 To make the paper-tube beads, cut six ½ × 6-inch pieces of Kraft paper. While wearing disposable gloves, brush a thin coat of sealer on both sides of each piece of paper. Begin at one narrow end and wrap each paper piece around a toothpick, forming a tight tube, as shown in **Diagram 1.**

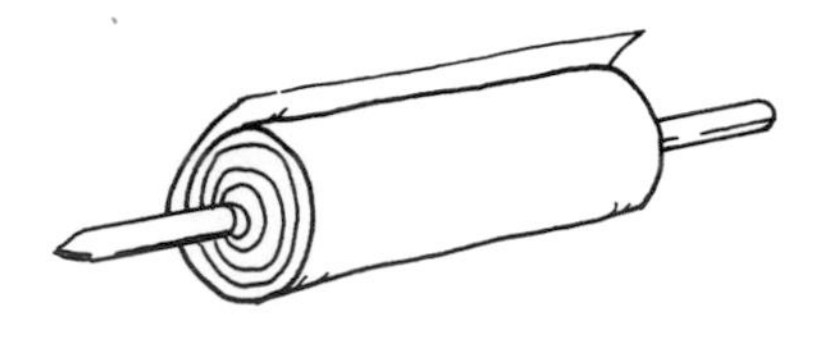

**Diagram 1**

2 Hold each paper end in place until the sealer sets. When each bead is dry to the touch on the surface but not yet hard, gently twist the toothpick to remove it from the bead. Use the center hole of each bead for stringing. Apply a second coat of sealer to the outer surface. Let it dry thoroughly. Repeat to make six small paper-tube beads.

3 To make the pleated-paper beads, cut five ½ × 6-inch pieces of Kraft paper. To crease the paper for pleating, fold each piece in half crosswise. Fold each half twice more, creasing each fold sharply so the piece is finally folded into eight sections, as shown in **Diagram 2.**

**Diagram 2**

4 Open out the paper strip and coat both sides of each paper with the sealer, making sure to wear disposable gloves. Refold each strip into the accordion shape. Hold the folded paper together until the sealer sets and keeps it together in the center. Use the large needle to punch a hole through the center of the pleats for stringing. Apply a second coat of the sealer to the outer surface. Let it dry thoroughly. Repeat this step to make five pleated-paper beads.

5 Using the large needle, string the tiger tail through one crimp bead, through the loop on one side of the clasp, and back through the crimp bead, as shown in **Diagram 3.** Flatten the crimp bead with the needle-nose pliers to fasten the clasp on the wire.

**Diagram 3**

6 Thread a faceted bead on the tiger tail. Refer to **Diagram 4** to string the next bead sequence. Referring to the photograph on page 91, continue to string this sequence for the remaining beads; end with a faceted bead.

**Diagram 4**

7 Fasten the other side of the clasp and the second crimp bead in the same way as in Step 5. Trim the excess tiger tail.

## Tube-Bead Bracelet

**Size:** As desired

### Materials

- ❄ Brown Kraft paper or grocery bag
- ❄ Round toothpicks
- ❄ ½ yard of tiger tail plastic-coated twisted wire
- ❄ 2 crimp beads
- ❄ 1 barrel clasp
- ❄ Ten 10mm disc beads, such as The Beadery No. 854*
- ❄ Five 10mm fluted antiqued beads, such as The Beadery No. 963*
- ❄ Four 8mm round beads, such as The Beadery No. 715*
- ❄ Eight 8mm corrugated disc beads, such as The Beadery No. 856*

**See the "Buyer's Guide" on page 176.*

### Directions

1 To make the paper-tube beads, cut six ½ × 6-inch pieces of Kraft paper. While wearing disposable gloves, brush a thin coat of sealer on both sides of each piece of paper. Begin at one narrow end and wrap each paper piece around a toothpick, forming a tight tube, as shown in **Diagram 1** of "Pleated-Paper Bracelet" on the opposite page.

2 Hold each paper end in place until the sealer sets. When each bead is dry to the touch on the surface but not yet hard, gently twist the toothpick to remove it from the bead. Use the center hole of each bead for stringing. Apply a second coat of sealer to the outer surface. Let it dry thoroughly. Repeat to make six small paper-tube beads.

3 Using the large needle, string the tiger tail through one crimp bead, through the loop on one side of the clasp, and back through the crimp bead, as shown in **Diagram 3** of "Pleated-Paper Bracelet." Flatten the crimp bead with the needle-nose pliers to fasten the clasp on the wire.

4 Using the pliers and referring to the **Stringing Diagram** for the bead sequence, use the large needle to string the beads on the tiger tail. End with a disc, fluted beads, and a disc.

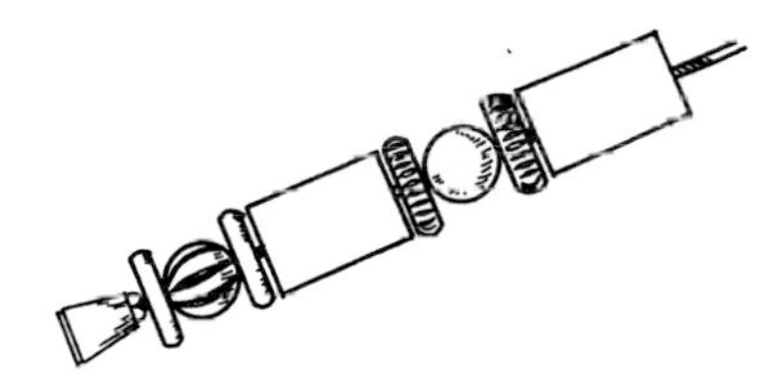

**Stringing Diagram**

5 Fasten the other side of the clasp and the second crimp bead in the same way as at the beginning. Trim the excess tiger tail.

## Colored-Paper Bracelet

**Size:** As desired

### Materials

- ❄ Glossy color pages from magazines or colored origami paper
- ❄ Nine ½-inch-diameter wooden beads
- ❄ Wooden skewers
- ❄ Wire rack
- ❄ Black elastic cord
- ❄ 9 silver pony beads

### Directions

1 Tear the colored paper into small pieces.

2 While wearing disposable gloves and holding the bead on a wooden skewer, brush a thin coat of sealer over the surface of the wooden bead. Press the torn paper pieces onto the surface of the bead, working from the center out to the edges. Use your fingers to smooth the paper around the curves and to eliminate any bubbles. Add layers of paper pieces, overlapping the edges and brushing on a coat of sealer before applying each additional paper layer. Let the bead dry thoroughly between layers. Repeat this process using the remaining wooden beads.

3 Apply a final coat of sealer to the entire outer surface of the beads. Replace the skewers with clean ones. Let the beads dry thoroughly on the wire rack.

4 Estimate the recipient's wrist measurement, then double it and add 1 inch. Cut a length of elastic cord to that measurement and thread it through the needle. Fold the cord in half and string the beads, alternating the colored-paper beads with the pony beads.

5 Tie the ends of the elastic cord into a tight knot. Trim the cord ends and push the knot into one of the beads so the ends are not showing.

# FABRIC LUNCH BAGS

*Use an easy technique to apply a plastic coating to transform any piece of fabric into a long-lasting lunch bag. Choose fabric suitable for each person on your list. Children may enjoy painting a personal panel to decorate special gifts for their friends.*

# Vegetable Lunch Bag

**Size:** 3½ × 6 × 11 inches

## Materials

- Iron
- Two 11 × 14-inch pieces of iron-on flexible vinyl, such as Heat n Bond*
- Two 12 × 15-inch pieces of fabric
- Scissors and pinking shears
- Matching sewing thread
- Sewing machine
- Air-soluble marking pen
- 1-inch piece of Velcro

*See the "Buyer's Guide" on page 176.

## Directions

1 Following the manufacturer's directions, fuse each iron-on vinyl piece to the right side of each fabric piece. Trim each piece to 10½ × 13 inches.

2 With right sides facing, use a ½-inch seam allowance to sew the two pieces together along the long sides and narrow bottom, as shown in **Diagram 1.**

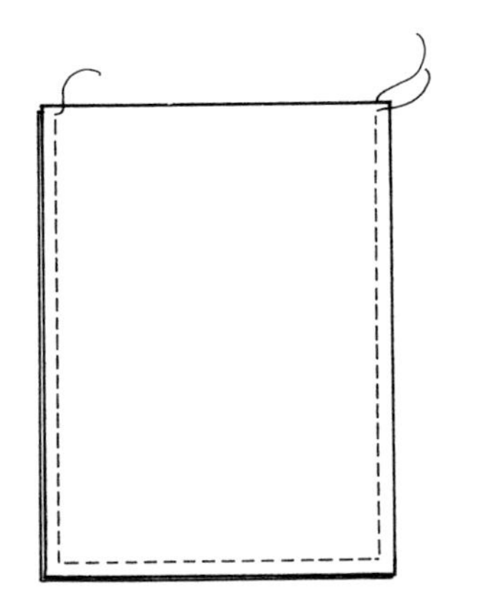

**Diagram 1**

3 Pull a lower corner of the bag out and flatten it to form a point. Using the marking pen, mark a seam 2¼ inches from the point; sew across the marked seam to form the corner, as shown in **Diagram 2.** Repeat to form a corner on the opposite side. Trim off each point about ½ inch from the stitching line.

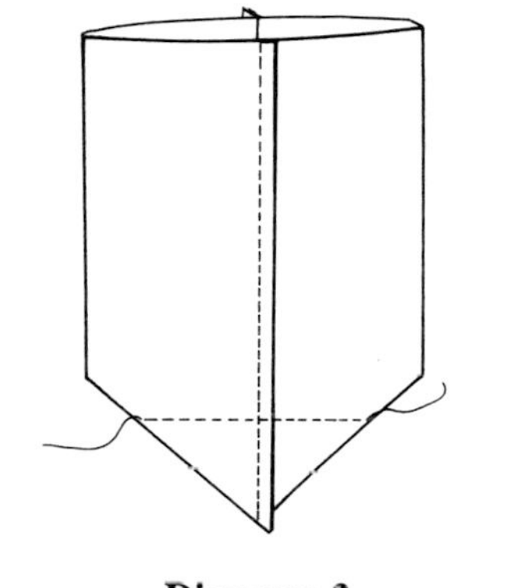

**Diagram 2**

4 Use the pinking shears to cut ½ inch off the top edge of the lunch bag for a decorative finish.

5 Fold the bag 1½ inches from the side seam, and sew a narrow and long ⅛ × 2½-inch dart at the fold, as shown in **Diagram 3.** Repeat on the opposite side of the same seam. Then repeat on the other side of the bag. Turn the bag right side out.

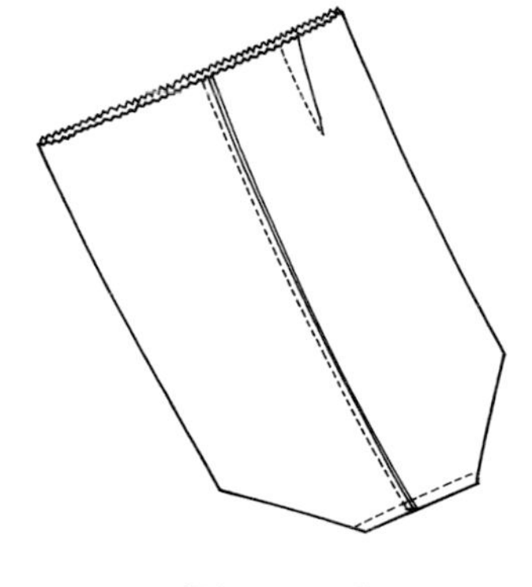

**Diagram 3**

6 Attach the hook (rough) side of the Velcro to the front of the bag, centered 3 inches from the top edge. Attach the loop (fuzzy) side of the Velcro to the back of the bag, centered ¼ inch from the top edge.

# Child's Lunch Bag

**Size:** 3½ × 6 × 11 inches

## Materials

- Iron
- 5 × 6-inch piece of paper-backed fusible web
- 5 × 6-inch piece of muslin
- Scissors and pinking shears
- Acrylic fabric paints in assorted colors
- Small amount of embroidery floss and an embroidery needle
- Two 12 × 15-inch pieces of fabric
- Two 11 × 14-inch pieces of iron-on vinyl, such as Heat n Bond*
- Matching sewing thread
- Sewing machine
- Air-soluble marking pen
- 1-inch piece of Velcro

*See the "Buyer's Guide" on page 176.

## Directions

1 Following the manufacturer's directions, fuse the paper-backed web to the wrong side of the muslin piece. Use the pinking shears to trim the fused muslin piece to 4½ × 5¼ inches.

2 Decorate the muslin piece with the acrylic paints as desired. Use the embroidery floss to sew a line of straight stitching along the outer edges of the piece. Remove the paper backing from the web and fuse the muslin piece to the center of one of the 12 × 15-inch fabric pieces. Following the manufacturer's directions, fuse a vinyl piece to the right side of the fabric, covering the decorated muslin. Fuse the second vinyl piece to the right side of the remaining fabric piece.

3 Follow Steps 2 through 6 of the "Vegetable Lunch Bag" to complete the "Child's Lunch Bag."

# SCENTED GIFT SACHETS

*In a few minutes, you can turn bits and snips of beautiful craft supplies into inexpensive yet elegant sachets. Search through your closet for frilly ribbons too short to go around a package, bits of metallic cord, and pretty artificial flowers and leaves. You can quickly sew up the ribbon pouches, fill them with fragrant potpourri, and add a trim to create last-minute gifts.*

## MATERIALS

For all the sachets:
- ❄ Scissors
- ❄ 20-inch length of 4½- to 5-inch-wide ribbon, fabric, or tulle
- ❄ Hand-sewing needle and thread, or sewing machine
- ❄ Potpourri
- ❄ Rubber band
- ❄ Artificial roses, other flowers, buds, and leaves with stems attached
- ❄ Scraps of ribbon, cord, and pregathered lace
- ❄ Hot glue gun and glue sticks

## PREPARING THE BAGS

### DIRECTIONS

1 Fold the ribbon or fabric in half lengthwise with right sides facing. Sew the side seams to form a sachet bag, using a ¼-inch seam allowance. Turn the sachet right side out.

2 Stuff the bag about two-thirds full with potpourri. For the tulle sachet, fill the bag with brightly colored potpourri since it will show through the sheer fabric.

3 Fold the top edge in to meet the potpourri and, with your fingers, gather the opening closed. Secure it with a rubber band.

## BROCADE SACHET

### DIRECTIONS

1 Repeat Steps 1 through 3 under "Preparing the Bags."

2 Group a number of small roses into a nosegay. Add a few leaves around the edges. Twist the stems together to secure. Insert the nosegay into the top opening of the sachet.

3 Tie a knot in each end of a 12-inch-long cord to stop fraying.

4 Knot the cord tightly around the gathers at the neck of the sachet, leaving the ends at different lengths. Using ribbon or a brocade scrap, tie a tiny bow over the cord knot.

## TULLE SACHET

### DIRECTIONS

1 Repeat Steps 1 through 3 under "Preparing the Bags."

2 Using a ⅜- to ⅝-inch-wide ribbon, make an 11- or 12-loop bow without a center "knot." Each loop should be about 2 to 2½ inches long.

3 Dab hot glue at the center gathers of the bow. Center the bow on the front of the sachet at the gathered neck, pressing glue into the gathers of the sachet.

4 Glue a length of 1½-inch-wide pregathered lace into a circle over the looped ribbon. Arrange several small leaves in the center of the lace and glue them in place. Glue small roses over the leaves.

## CLUNY LACE SACHET

### DIRECTIONS

1 Repeat Steps 1 through 3 under "Preparing the Bags."

2 Sew lengths of cluny lace together to form a piece about 7 inches square. Gather the top edge of the lace square and hand tack it to the sachet over the rubber band.

3 Fold a 3-yard length of narrow ribbon back and forth to form three 1-yard lengths. Do not cut the ends at this time.

4 Wrap the folded ribbon around the gathers at the neck of the sachet bag and tie it into a bow. Separate the loops of the bows and pull them to different lengths.

5 Cut one set of long loop ends. Glue several rose leaves and buds at the center of the bow. Glue a single large rose in the center of the leaves and buds.

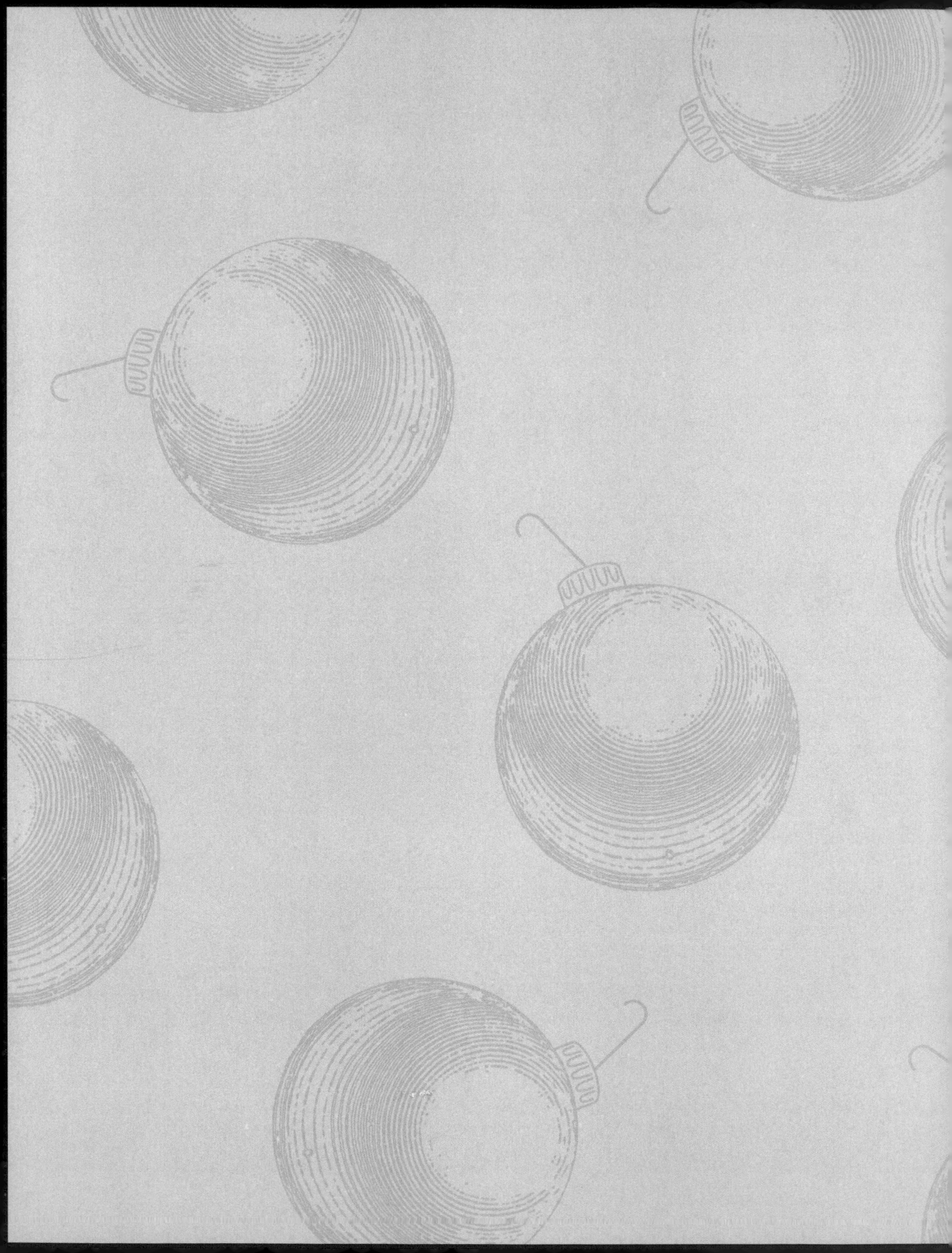

*Chapter Four*

# Gifts for Friends

*Thoughts of friends make the holidays brighter, so rekindle friendships with Christmas gifts you made yourself. This selection of projects includes labors of love like a hearth-warming rag rug and easy-to-craft holiday wreaths to decorate a neighbor's door. You'll also discover a woodland birdhouse and a friendly cross-stitch sampler to keep you in touch with friends near or far. Your friends will cherish these gifts filled with good wishes, glad tidings, and warm sentiments.*

# HOLIDAY WREATHS

*A wreath makes a perfect gift! Coated with glittering glaze, dime-store cookie cutters take on the look of precious metals. Tiny wrapped packages suggest one of the most delightful traditions of the season—gift giving. Use classic colors for the wreath or tailor the colors toward those used in the recipient's home-decorating scheme.*

## PACKAGE WREATH

**Size:** 16-inch diameter

### MATERIALS

- Ruler
- Serrated knife
- 12 × 36-inch sheet of 1-inch-thick Styrofoam
- Scissors for cutting paper
- Holiday wrapping papers
- Glue stick and fabric glue
- 16 yards of gold metallic package cord
- Thin florist's wire and wire cutters
- 16-inch-diameter wreath
- Gold mesh florist's bow

### DIRECTIONS

1 Use the serrated knife and ruler to cut the Styrofoam into about 45 blocks for the package shapes. Cut an assortment of blocks in the following sizes: 1½ inches square, 1¾ × 2½ inches, 2 inches square, 1½ × 1¾ inches, and 1¼ × 2¾ inches.

2 Cut the wrapping paper to size, and wrap each Styrofoam block with the paper, using the glue stick to glue the paper edges and corners in place. Do not use tape because it will show.

3 Tie a length of the gold metallic cord around the wrapped package and make a small bow at the top. Place a dab of fabric glue on the ends of the cord to prevent fraying, then dab glue on the knot to secure it.

4 Cut a 6-inch length of wire and wrap the center of it around the cord at the bottom of each package. Use the ends of the wire to attach the packages to the wreath.

5 Attach the bow to the wreath using the ends of the wire.

# Cookie Cutter Wreath

**Size:** 16-inch diameter

## Materials

- ❄ 26 assorted cookie cutters
- ❄ 1-inch-wide foam brush
- ❄ Assorted metallic paints, such as Plaid Folk Art Metallic Acrylic Paints in Amethyst, Peach Pearl, Rose Shimmer, Champagne, and Aquamarine*
- ❄ Thick white craft glue
- ❄ Silver confetti glitter
- ❄ Thin florist's wire and wire cutters
- ❄ 16-inch-diameter wreath
- ❄ White mesh florist's bow

*See the "Buyer's Guide" on page 176.

## Directions

1 Divide the cookie cutters into five groups. Use the foam brush to paint all the surfaces of each group with one of the paint colors; apply at least three coats of paint. Let the paint dry thoroughly.

2 Dilute the glue and apply a thin coat to the inside and outside of each cookie cutter. While the glue is still wet, sprinkle the glitter onto the glued surfaces. Let the glue dry thoroughly, then shake off any excess glitter.

3 Cut an 8-inch length of wire and wrap the center of it around each cookie cutter. Use the ends of the wire to attach the cookie cutters to the wreath. If the cookie cutters do not hang properly with one wire, attach a second wire directly across from the first wire.

4 Attach the bow to the wreath using the ends of the wire.

## How to Tie a Florist's Bow

❄

**You will need about 3 yards of 2- to 3-inch-wide ribbon, weatherproofed if the bow will be outdoors, and a 10-inch length of floral wire.**

**1. Leaving a tail about 10 inches long, make a 4½- to 5-inch loop. Gather the ends of the loop together tightly. Make another loop opposite the first and gather the ends. The piece will now look like a propeller gathered in the middle. Make a second and third set of loops to either side of the first set, gathering each as before.**

**2. Bend the floral wire in half and wrap it tightly around the gathered sections of the ribbon. Twist the wires together at the back to hold the ribbon loops in place, but do not trim the wire ends.**

**3. To form the knot, bring the longer ribbon tail to the front of the bow. Place your thumb over the wire on the front of the bow. Wrap the ribbon over your thumb, gather it up under your thumb, pull the ribbon to the back of the bow, and secure it between the two wire ends. Twist the wire ends tightly again. Adjust the loops evenly around the knot. Trim the ends of the ribbon as desired. Use the ends of the wire to secure the bow to the wreath.**

# STAMP-DECORATED BOX AND FRAME

*These coordinating desk accessories will add color and a personal note to your friends' home offices or business areas. They may even be a reminder to drop you a line! Buy a packet of canceled foreign stamps in a collectibles store or inexpensive variety packs at a hobby store to add to those saved from your own correspondence.*

## STAMP FRAME

**Size:** To fit a 5 × 7-inch photograph

### MATERIALS

- ❄ Frame with 2-inch-wide molding to fit a 5 × 7-inch photograph
- ❄ Paintbrush
- ❄ Flat black acrylic paint
- ❄ Paper
- ❄ Pencil
- ❄ Package of canceled postage stamps
- ❄ Small glue brush
- ❄ Thick white craft glue
- ❄ Acrylic high-luster varnish

### DIRECTIONS

1 If the frame has a glass insert, remove it before proceeding.

2 Paint the front of the frame molding with the black acrylic paint. Let the paint dry thoroughly.

3 With the pencil, outline the frame molding on the piece of paper. Arrange the stamps on this paper-frame outline until you have a pleasing design. Place a triangular stamp at each corner of the frame. Place some stamps at a slant and overlap others.

4 Use the glue brush to apply a coat of glue to the backs of the stamps, then glue them in place on the frame. Glue one stamp at a time, removing it from the planned arrangement and placing it in the same position on the frame. After all the stamps have been glued in place, smooth over the entire surface of the frame with your finger to make sure each stamp adheres completely. Reglue any stamps if necessary. Let the glue dry thoroughly before proceeding.

5 Apply three coats of varnish to seal the front of the frame, allowing each coat to dry thoroughly before applying the next.

6 Reassemble the frame once the varnish is completely dry.

## STAMP BOX

**Size:** 4-inch diameter

### MATERIALS

- ❄ 4-inch-diameter wooden box with lid
- ❄ Pencil
- ❄ Craft knife
- ❄ Emery board
- ❄ Flat black acrylic paint
- ❄ Paintbrush
- ❄ Small glue brush
- ❄ Thick white craft glue
- ❄ Package of canceled postage stamps
- ❄ Acrylic high-luster varnish

### DIRECTIONS

1 With the lid on the box and using a pencil, mark the position of a ⅛ × 1-inch slot for dispensing stamps on the side of the box bottom, as shown in **Diagram 1.** Use the craft knife to cut out the slot, then file the edges of the slot smooth with the emery board.

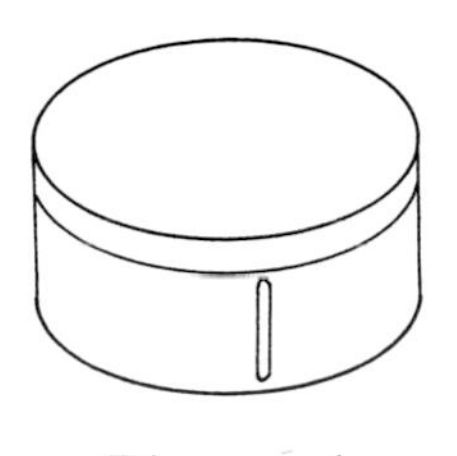

**Diagram 1**

2 Paint the outer and inner surfaces of the box bottom and lid with the black acrylic paint. Let the paint dry thoroughly.

3 Use the glue brush to apply a coat of glue to the backs of the stamps. Then glue the stamps to the sides of the box bottom and lid, allow the stamps to extend beyond the box and lid edges by ¼ inch, as shown in **Diagram 2.**

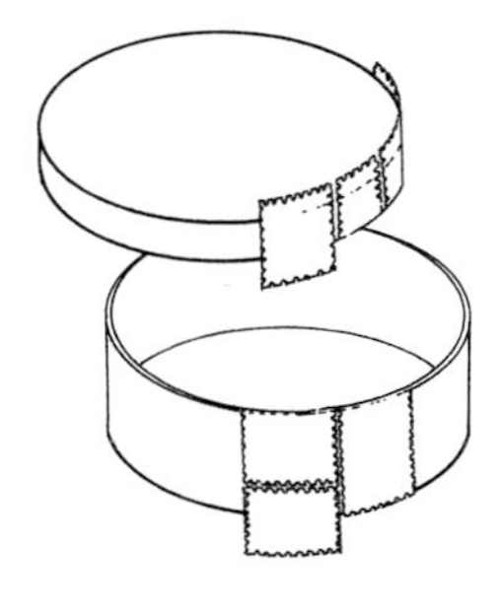

**Diagram 2**

4 Trim the corners of the stamps and cut V-shaped notches in the extended edges; fold the stamp edges flat onto the top of the lid and the bottom of the box, as shown in **Diagram 3.**

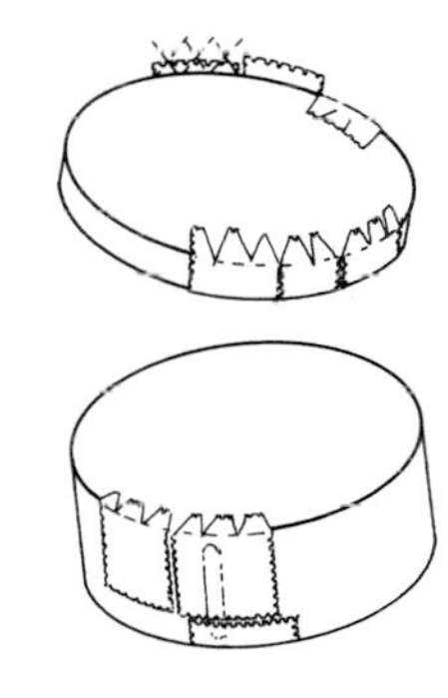

**Diagram 3**

5 Cover the bottom of the box and the top of the lid with stamps, covering the notched stamp edges as well. Trim off any excess stamp edges. After all the stamps have been glued in place, smooth over the entire surface of the box with your finger to make sure each stamp adheres completely. Reglue any stamps if necessary and let the glue dry. Cut away the stamp material that covers the dispensing slot.

6 Repeat Step 5 of the "Stamp Frame" to finish the box.

# TRIMMED PILLOWCASES

*Give the gift of one-of-a-kind bed linens. Inspired by Celtic designs, the trim is created with ordinary single-fold bias tape. White adds an elegant touch to colors while pastels color-keyed to the bedroom add a personal touch to white. For a really special gift, repeat the design on the top hem of a matching sheet or around the ends of a bolster pillow.*

**Size:** 3⅜-inch-wide tape design

## MATERIALS

- ❄ Pencil
- ❄ Lightweight paper
- ❄ Standard-size pillowcase in a color to contrast white bias tape
- ❄ Water-soluble marking pen
- ❄ Scissors
- ❄ White sewing thread
- ❄ Hand-sewing needle
- ❄ 3 yards of white single-fold bias tape
- ❄ Steam iron

## DIRECTIONS

1 Trace the **Celtic Pattern** below, including the dotted lines, onto the lightweight paper.

2 Tape the pattern to a sunny window. Place the hemmed edge of the pillowcase over the pattern and use the water-soluble pen to draw the design lines onto the hem of the pillowcase. Reposition the pillowcase edge to repeat the pattern around the entire edge of the pillowcase, joining the pattern at the dashed lines, as shown in **Diagram 1.**

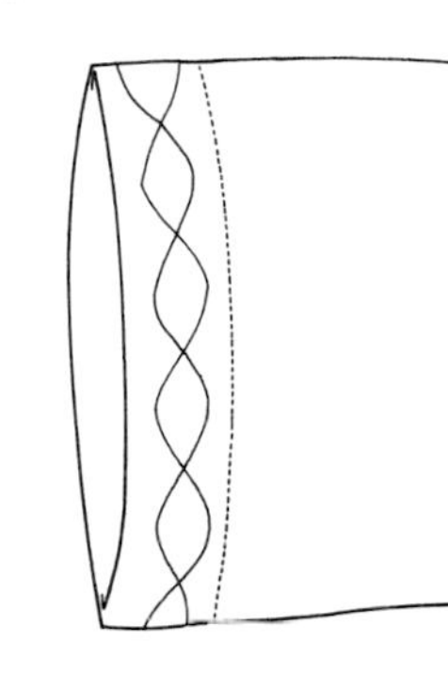

**Diagram 1**

3 Mark a second set of design lines on the hemmed edge of the pillowcase, placing them so that the center point of the wide curve of the second set of lines is located at the crossover point of the first set of lines. Repeat the pattern around the entire edge of the pillowcase, joining the pattern at the dashed lines, as shown in **Diagram 2.**

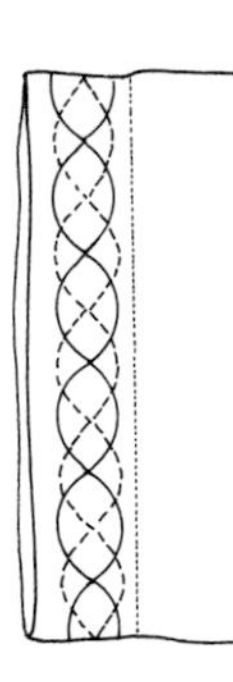

**Diagram 2**

4 Baste a length of bias tape over one of the design lines, working with one continuous line of the bias tape at a time and easing the tape around the curves so that it lies flat. Overlap the ends of the tape where they meet, turning under ¼ inch on the top tape end and basting it down. Press the tape thoroughly with a steam iron to smooth it into place. Slip stitch the edges of the tape in place.

5 Repeat Step 4 to baste, then slip stitch lengths of the bias tape over the three remaining lines of the design.

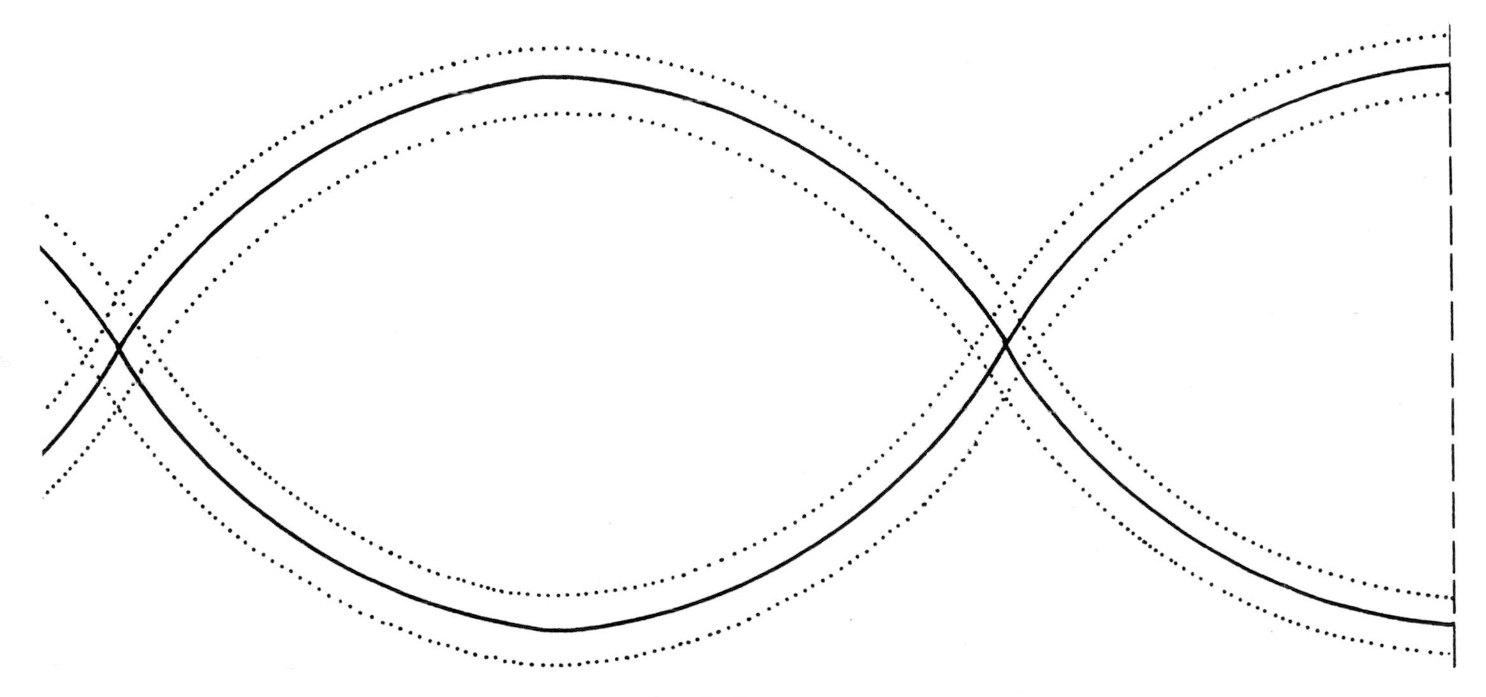

**Celtic Pattern**

# COILED RAG BASKETS

*Fabric strips, a large blunt needle, and stiff coiling are all that's needed to create decorator gifts quickly and easily. Choose fabrics to complement a certain decor or stick to neutral country colors for a universal appeal. After a few quick rounds, you'll be surprised at how fast these projects zip along.*

## MATERIALS

For both baskets:
❄ Heavy scissors
❄ 22 yards of ¾-inch coiling
❄ Masking tape
❄ Ruler
❄ Large needle

# BASKET-MAKING BASICS

## DIRECTIONS

1 Select cotton or poly/cotton fabrics as indicated for the "Country Basket" or the "Handled Basket" on page 108. Be sure to prewash the fabrics before tearing them into strips.

2 To tear the strips, fold the fabric in half lengthwise and clip into the folded edge at 1-inch intervals, as shown in **Diagram 1.** Tear the fabric across the width toward the selvages. You can also use a rotary cutter or scissors to cut the strips.

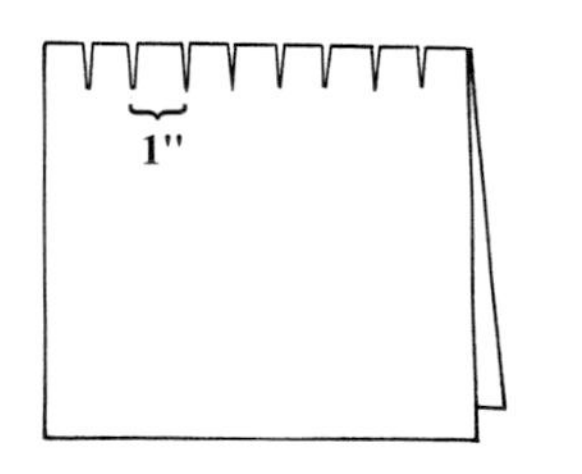


**Diagram 1**

3 Use heavy scissors to trim the end of the coiling to a tapered point. Cut each of the three twisted plies in the coiling separately for easier cutting, making the second ply 1 inch shorter and the third ply 2 inches shorter, as shown in **Diagram 2.** Holding the three plies together, wrap the masking tape around the end to hold the tapered plies securely together.

**Diagram 2**

4 Thread one of the fabric strips about 4 inches onto the large needle. Begin winding the other end of the strip around the coiling, starting about 4 inches from the tape-wrapped end; wrap it over the tail end of the fabric strip to hold it firmly in place, as shown in **Diagram 3.** When wrapping, overlap the edges of the fabric strips to completely cover the coiling and always pull the wraps tightly against the coiling. Pull the connecting wraps very tightly and always wrap them around twice.

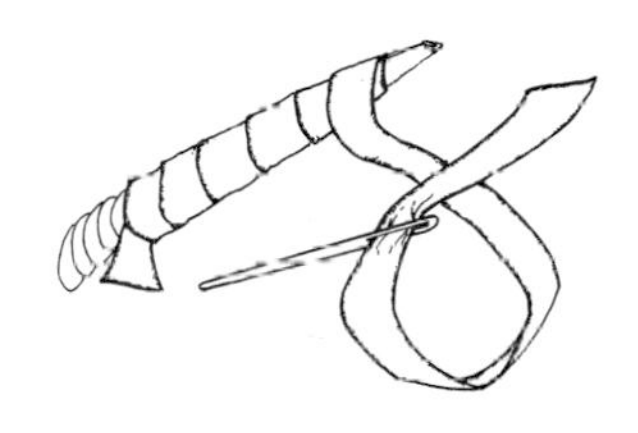

**Diagram 3**

5 Referring to **Diagram 4,** bend the end of the coiling to make a loop, leaving a hole at the center. Continue to wrap the fabric strip around the coiling, including the taped and tapered point, to hold it in place.

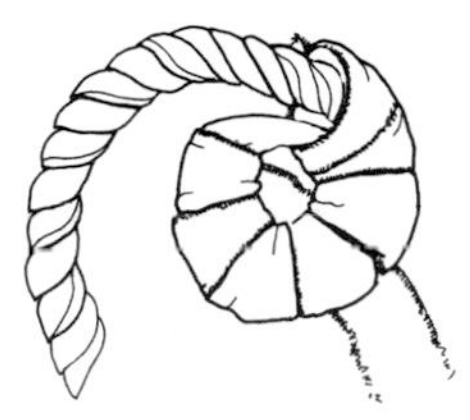

**Diagram 4**

6 When the center loop has been covered with wraps, continue to wrap the outer coiling for four to six more wraps. Push the needle through the center loop, bending the coiling to form a circle, as shown in **Diagram 5.**

**Diagram 5**

7 Continue wrapping the outer coiling three to four times. To make a joining stitch to the wrapped coiling, push the needle between the coilings and wind the strip around two coils instead of one. Repeat these basic steps (several wraps around the coiling followed by a joining stitch to connect the coiling) to make the basket shape.

8 To add a new fabric strip at the end of the old one, lay about 2 inches of the beginning and ending tails along the coiling. Wrap over both tails with the new strip, as shown in **Diagram 6.**

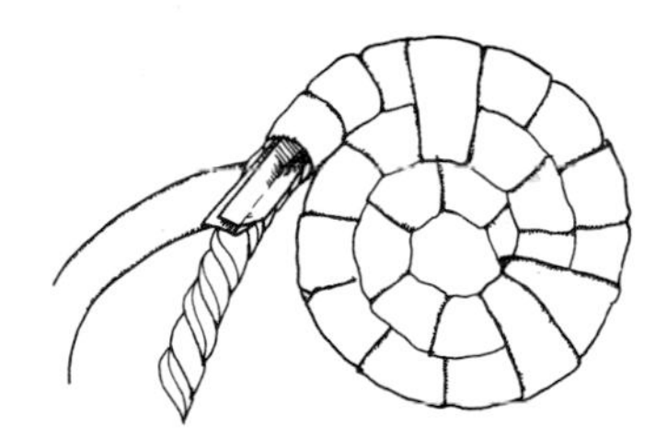

**Diagram 6**

9 Wrap the coilings in a flat shape for the basket bottom. After about four rounds, add more strength to the basket by making a tight knot around the joining stitch, as shown in **Diagram 7** on page 108. When the basket bottom is the size desired, shape the basket sides by working the wrapped coilings on top of one another.

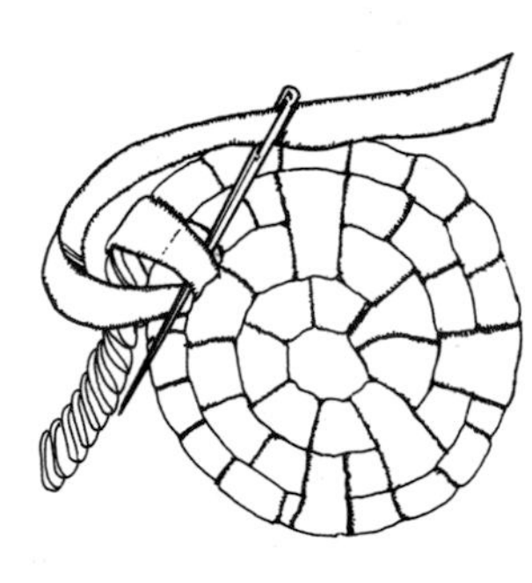

Diagram 7

**10** If needed, splice or add more coiling by tapering the end of the old coiling and the beginning of the new coiling. Then overlap the tapered ends and wrap them with masking tape to hold them securely together, as shown in **Diagram 8.**

Diagram 8

**11** To finish the coiling at the end of the basket, use the heavy scissors to taper the ends of the coils as you did at the beginning of the basket. Wind the fabric strip around the tapered ends until the last coil smoothly joins the basket edge, as shown in **Diagram 9.** Pull the fabric strip back under the last three wraps to secure the end, then trim off the remaining tail of the fabric wrap.

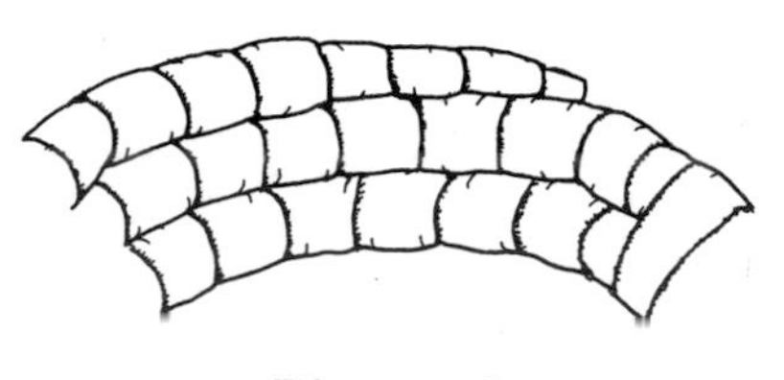

Diagram 9

## Country Basket

**Size:** 11 × 14 inches

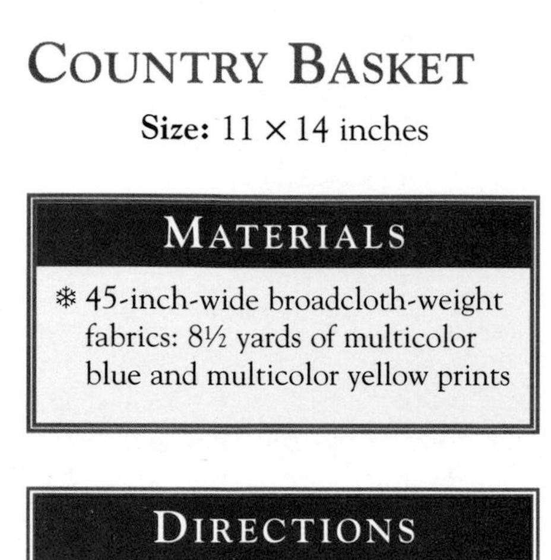

### Materials

- 45-inch-wide broadcloth-weight fabrics: 8½ yards of multicolor blue and multicolor yellow prints

### Directions

**1** Follow the "Basket-Making Basics" directions on page 107 to prepare the fabric strips and wrap the coilings for the basket shape.

**2** Begin with a circular bottom of 9 rounds, alternating the fabrics. Work the sides straight up with 12 rounds of the same fabrics.

## Handled Basket

**Size:** 6 × 14 inches

### Materials

- 45-inch-wide broadcloth-weight fabrics: 4½ yards of multicolor blue and multicolor yellow prints
- 2 wire coat hangers
- Pliers

### Directions

**1** Follow the "Basket-Making Basics" directions on page 107 to prepare the fabric strips and wrap the coilings for the basket shape.

**2** Begin with a circular bottom of six rounds, alternating the fabrics. Work the sides angled out with seven rounds of the same fabrics.

**3** On the last round of the basket, make the handle by bringing the coiling up and across the basket in a 24-inch arched shape. Use the pliers to cut and shape the two coat hangers to the same arch shape, bending the ends flat, as shown in **Diagram 1.**

Diagram 1

**4** Tape one wire arch to the coil ing, inserting the wire ends in the coiling, and wrap the wire with the fabric strips. Fold the coiling back across to the other side where you start at the handle. Tape the second wire arch to this coiling and wrap it with the fabric strips, wrapping over the first handle in several places, as shown in **Diagram 2.**

Diagram 2

**5** Continue wrapping the coiling to finish the last round of the basket. End the coiling as usual, but do not cut the fabric strip—wrap it around to the second side of the handle and secure it tightly with the fabric strip.

**6** Bend the ends of the arches around the coilings and cover them with fabric strip wrappings.

# FRIENDLY NEIGHBOR CROSS-STITCH SAMPLER

*Imagine the delight with which this sentimental sampler will be greeted! It makes your feelings abundantly clear through both the message and the stitching time involved.*

**Size:** 14 × 20½-inch cross-stitch area

## Materials

- Sewing machine
- Matching sewing thread
- Scissors
- 30 × 36-inch piece of Charles Craft Linaida 14-count cross-stitch fabric*
- Contrast basting thread
- Hand-sewing needle
- Size 22 or 24 tapestry needle
- 1 skein of embroidery floss for each color listed in the **Color Key** (unless otherwise indicated)

**See the "Buyer's Guide" on page 176.*

## Directions

**1** Zigzag the edges of the cross-stitch fabric to prevent raveling. Use the basting thread to hand sew a line of running stitches to mark the vertical and horizontal centers of the cross-stitch area.

**2** Follow the **Friendly Neighbor Cross-Stitch Sampler Chart** on pages 110 through 113 and the **Color Key** to cross-stitch the design in the center of the fabric, using the tapestry needle and two strands of floss to work the cross-stitches. Work the cross-stitches first, then work all the backstitching with two strands of black floss.

## Color Key

| | Color | Anchor |
|---|---|---|
| ✚ | White | 1 |
| ■ | Black | 403 |
| ʋ | Christmas Red | 9046 |
| • | Deep Canary (2 skeins) | 291 |
| o | Dk. Carnation | 57 |
| ✖ | Dk. Burnt Orange | 332 |
| / | Dk. Parrot Green | 239 |
| \ | Imperial Blue (3 skeins) | 410 |

Friendly Neighbor Cross-Stitch Sampler Chart

Shaded area indicates overlap from previous page.
Lower left corner of chart

Shaded area indicates overlap from previous page.

Friendly Neighbor Cross-Stitch Sampler Chart

Shaded area indicates overlap from previous page.

# HOLIDAY RAG RUG

*Imagine the look on your friends' faces when they open this package— marked "open early"— they'll have a whole season to enjoy this fabulous rug! Worked in a very simple variation of needlepoint, the rug is made of torn fabric strips. Finish it off with three rounds of braided strips.*

**Size:** 17½ × 29 inches

## Materials

- ❄ Cotton fabrics for the needlepoint center: 1⅛ yards each of solid ecru and green Christmas print; ½ yard of red Christmas print; ¼ yard each of dark brown and tan; and ⅛ yard each of bright yellow and bright blue
- ❄ Cotton fabrics for the braided rug border: 1 yard each of tan print and red and green Christmas prints
- ❄ Scissors, pencil, ruler, and T-pins
- ❄ Masking tape
- ❄ 17½ × 29-inch piece of 3.3 or 3.5-count rug canvas
- ❄ Large tapestry needle
- ❄ Rug braiding tools: metal fabric folding tips, spring clamp or clothespin, and lacing needle*
- ❄ Buttonhole twist or strong thread
- ❄ Medium-size crochet hook

*See the "Buyer's Guide" on page 170.

## Directions

### Preparing the Fabric Strips

**1** Select cotton or poly/cotton fabrics and prewash them before tearing them into strips.

**2** To tear the strips, fold the fabric in half lengthwise and clip into the folded edge at 1-inch intervals. Tear the fabric across the width toward the selvages. You could also use a rotary cutter or scissors to cut the 1-inch strips. Tear the fabric strips as you need them since the remaining fabric will be used for the braiding. (If you cut the strips wider than 1 inch, allow for extra fabric yardage.)

### Stitching the Design

**1** Use the masking tape to tape or bind the edges of the rug canvas to prevent raveling. Mark the horizontal and vertical centers of the canvas. Use these as a reference for placing the design.

**2** Thread a fabric strip onto the needle. Do not work with too long a strip or the fabric edges will become too frayed and worn as the stitches are worked. To begin, lay the tail flat on the back of the canvas and stitch over it. To end, run the strip under four or five stitches.

**3** Using the continental stitch, as shown in the **Continental Stitch Diagram,** and following the

**Holiday Rag Rug Chart** below, work the design on the rug canvas. Stitch one row horizontally from right to left and the next row from left to right to achieve the herringbone texture for the background. Follow the chart for color changes, working areas of color one at a time. Stitch the horse and sleigh design first, working from the center out, then stitch the background.

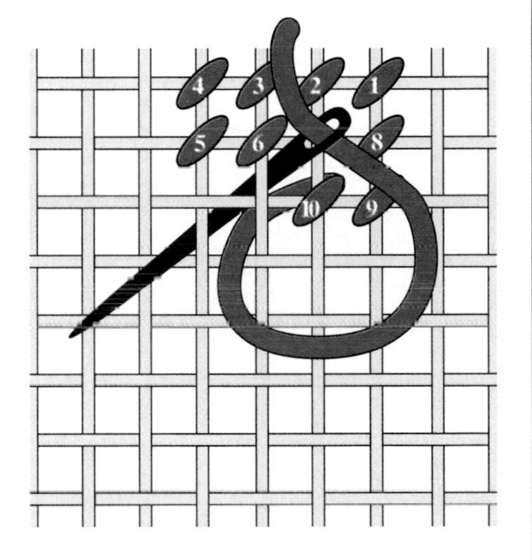


**Continental Stitch Diagram**

4 Allow enough of the remaining canvas to stitch the four rows of the needlepoint border, then add 1 inch to each edge, and trim the canvas to those dimensions. Fold back the 1-inch hem along the four edges of the canvas piece. Complete the stitching of the border pattern, stitching through both layers of canvas to finish the edge.

## *Braiding the Rug Border*

1 Cut or tear the fabrics for the border into 1½-inch-wide strips. Seam the fabric strips together on the bias for a long, continuous strip. You will need to braid about a 2½-yard length of each color.

2 Slide a metal fabric folding tip onto one end of each of three different fabric strips. Using the T-pins, pin this end of the three strips together on the work surface.

3 Using the spring clamp or clothespin to hold the beginning ends of the braid together, braid the strips, sliding the metal tips along to fold the fabric edges.

4 After one braid is completed, sew it around the outer edges of the needlepoint center, stitching through the back of the braid to hide the thread. Ease the braid around each corner so the braid lies flat. Trim the braid ends, leaving 2 to 3 inches to finish. Remove the metal tips. Use the crochet hook to pull the ends of the strips into the braid to complete the weave. Trim any excess strips and sew the ends in place on the wrong side of the braid.

5 Braid two more strips to fit around the edge of the rug, sewing each in turn to the edge and finishing the fabric ends in the same way as the first braid.

**Holiday Rag Rug Chart**

# TWIG-AND-LEAF BIRDHOUSE

*This "tweet" little home would make the perfect gift for a bird-watching buddy. You can create a birdhouse of any size—just collect straight twigs in a variety of lengths. For variety of texture, shingle the roof with "petals" from dried pinecones.*

**Size:** As purchased

## MATERIALS

- ❄ Sandpaper
- ❄ Wooden birdhouse, such as Walnut Hollow Farm's Medium Cloud Cabin*
- ❄ Paintbrush
- ❄ Redwood brown acrylic paint
- ❄ Hot glue gun and glue sticks
- ❄ Assorted twigs (as straight as possible)
- ❄ Hand pruners or small saw for cutting the twigs
- ❄ Dried eucalyptus leaves
- ❄ 2-inch-high craft bird

*See the "Buyer's Guide" on page 176.

## DIRECTIONS

1 Lightly sand the birdhouse, if needed, so the paint will adhere better. Apply a coat of paint to all the outer surfaces of the house, including the underside of the roof eaves. Let the paint dry thoroughly.

2 Use the hot glue gun to glue the twigs to the front, back, and sides of the birdhouse as follows: Begin at the base of the house and alternate gluing the twigs around the four sides so they cover the surface; pile them log cabin–style up to the roof, as shown in the **Twig Diagram.** Break or cut the twigs into varying pieces to get lengths as straight as possible, with the twigs extending about ¼ inch from the house corners so the "logs" will overhang at the corners. Cut the twigs to fit around the round opening on the front of the birdhouse.

3 Glue individual eucalyptus leaves in rows to cover the roof. Begin the first row along the lower edge of each side of the roof, overlapping the sides of the leaves slightly. Continue to glue rows of leaves to the roof, lapping each row over the previous row and ending at the peak of the roof.

4 Break or cut a 1½-inch-long twig for the perch. Glue it in place on the front of the birdhouse about 1 inch below the round opening and nestle it between two twigs. Glue the craft bird to the perch.

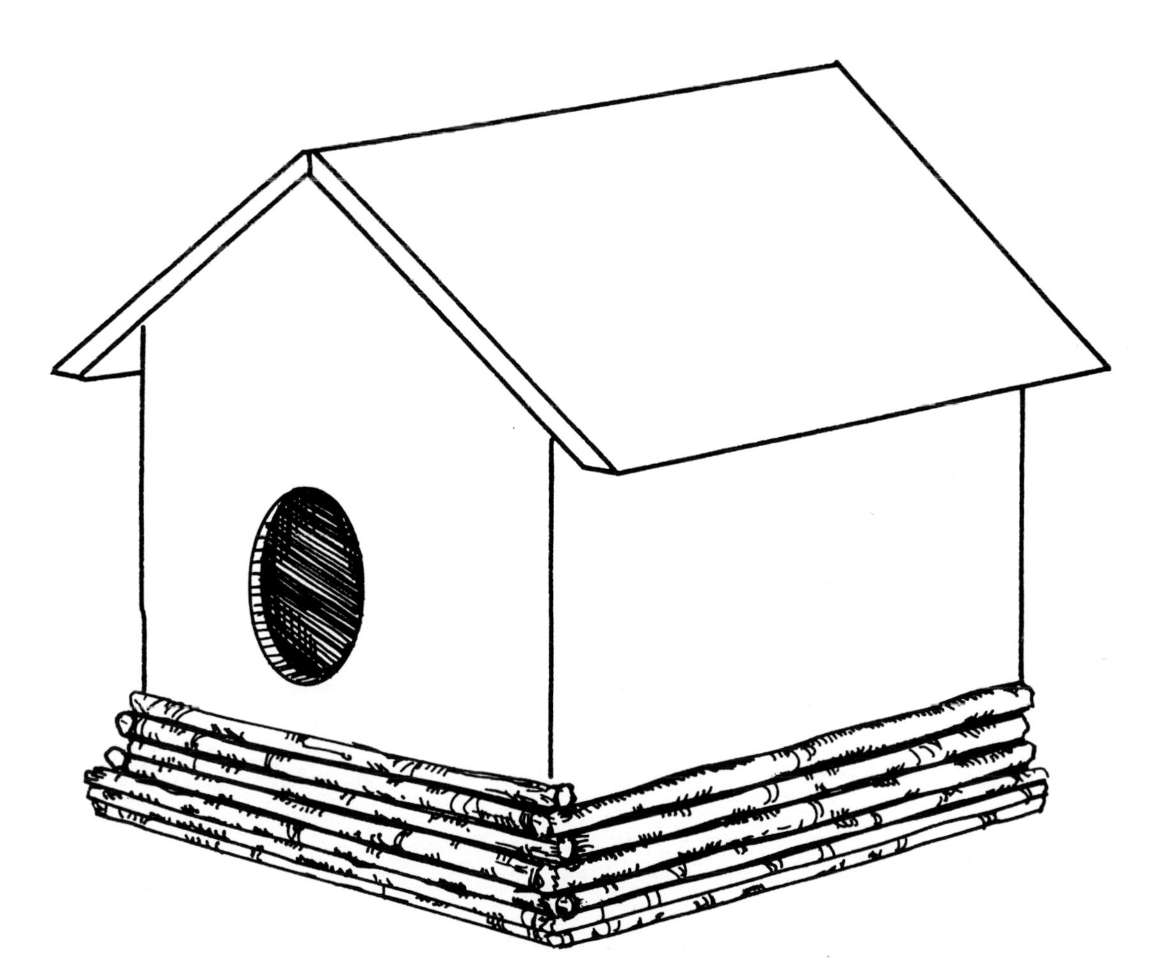

**Twig Diagram**

*Chapter Five*

# Secret Santa Gifts

*Thinking about others who do not share in our good fortune is an important part of the Christmas season. These gifts are geared toward the homebound, those with special needs, and children who are unlikely to receive toys from Santa. All were designed with simplicity in mind and use readily available supplies. You and your family can spend evenings completing these thoughtful little tokens, and the gift recipients will treasure your thoughtfulness.*

# TRADITIONAL BOARD GAMES

*Traditional board games are easy to make and great fun for the recipients. Whether you choose to face off for a little battle of backgammon, settle down for a checkers tournament, or brush up on your geography with a map puzzle, we have a board for you. If those checker pieces look familiar, they should! They're made from juice-drink bottle caps.*

# Backgammon Board

**Size:** 17¼ × 18½ inches

## Materials

- ❄ Sandpaper
- ❄ 17¼ × 18½-inch piece of ¼-inch interior-grade hardwood-backed plywood
- ❄ 2-inch-wide foam brush
- ❄ White acrylic paint
- ❄ Gold, red, and black acrylic paints
- ❄ Pencil
- ❄ Ruler
- ❄ Two 8 × 11-inch pieces of stencil Mylar
- ❄ Stencil brush
- ❄ Craft knife
- ❄ Electric or hand saw
- ❄ 8-foot length of ¼ × ¾-inch wooden furring strip
- ❄ White carpenter's glue
- ❄ Wood clamps
- ❄ 2 pairs of regulation dice
- ❄ ¾ × ¾-inch doubling cube
- ❄ 32 plastic gaming chips, 16 black and 16 white

## Directions

1 With the sandpaper, sand both sides of the plywood smooth.

2 Use the foam brush to paint both sides of the plywood with a base coat of white acrylic paint, allowing the paint to dry thoroughly. Always let each coat of paint dry thoroughly before proceeding.

3 Using the less porous, smoother side of the plywood for the face side of the game board, paint this side with a coat of gold acrylic paint. If necessary, apply a second coat of paint for an even finish.

4 With the pencil and ruler, draw a straight line across the width of one piece of stencil Mylar, about ¾ inch from one long edge. Using the **Triangle Pattern,** trace three 6½-inch-long triangles onto the Mylar, spacing the triangles 1¼ inches apart and lining up the triangle bases along the straight line. Using the craft knife, cut the triangles from the Mylar. Make another stencil the same way. You will use one stencil for each of the board's alternating red and black triangle designs.

5 Refer to the photograph on the opposite page and lightly mark the perimeter of the painted plywood board for the placement of a ¾-inch-wide furring strip frame and the center strip of the backgammon game board.

6 Use the stencil patterns and the stencil brush to paint the red and black triangle designs inside the marked areas of the plywood board. Place the bases of the triangles along the top and bottom marked frame edges. Use one stencil for each color and paint one color at a time. Allow the first color to dry thoroughly before painting the second color. If necessary, apply a second coat of paint for an even finish. Note that the black triangles face the red triangles across the board.

7 Using the saw, cut two 17¼-inch lengths of furring strip for the top and bottom of the frame and three 17-inch lengths of furring strip for the sides and center of the frame. Check these measurements before cutting to be sure the cut pieces will fit the edges and center of the plywood board. Paint each piece black and let them dry thoroughly. If necessary, apply a second coat of paint.

8 Use the carpenter's glue to affix the furring strips in place. Use the wood clamps to hold the strips in place until the glue dries.

9 Gather the dice, doubling cube, and gaming chips to complete the backgammon game.

**Triangle Pattern**

# CHECKERBOARD

**Size:** 18 × 20¼ inches

## MATERIALS

- Sandpaper
- 18 × 20¼-inch length of ¼-inch interior-grade hardwood-backed plywood
- 1-inch-wide foam brush
- White acrylic paint
- Pencil
- Ruler
- Red, gray, and black acrylic paints
- Piece of 8 × 11-inch stencil Mylar
- Stencil brush
- Craft knife
- Masking tape
- Miter box and saw
- 8-foot length of ⅞-inch corner guard wood trim for edging
- White carpenter's glue
- Wood clamps
- 24 twist-off juice-drink bottle caps
- 1 pound of dry water putty
- 2-inch putty knife

## DIRECTIONS

1 With the sandpaper, sand both sides of the plywood smooth.

2 Use the foam brush to paint both sides of the plywood with a base coat of white acrylic paint. Let the paint dry thoroughly. Always let each coat of paint dry thoroughly before proceeding.

3 Use the less porous, smoother side of the plywood for the face side of the game board. With the pencil and ruler, lightly mark an outline of a 14-inch square in the center of the face side of the board. Paint this square red.

4 Draw a grid of fifteen 1¾-inch squares on the stencil Mylar (five squares high × three squares wide). Using the craft knife, cut out the marked alternate squares from the stencil, as shown in the **Checkerboard Stencil Diagram.**

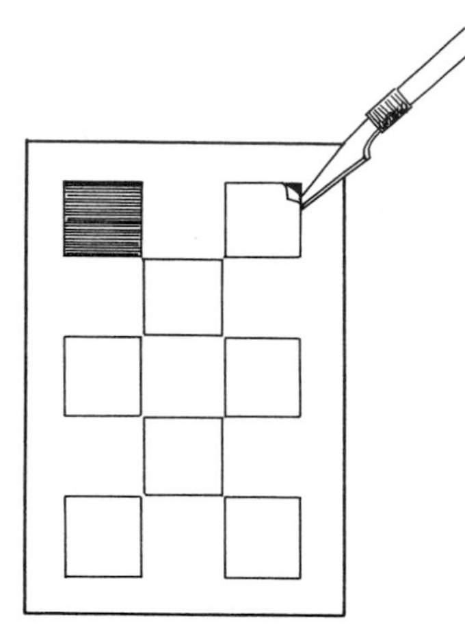

**Checkerboard Stencil Diagram**

5 Lightly mark the placement of 1¾-inch squares in an eight-square × eight-square checkerboard on the large red square. Mark the alternate squares to be painted black. Use the stencil pattern and the stencil brush to paint the black squares on the board. Rotate the stencil around the board to finish all the squares.

6 When the paint is dry, use masking tape to mark off the area around the checkerboard design. Paint the outer edges of the game board with gray paint, as shown in the photograph on this page.

7 Using the miter box and saw, cut four pieces of the corner guard trim to fit around the outer edges of the plywood board. Check your measurements to be sure the cut pieces will fit the edges like a frame. Paint each piece red and let it dry thoroughly.

8 Use the carpenter's glue to affix the trim pieces around the board. Use wood clamps to hold the trim in place until the glue dries.

9 Wash the twist-off caps. Mix the water putty with water to a sour cream–like consistency. Use the putty knife to fill the underside of the caps with the putty, smoothing the putty even with the edge of the cap. Let the putty dry overnight. Paint 16 filled caps black and 16 caps white, painting all the surfaces of the caps.

## Map Puzzle

**Size:** 20 × 30 inches

### Materials

- Sandpaper
- 20 × 30-inch piece of ¼-inch interior-grade hardwood-backed plywood
- 1-inch-wide foam brush
- Pointed artist's brush
- White latex paint
- Spray varnish
- 20 × 30-inch map of the United States, or as desired
- Scissors
- Two 16 × 20-inch pieces of ¼-inch-thick stick-on foam core board
- Craft knife
- Pencil
- Green and blue acrylic paints
- 2-inch-wide purple duct tape

### Directions

1 With the sandpaper, sand both sides of the plywood smooth.

2 Use the foam brush to paint both sides of the plywood with a base coat of white latex paint. Let the paint dry thoroughly. Always let each coat of paint dry thoroughly before proceeding.

3 Spray a coat of varnish on the face side of the map to stiffen the paper. Let the varnish dry thoroughly before proceeding.

4 Cut the map into two sections to fit onto the pieces of your foam core board, using state boundaries as a dividing line. Peel away the protective sheets from the foam core board. Adhere a map section to a piece of foam core board. Make sure the map is smooth and attached on all of the edges by applying gentle pressure with your hand, working from one side of the adhered section toward the other side.

5 Using the craft knife, carefully cut along the map perimeter on each foam piece. Use a sawing motion when cutting the foam core board. If desired, simplify the edges of the map pieces to make a smoother puzzle.

6 Position the two map pieces on the plywood board. Use the less porous, smoother side of the plywood for the face side of the puzzle. Use a pencil to outline the perimeter of the map onto the board.

7 Use the artist's brush and the acrylic paints to paint the map area green and the border areas blue. Mark a pencil line ½ inch from each of the four edges of the plywood board. Tape the four edges of the plywood board with the duct tape, using the pencil line to keep a straight edge.

8 Using the craft knife, cut apart the states to make the puzzle pieces. Where needed, simplify the shapes of the states along intricate borders to make a smoother puzzle piece. Do not cut apart individual small states; instead, combine several of them into one larger piece.

# KNITTED BED SOCKS

*Wearing socks to bed may be an old-fashioned idea, but it's a good one, adding toasty comfort on frosty nights. These one-size, unisex socks make perfect gifts for people of all ages. They knit up quickly in a chunky weight, mohair-type yarn and are light enough to slide into slippers in the morning.*

**Size:** One size fits all

## Materials

- ❄ Two 3-ounce/85-gram balls of Lion Brand Jiffy yarn in desired color*
- ❄ Pair of size 10½ knitting needles

*See the "Buyer's Guide" on page 176.*

## Directions

### Checking the Gauge

To make sure the finished size of the socks will be correct, take time to check your gauge. Here the gauge is 9 stitches and 9 rows = 2 inches. (See "Checking Gauge" on page 61.)

### Making the Bed Socks

1 Begin the knitted socks by casting on 36 stitches.

2 Row 1: * Knit 1 stitch, purl 1 stitch; repeat from the * across all the stitches on the needle. Repeat Row 1 until the piece is 3 inches long.

3 To work the next pattern row: * Knit 2, purl 2; repeat from the * across all the stitches on the needle. Repeat this pattern row for 14 inches—the piece will measure 17 inches.

4 Work in stockinette stitch (knit 1 row, purl 1 row) for 4 rows.

5 To work the first toe-shaping decrease row: * Knit 2, knit 2 together; repeat from the * across all the stitches on the needle (27 stitches). Next row: Purl.

6 To work the next toe-shaping decrease row: * Knit 1, knit 2 together; repeat from the * across all the stitches on the needle (18 stitches). Next row: Purl.

7 To work the next toe-shaping decrease row: * Knit 2 together; repeat from the * across all the stitches on the needle (9 stitches).

8 Bind off all the stitches. Cut the yarn, leaving a length of yarn long enough for sewing the entire side seam.

9 Sew the center back seam and across the toe seam, then turn the sock right side out; refer to the **Sewing Diagram** below.

10 Make the second sock in the same manner, repeating Steps 1 through 9.

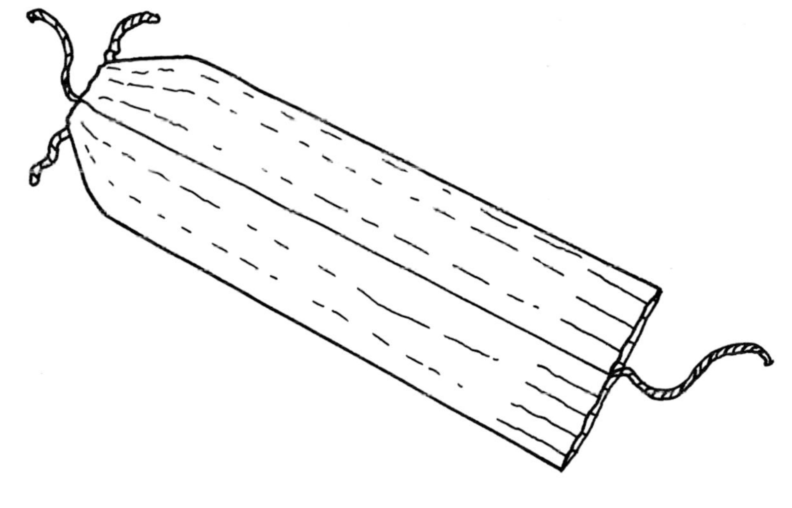

**Sewing Diagram**

# COTTAGE COOKIE JAR

*A bit of simple carpentry and a splash of colorful paint transform a classic wooden birdhouse into a charming kitchen accent. Fill the house with favorite cookies for a second treat. It's the perfect way to say, "From our house to yours with affection."*

**Size:** As purchased

## MATERIALS

- Sandpaper
- Wooden birdhouse, such as Walnut Hollow Farm's Large Cloud Cabin*
- Small hammer
- Pliers
- Small scrap of thin wood
- Carpenter's glue
- Foam brush
- Assorted acrylic paints: cream, bright pink, peach, sky blue, bright green, black, and gold
- Pair of 1¼-inch brass hinges
- Screwdriver
- Craft saw
- 60 wooden craft sticks (tongue-depressor size)
- Pencil
- Hot glue gun and glue sticks
- Tracing paper
- Small, pointed artist's brush
- Saucers or palettes
- Small natural sponge
- High-luster varnish

*See the "Buyer's Guide" on page 176

## DIRECTIONS

1 Lightly sand the birdhouse, if needed, so the paint will better adhere to the surface.

2 Remove one side of the roof from the house: Use the hammer on the underside of the roof to tap apart the nailed edges, freeing the roof half. Use the pliers to remove any nails that are exposed.

Sand the edges of the scrap of wood smooth. Use the carpenter's glue to glue the scrap over the entrance hole from the inside.

3 Using the foam brush, apply a coat of cream paint to the inner and outer surfaces of the house, including both sides of the separate roof piece. Let the paint dry thoroughly before proceeding.

4 Attach the hinges to the roof about 1¼ inches in from each end, as shown in **Diagram 1.** Attach the loosened side of the roof to the other side of the hinges so that the roof fits back in the original position. Apply a coat of bright pink paint to both roof sections and let them dry thoroughly.

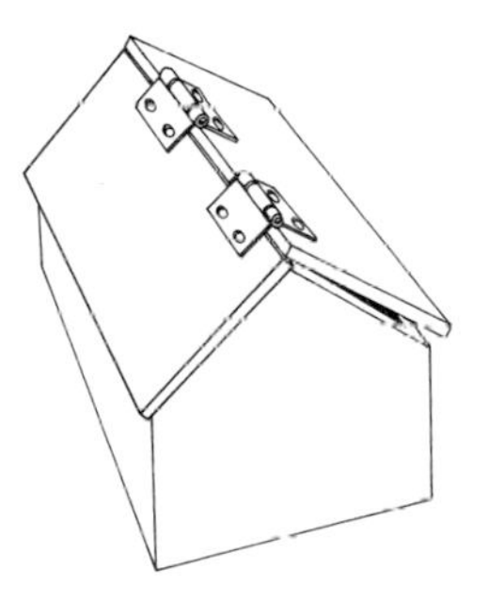

**Diagram 1**

5 Using the craft saw, cut off a 1⅜-inch piece from each end of the craft sticks for the shingles. Paint both sides of each shingle peach and let dry thoroughly.

6 Beginning at the peak of the roof, use the pencil to lightly mark four lines ¾ inch apart along each side of the roof for shingle placement. Use the hot glue gun to glue the shingles in rows to cover the roof, matching the straight edge of each shingle with the marked line on the roof, as shown in **Diagram 2.** Begin the first shingle row along the lower edge of each side of the roof. Continue to glue the rows of shingles to the roof, matching the ends of the shingles with the marked lines so that each row overlaps the previous row. End at the peak of the roof, leaving the pins of the hinges free so that the roof will open.

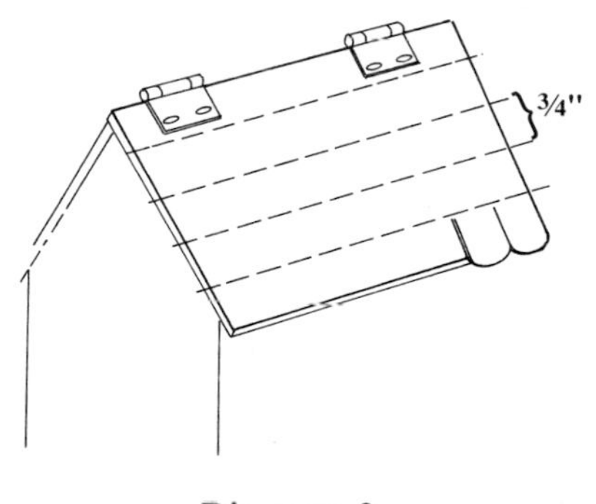


**Diagram 2**

7 Place the paints on their own saucers. Use the sponge to dab peach paint on the walls of the cottage for a stucco look. Lightly pencil in the window, shutters, door, and bushes on the four sides of the cottage, as shown below in the **Cottage Decorating Diagram.**

8 Use the small brush to paint the sky blue windows, peach shutters and doors, and bright green lower bushes. Mix a small amount of cream paint with the bright green to get a lighter shade of green and paint the upper bushes. Paint the heart on the door with sky blue. Outline the windows, shutters, and door with black paint. Refer to the photograph on the opposite page to paint the multicolored flowers, then outline each one with black paint. Paint the base of the house with bright pink.

9 Coat the entire cottage with one or two coats of high-luster varnish. Let dry thoroughly.

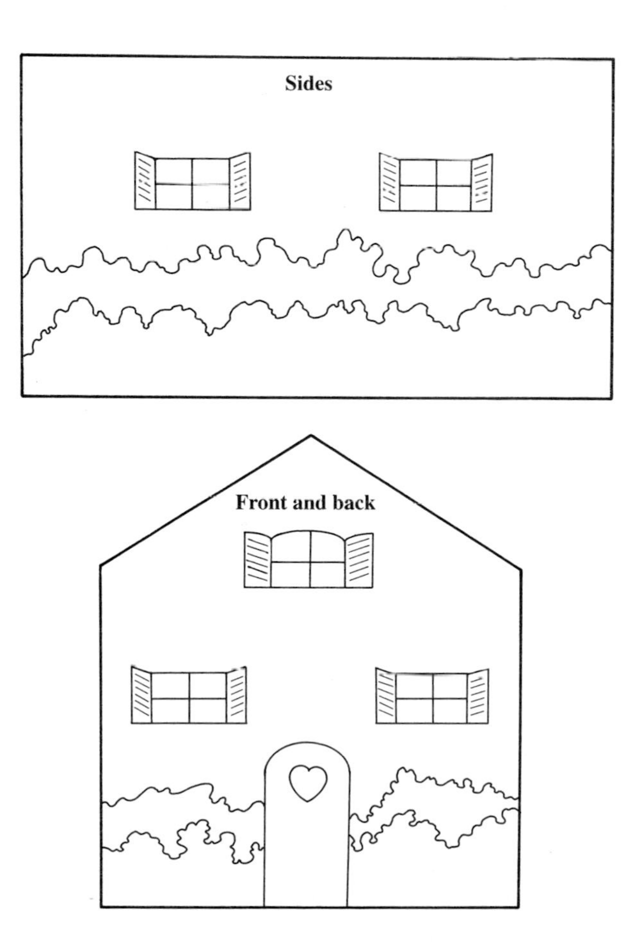


**Cottage Decorating Diagram**

# RAG DOLL DUO

*It's quite amazing how these little dolls take on personalities of their own. Even the smallest variation in materials creates a whole new character. Children in difficult situations, or any child for that matter, appreciate the simple detailing and soft, huggable quality of these dolls. A child's imagination will bring these characters to life.*

# Little Girl

**Size:** About 9 inches tall

## Materials

- Tracing paper
- Pencil
- Scissors
- 12 × 20-inch piece of pink gingham
- Water-soluble marking pen
- Sewing machine
- Matching sewing thread
- Polyester fiberfill
- Hand-sewing needle
- 55 yards of pink yarn
- 9-inch-wide piece of cardboard
- Pins
- Large-eyed needle
- 9 × 14-inch piece of floral print
- 2 yards of narrow, pink, double-fold bias tape

## Directions

1 Trace the **Dress** and **Rag Doll Body** patterns on pages 130 and 131 onto the tracing paper. Each pattern includes a ¼-inch seam allowance. Cut out the pattern pieces.

2 Cut two bodies from the pink gingham. Transfer the markings onto the fabric with the water-soluble marking pen. With the right sides facing and using a ¼-inch seam allowance, sew the two body pieces together, leaving an opening for turning. Clip the seam allowance along the curves and turn the body right side out. Stuff the body firmly with the polyester fiberfill and slip stitch the opening closed.

3 To make the little girl's hair, wrap the yarn 100 times around the piece of cardboard. Cut the yarn loops at one end of the cardboard. Open the yarn strands and lay them flat, removing the cardboard and keeping the yarn strands together. Place the strands on a piece of tracing paper, arranging them into a 4-inch-wide hank. To make the part for the hair, use a medium-length straight stitch to machine sew through the center of the yarn hank, as shown in **Diagram 1.** Sew twice along the hair part to secure the yarn strands, then peel the paper away from the yarn.

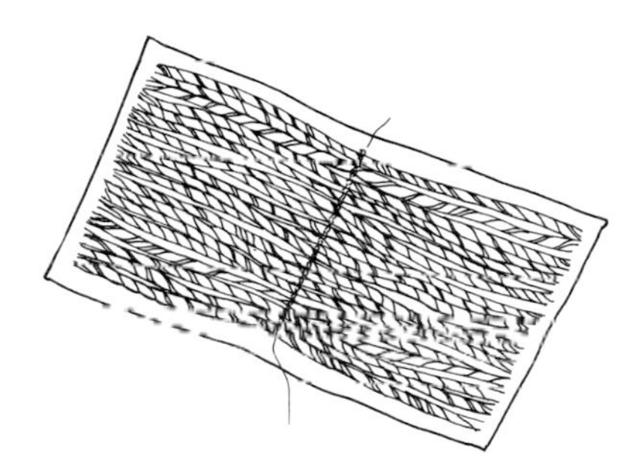

**Diagram 1**

4 Pin the hair part along the center of the head with the front of the part about 1 inch down from the head seam. Pin the remainder of the part along the back of the head. Referring to **Diagram 2,** hand sew the hair to the head along the part using a backstitch.

**Diagram 2**

5 Thread the large-eyed needle with a length of yarn. Sew through the side of the head at the neck and tie the yarn ends around the hair strands to shape a ponytail. Repeat for the ponytail on the other side of the head.

6 Cut two dresses from the floral print. Sew a length of bias tape along the top edge of each piece. With the right sides facing and using a ¼-inch seam allowance, sew one side seam. Bind the entire hem edge of the dress, then sew the remaining side seam, including the hem binding, as shown in **Diagram 3.**

**Diagram 3**

7 Cut two 19-inch lengths of bias tape for the armholes. Place a mark at the center of each piece. Pin a piece to each armhole edge, aligning each mark with the side seam. Ease the bias tape to fit around the armhole curve at the side seam, as shown in **Diagram 4.** Sew the bias tape to the armhole edge, leaving the ends of the tape free at each end for ties. Place the dress on the doll and tie the tape into a bow at each shoulder.

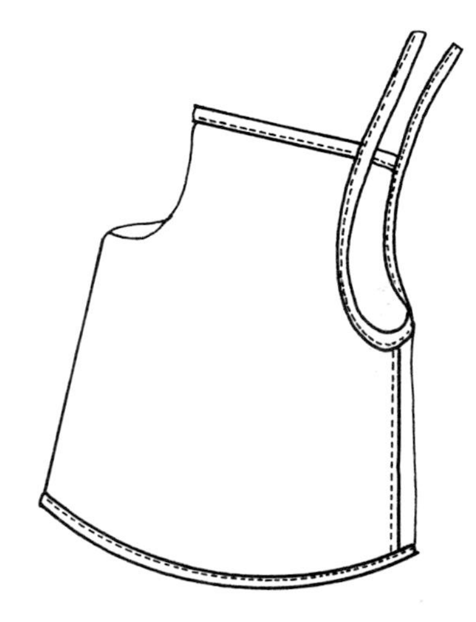

**Diagram 4**

*Chapter Six*

# Gifts for VIPs

*Teachers, baby-sitters, delivery persons—they all touch our lives throughout the year. Remember them at Christmastime with a handcrafted gift. Your child's favorite teacher will be happy to carry papers in an academically inspired tote bag. Show your appreciation to a sitter with a charming woven ribbon purse. Leave a handmade gift envelope with a tip for delivery persons. You'll find ideas for all those who help make your days special.*

# TEACHER'S GOLDEN RULE TOTE

*Combine the tools of the trade with I-appreciate-you apples to tell a special teacher how much you think of her. If desired, you could repeat the simple-to-paint design on a T-shirt or on a mini tote or book bag. With a gift like this, you'll be the apple of the teacher's eye.*

**Size:** 13-inch-square design

## MATERIALS

- Masking tape, ruler, and pencil
- 18-inch-square canvas tote
- Tracing paper
- Dressmaker's tracing paper
- 16-inch square of foam core board or corrugated cardboard
- Acrylic paints in bright pink, peach, red, light blue, bright green, and yellow, such as Delta Ceramcoat* and Duncan Decorator Acrylics*
- Black dimensional writer, such as Duncan's dimensional writer*
- Saucers or palettes
- Textile medium
- ⅜-inch flat and small, round, pointed paintbrushes

*See the "Buyer's Guide" on page 170.

## DIRECTIONS

**1** Use the masking tape to outline a 13-inch square in the center of the front of the canvas tote. This square indicates the location of the design.

**2** With the ruler and pencil, trace the **Golden Rule Tote Pattern** on the opposite page onto a 14-inch square of tracing paper, centering the ruler-bordered section of the design on the paper. Complete the design by rotating the pencils around the center of the design to repeat them at each of the three remaining corners, as shown in the **Placement Diagram.** Then in the top left and bottom right corners, add the remaining apple motifs by tracing the center apple.

**Placement Diagram**

3 Place the dressmaker's tracing paper, color side down, on the front of the tote. Next, place the pattern on top of the dressmaker's paper, centering it within the taped area. Use the pencil to draw over all the design lines again, transferring the pattern onto the fabric.

4 Remove the tracing paper pattern. Insert the foam core board or cardboard inside the tote to prevent the paint from bleeding through to the back of the tote.

5 Place each paint color on a saucer or palette, then mix the textile medium with each paint color, following the manufacturer's directions.

6 Begin painting the design from the center out. Use the flat brush for the large areas and the pointed brush for the small areas. Paint the outer edge of each shape first, then fill in the center. Always let each color dry thoroughly before painting next to it with another color. A suggested painting order is to begin by painting the red center apple, the yellow rulers, the red corner squares, the blue pencils, the pink pencil erasers, the flesh pencil tips, the green apples, and ending with the apple hearts and stems in bright yellow, blue, and red.

7 For a professional finish, use the black dimensional writer to outline each shape, including the ruler markings.

8 After all the paints are thoroughly dry, remove the foam core board from the tote.

**Golden Rule Tote Pattern**

# FRAMED APPLE PICTURE

*Even the youngest scholar will be able to help with this no-sew present for the teacher. Fusible fleece adds depth to the fabric, and dimensional paint adds the look of handstitching. The painted and stamped frame requires little woodworking experience—just use wooden strips, glue, and a few small clamps.*

**Size:** 14½ × 22⅛ inches

## MATERIALS

- Tracing paper
- Pencil
- Scissors and pinking shears
- ½ yard of paper-backed fusible web
- Iron
- 9 × 13-inch piece of fusible fleece
- 7 × 14-inch piece of tan print fabric, such as from V.I.P. Fabrics*
- 6-inch square each of 2 different red print fabrics
- Assorted fabric scraps: 3 of red plaid, 2 of green print, and 1 of brown print, such as from V.I.P. Fabrics*
- 12 × 19-inch piece of red check fabric, such as from V.I.P. Fabrics*
- Black dimensional fabric paint
- 9½ × 17⅛-inch piece of foam core board
- Carpenter's glue
- Ruler
- 12 feet of ¼ × 2⅝-inch wooden trim
- Miter box and saw
- 2-inch foam brush
- Maple stain varnish
- Slate blue acrylic paint
- Paper towels
- Clamps
- Set of ¾-inch-high capital-letter rubber alphabet stamps
- Green stamp pad

**See the "Buyer's Guide" on page 176.*

## DIRECTIONS

### MAKING THE APPLE PICTURE

1 Trace the patterns on page 142 onto tracing paper and cut them out. Use the patterns to mark two apples, two small hearts, one large heart, three leaves, and two stems (with one in reverse) on the paper side of the fusible web. Cut the shapes from the web, leaving ¼ inch extra outside the marked lines. Cut a 6¾ × 13¾-inch rectangular piece from the remaining web.

2 Following the manufacturer's directions, fuse the fleece to the wrong side of the large heart, one leaf, and one small heart.

3 Following the manufacturer's directions, fuse a 6¾ × 13¼-inch piece of the fleece to the wrong side of the tan print.

4 Fuse an apple to the wrong side of each of the two 6-inch red print squares. Fuse the leaf with the fleece from Step 2 onto one green print piece. Fuse a second leaf onto the same green print piece and one leaf onto the second green print piece. Fuse the two stems onto the brown print. Fuse the large heart with the fleece and the small heart with the fleece onto two different red plaids. Fuse the remaining small heart to the remaining red plaid. Fuse the 6¾ × 13¼-inch piece of web to the wrong side of the tan print–fleece piece.

5 Use the pinking shears to cut two 6½-inch squares from the tan print–fleece piece. Use the scissors to cut out the remaining shapes.

6 Refer to the photograph on the opposite page to center the two tan print–fleece squares on the 12 × 19-inch piece of red check, with the squares about 1 inch apart. Fuse the squares in place.

7 Fuse an apple to each tan print square. Fuse the large heart in the center of one apple and a small heart on each apple, as shown in the photograph. Fuse the stems and leaves in place, attaching the leaf with the fleece last.

8 Press the entire piece from the wrong side to completely secure the fused pieces.

9 Use the dimensional fabric paint to add the "stitches" along the outlines of the fused pieces, as shown in the photograph.

10 Mount the fabric picture onto the foam core board by centering the design and wrapping the edges of the fabric to the wrong side of the foam core board. Stretch the fabric taut on the foam core board and glue the edges in place with carpenter's glue.

### MAKING THE FRAME

1 Using the miter box and saw, cut the wooden trim into eight lengths for the two frame sections: Cut two 16⅞-inch lengths and two 14½-inch lengths for the front section; cut two 9¼-inch lengths and two 22⅛-inch lengths for the back section.

2 Apply a coat of varnish to the front, sides, and ends of each front frame piece. Apply a coat of the maple stain varnish to the sides and ends only of each back frame piece, since only these areas of the back frame will show. Let the varnish dry for at least three hours. Paint the varnished sections of the trim pieces with the blue acrylic. Before the paint is completely dry, use the paper towel to wipe off some of the blue so the wood grain shows through. Let the remaining paint dry thoroughly.

3 Referring to **Diagram 1,** place the front frame pieces face down on a flat surface and glue them together.

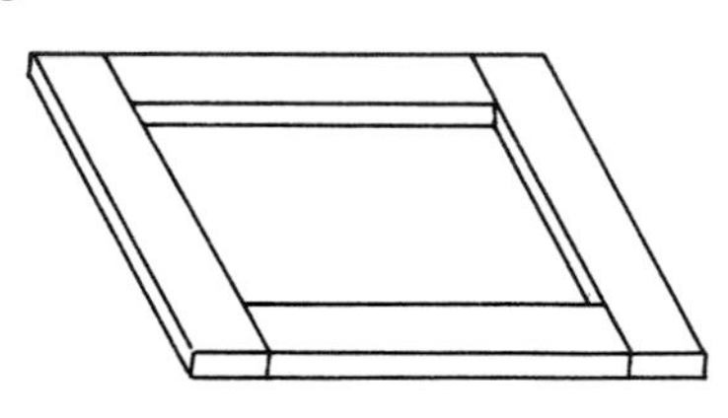

**Diagram 1**

4 Apply a thin coat of glue to the top side of these frame pieces. Referring to **Diagram 2,** place the assembled back frame pieces face side down onto the front frame pieces. Use the clamps to hold the frames in place until the glue is thoroughly dry.

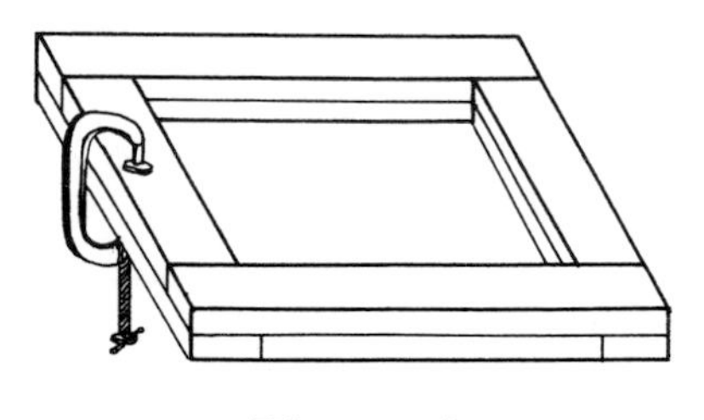

**Diagram 2**

5 Use the rubber stamps and green stamp pad to stamp the edges of the front of the frame with a motto. Stamp "A P P L E S" along the top, stamp "F O R" along the left side, stamp "T H E" along the right side, and stamp "T E A C H E R" along the bottom, as shown in the photograph on page 140. Space the letters about 1 inch apart and stamp them slightly askew.

6 Place the right side of the apple picture against the back of the frame, as shown in **Diagram 3.** Then carefully glue the picture into position.

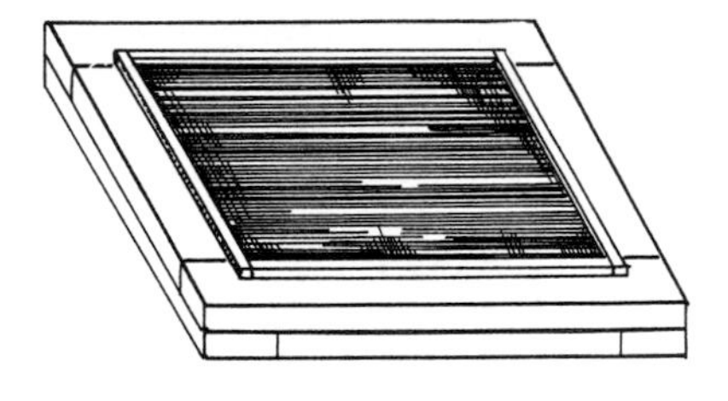

**Diagram 3**

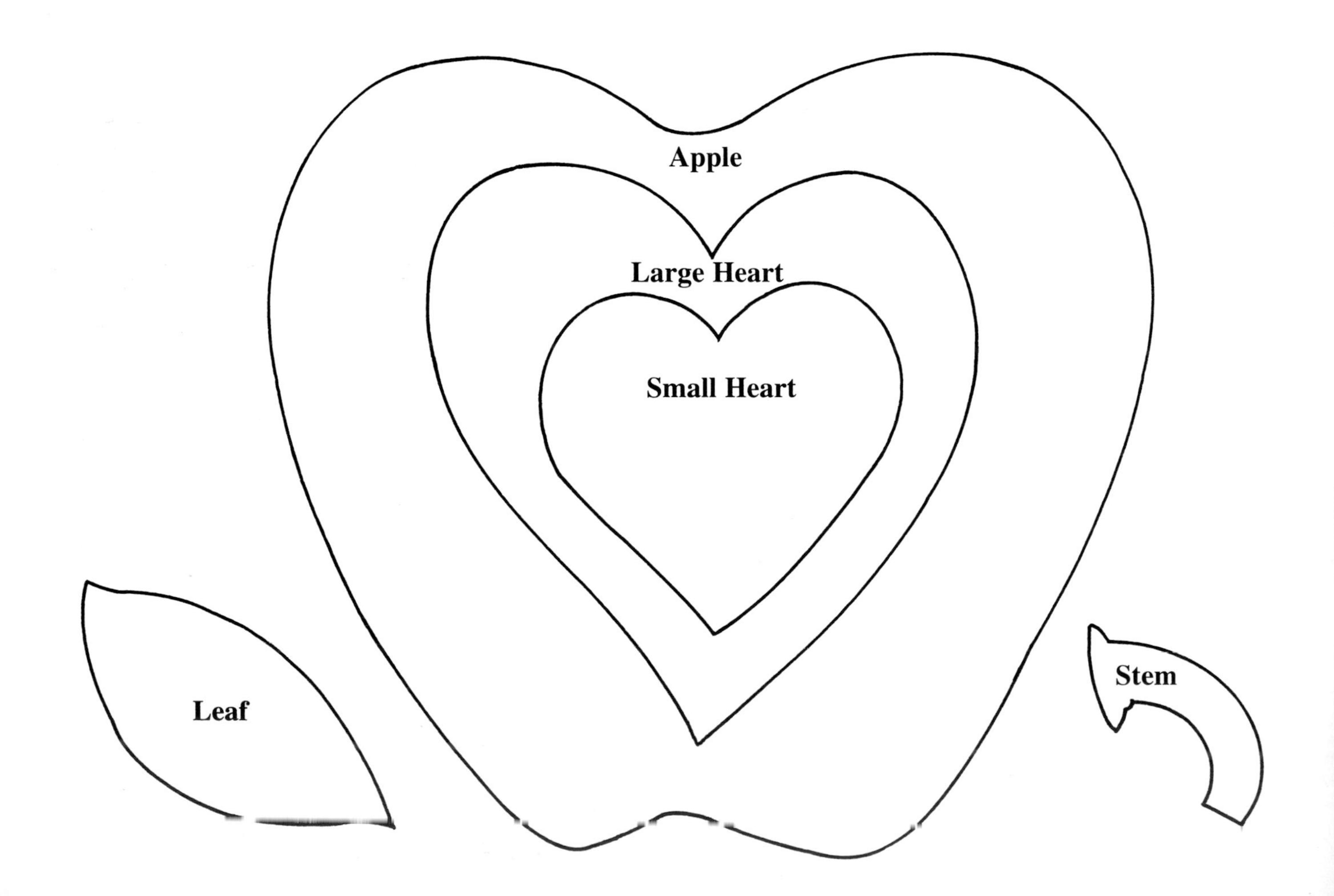

# WOVEN-RIBBON SHOULDER BAG

*Add an air of holiday excitement to your baby-sitter's outings. A shoulder bag woven of sparkling ribbons is the perfect party accessory. Choose colors to complement her coloring or her festive new outfits.*

**Size:** 5½ × 10 inches, with a 2½-inch-deep bottom

## Materials

- 14 × 17-inch piece of foam core board
- Aluminum foil
- Scissors
- Offray wire-edged ribbons: 3 yards of ⅞-inch-wide gold, 2¾ yards of ⅞-inch-wide ivory moiré, and 6½ yards of ⅝-inch-wide rose*
- Rustproof straight pins
- 12 × 15-inch piece of lightweight fusible interfacing
- Iron
- 12 × 15-inch piece of ivory fabric for the lining
- 9-inch ivory zipper
- Sewing machine
- Ivory thread
- Hand-sewing needle
- 2 large metallic gold tassels
- Fabric glue
- Gold thread
- 1 yard of ¼-inch-diameter metallic gold cording
- Thick white craft glue

*See the "Buyer's Guide" on page 176.

## Directions

**1** Cover one side of the foam core board with aluminum foil. Cut nine 12-inch lengths of rose ribbon and eight 12-inch lengths of ivory ribbon. Alternating the ribbon colors and beginning and ending with the rose ribbon, pin the ribbon lengths vertically along the 14-inch side of the foil-covered foam core board, as shown in **Diagram 1** on page 144; place the lengths right next to each other.

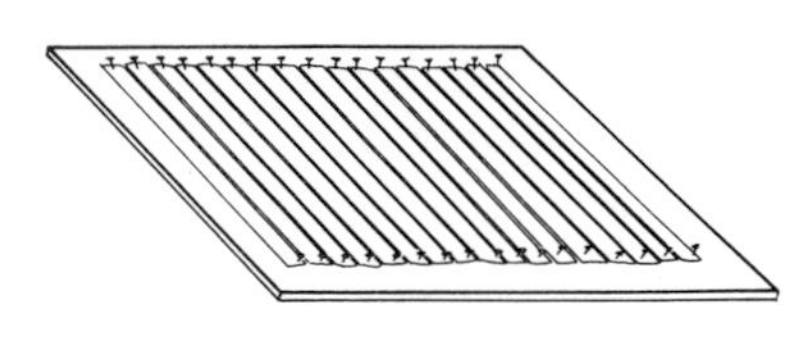

**Diagram 1**

2 Cut eight 15-inch lengths of rose ribbon and seven 15-inch lengths of gold ribbon. Beginning and ending with the rose, weave these ribbons horizontally, over and under the vertical lengths and right next to each other, as shown in **Diagram 2.** Unpin the short lengths at one end, as needed, to ease the weaving. Repin all the ends when the weaving is finished to square up the corners. Remove the woven ribbon fabric from the foam core board.

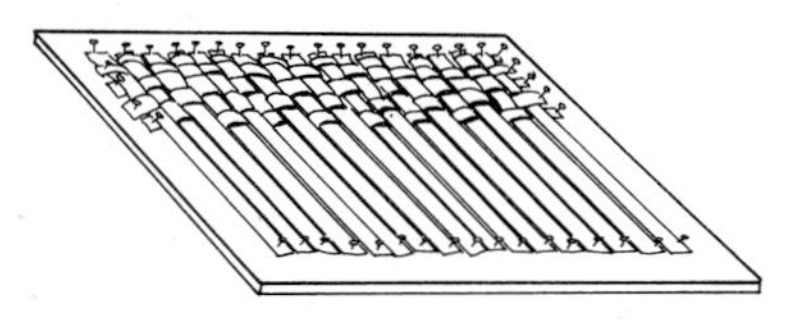

**Diagram 2**

3 Place the interfacing, fusible side down, on the woven ribbons. Remove the pins and fuse the interfacing in place following the manufacturer's directions to create the ribbon fabric. Trim the ribbon ends even with the interfacing.

4 Place the lining on a flat surface with the right side facing up. Referring to **Diagram 3,** place the zipper right side up along one short edge of the lining, carefully matching the edges. Place the woven ribbon fabric face down on the zipper and lining, matching the edges. Sew along this short edge close to the zipper teeth.

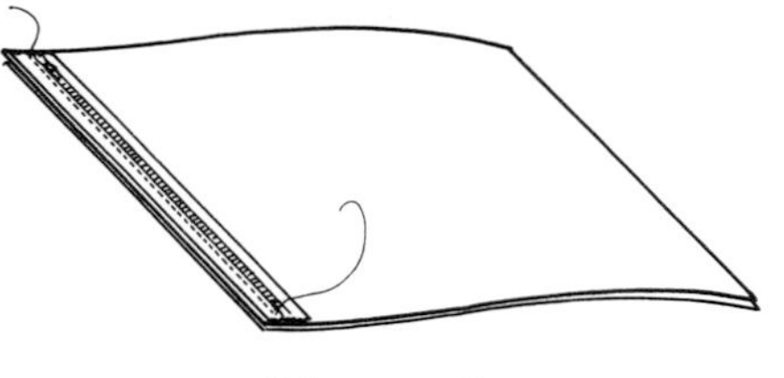

**Diagram 3**

5 Press ¼ inch to the wrong side on both the lining and woven ribbon fabrics along the opposite short edge. Using a ½-inch seam allowance, sew along both long edges, as shown in **Diagram 4.**

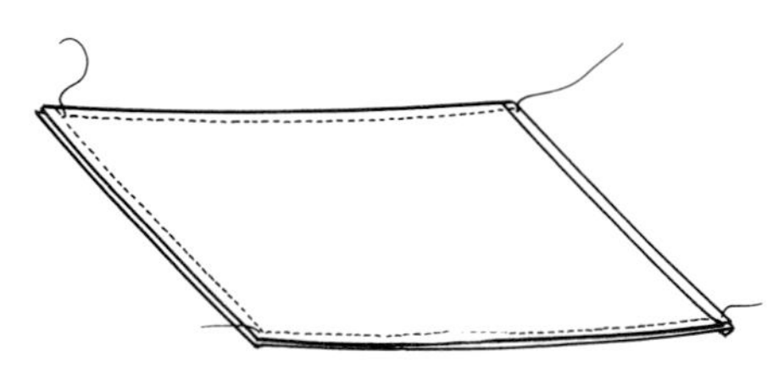

**Diagram 4**

6 Turn the fabrics right side out. Fold the purse in half crosswise to create a rounded bottom. Insert the free zipper edge between the pressed folds of the lining and woven ribbon fabric and slip stitch the folded edges to the zipper.

7 Turn the purse wrong side out. Referring to **Diagram 5,** fold the side seams to create tucks for the purse bottom. Sew across each corner, approximately 1¼ inches from the point. Turn the purse right side out again.

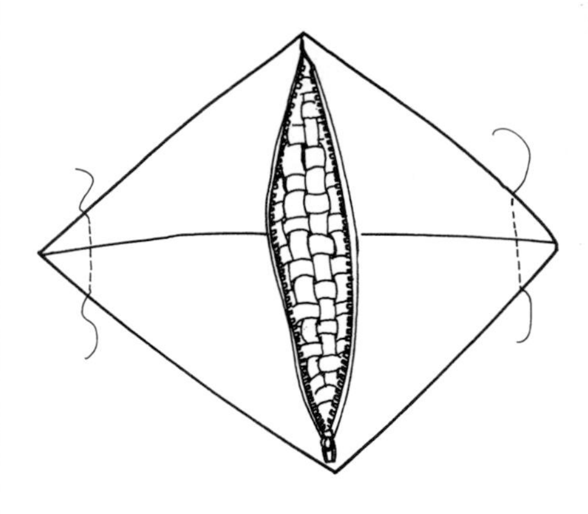

**Diagram 5**

8 To make the shoulder strap, tie a tassel 1 inch from each end of the decorative gold cording. Fold up each end of the cord and glue it in place. Wrap gold thread around the cording to cover each glued end. Attach the strap to the purse by tacking each end of cording to an upper corner of the purse.

9 After the purse is completed, you may find the ribbons have separated from the interfacing. Since the fusible interfacing was used to help construct the purse, its loosening will not affect the finished appearance.

# HIGH-FASHION ACCENTS

*Whether you choose to add barrettes, pin backs, or jacket clips, these rose-centered pieces will make perfect gifts. The glorious blooms are created with wired French ribbon and fused pearls. Gathering and folding are the only techniques you have to master to create these lovely roses. Delicate and Victorian-inspired as shown in soft peach, they would be dramatic fashion statements in true red or bright pink.*

# HANDMADE GIFT ENVELOPE

*A gift of cash or a gift certificate will be even more appreciated when it is delivered in a handmade envelope. Kids will enjoy making these simple gifts out of decorative paper and holiday shapes.*

**Size:** 4½ × 8½ inches

## Materials

- ❄ 8½ × 11-inch piece of decorative red paper
- ❄ Ruler
- ❄ Thick white craft glue
- ❄ Scissors and pinking shears
- ❄ Scraps of decorative paper in white, green, black, red, and orange
- ❄ Tracing paper

## Directions

**1** Fold up 4 inches on one short end of the red paper and glue it at the sides.

**2** Mark the center of the extending piece to create the pointed flap. Pink along the glued edges; then pink diagonally from the base of the flap to the center mark at the top edge, then back to the base of the flap on the other side.

**3** To make the snowman stamp, cut a 2 × 2½-inch piece of white paper. Cut a 1¾ × 2-inch piece of green paper. Glue the green paper to the center of the white paper. Use the full-size **Snowman Stamp** pattern to trace and cut out a white snowman; a black hat, eyes, and buttons; a red scarf; and an orange carrot nose. Glue the paper shapes to the stamp in the order listed. Fold down the envelope flap and glue the stamp on the point, with 1 inch extending below the flap.

## *Giving Gift Certificates*

❄

**It isn't always possible to give a personalized gift to someone you wish to remember. When that happens, think about giving a gift certificate. Many businesses offer them in a wide variety of denominations, and all offer the chance for a special splurge. In addition to the usual stores and services, you might consider giving the following certificates:**

- ❄ **Supermarkets**
- ❄ **Service stations**
- ❄ **Retail chains**
- ❄ **Beauty salons**
- ❄ **Bike shops**
- ❄ **Restaurants**

# EGGSHELL INLAY DESK SET

*Creating these very special desk accessories is time-involved and detailed, but the results speak for themselves. The look of a treasured heirloom is captured in this classic craft. If time doesn't permit making the entire set for your employer or coworker, just make the note holder or pencil cup as a small token of friendship.*

**Size:** To fit purchased accessories

## MATERIALS

- Eggshells
- Large-mouth glass jar with lid
- Chlorine bleach
- Paper towels
- Foam brush
- Navy acrylic paint
- Desk set pieces: pencil cup, blotter, and memo pad holder, such as canvas ones from Dalee Book Co.*
- Masking tape
- Ruler
- Pencil
- Thick white craft glue
- Scissors
- Single-edged razor blade
- Emery boards
- Soft cloth
- Matte sealer
- Cotton swabs
- Antique gold decorator's gilt metallic wax

*See the "Buyer's Guide" on page 176.*

## DIRECTIONS

1 Clean the eggshells with warm soapy water and rinse well. Place them in the glass jar and pour in enough bleach to completely cover the eggshells. Place the lid on the container and let the shells soak for two days.

2 After two days, drain off the bleach and thoroughly rinse the shells with water. Set the shells on paper towels to dry. Crack and flatten the shell pieces. Save all the shell pieces; even the smallest piece can be used to fill in a space in the inlay area.

3 Using the foam brush, brush a coat of navy acrylic paint on the outer surfaces of the desk accessories where the inlay is to be placed. Let the paint dry thoroughly before proceeding.

4 Use the masking tape, ruler, and pencil to mark the edges of the gold-color diamond shapes on the desk pieces, as shown in the photograph on page 149. Outline a 1-inch diamond on the pencil cup, three 2-inch diamonds spaced about ⅜ inch apart on each end of the blotter, and one 1-inch diamond on the top of the memo pad holder.

5 Use pieces of shell to fill each diamond shape. Apply a thin coat of glue to the back of a shell piece and press it firmly in place within the taped areas. Allow the shell to crack to create the fine web of cracks that define the technique. Continue to glue shell pieces to fill the taped spaces, shaping the shell edges with a scissors, razor blade, or an emery board as needed to fit the designated spaces. Let the filled diamonds dry thoroughly before you proceed.

6 Use the razor blade to trim the shells along the sides of the diamond for a clean edge. Carefully remove the masking tape.

7 Leaving a ⅛-inch margin around the sides of the diamond shape to allow the background color to show, glue shells to cover the remainder of the surface to be inlaid. Let the edges of the shell pieces extend beyond the edges of the item; they will be trimmed later. Let the item dry overnight.

8 Use a soft cloth to clean off any glue residue from the surface of the shells. Apply a coat of matte sealer and let it dry thoroughly.

9 Use the razor blade or scissors to trim the shell edges that extend beyond the edges of the item. File any rough edges with the emery board. Retouch any navy-painted areas if needed and let the paint dry thoroughly.

10 Apply a second coat of matte sealer.

11 Following the directions from the manufacturer, use a cotton swab to carefully apply the metallic wax to the diamond shapes. Let the wax set for a short time. Apply a third coat of sealer.

# CORK FEEDING MATS

*A special gift mat will highlight your affection for your kitty or pooch. Since most pets can use your help in the neatness department, these place mats are made from cork to stay put and are large enough to catch inevitable spills. Paint the mats with cute, pet-inspired motifs.*

## Pet Collar Mat

**Size:** 12 × 18 inches

### Materials

- Thick white craft glue
- Two 12 × 18-inch pieces of ⅛-inch cork
- Tracing paper and pencil
- Scissors
- Pop-up craft sponge
- Compass
- Saucer or palette
- Silver acrylic paint
- Paintbrush
- Black, permanent marking pen

### Directions

1 Use the craft glue to glue the two pieces of cork together to make a ¼-inch-thick mat.

2 Trace the **Chain Link Pattern** onto the tracing paper. Cut out the shape and use the pencil to outline it on the pop-up sponge. This will be the stamping sponge. Cut out the sponge and wet it so it expands. Squeeze out any excess water.

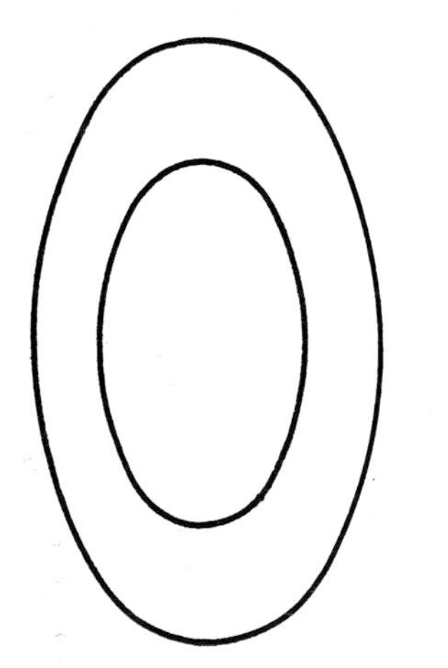

**Chain Link Pattern**

3 Use the compass to mark a 2½-inch-diameter "dog tag" circle on the cork mat 2 inches from the center top edge. The tag will connect to the links in the chain.

4 Place the paint on a saucer or palette. Dip the link-shaped sponge in the paint, then press it onto the cork with a light, even pressure. Stamp the chain links ¾ inch from the edge and around all four sides of the mat, overlapping each link about 1 inch, as shown in the photograph on page 151. Use the brush to paint the dog tag silver. Stamp a link to connect each end of the chain to the dog tag.

5 Use the marking pen to outline the dog tag and each chain link, omitting the link outline where it overlaps the connecting link, as shown in the **Link Diagram.** Letter the pet's name in the dog tag.

**Link Diagram**

## Dog Bone Mat

**Size:** 14 × 20 inches

### Materials

- Thick white craft glue
- Two 15 × 21-inch pieces of ⅛-inch cork
- Tracing paper
- Pencil
- Scissors
- Pop-up craft sponges
- Acrylic paints in yellow, red, blue, green, and black
- Saucers or palettes
- Paintbrush

### Directions

1 Use the craft glue to glue the two cork pieces together to make a ¼-inch-thick mat.

2 Referring to Step 2 of the "Pet Collar Mat" on this page, make a circle and a bone sponge stamp for each paint color.

3 Enlarge and trace the **Dog Bone Mat Quarter-Pattern** on page 154 onto a sheet of tracing paper. Cut out the shape and use it to outline the full dog bone shape on the piece of cork, as shown in the **Dog Bone Diagram.** Cut out the mat shape.

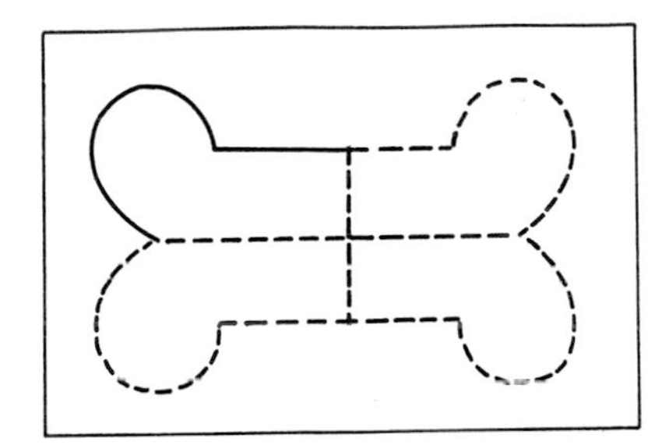

**Dog Bone Diagram**

4 Place the paints on the saucers or palettes. Dip a craft sponge into the acrylic paint, and then press it onto the cork with a light, even pressure. Use a different sponge for each color of paint. Stamp the bones and circles on the mat in a random fashion, as shown in the photograph on the opposite page. Use the paintbrush to fill in any areas skipped by the sponge stamp.

# Mice Mat

**Size:** 10 × 30 inches

## Materials

- Tracing paper
- Pencil
- Scissors
- Two 11 × 31-inch pieces of ⅛-inch cork
- Thick white craft glue
- Acrylic paints in bright pink, gray, and black
- Saucers or palettes
- Paintbrush

## Directions

1 Enlarge and trace the **Mice Mat Half-Pattern** on page 154 onto the tracing paper. Cut out the shape and use it to outline the two mice shapes on the piece of cork, as shown in the **Mice Diagram.** Using the pencil, mark the eye, nose, whisker, and tail shapes on the cork mat. Trace the **Ear Pattern** on page 154 as a separate pattern. Outline an ear shape for each mouse on the piece of cork. Cut out the ear shapes.

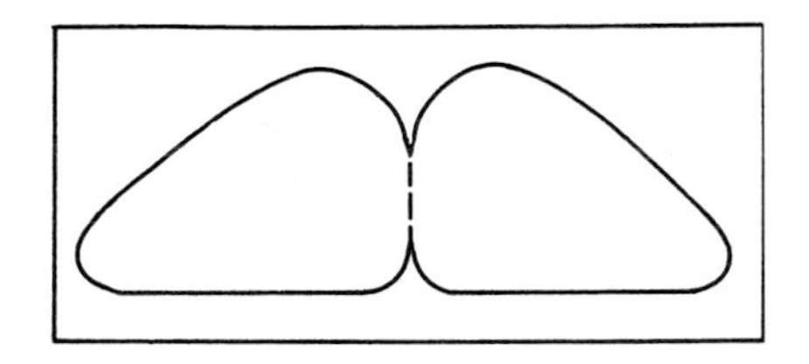

**Mice Diagram**

2 Use the craft glue to glue the second cork piece to the back of the first cork piece to make a ¼-inch-thick mat. Cut out the mat shape.

3 Place the paints on the saucers or palettes. Use the paintbrush to paint the tails and ears gray, the noses pink, and the eyes and whiskers black. Paint a thin black line between the mouse tails, as shown in the photograph below. Let the paints dry thoroughly.

4 Using the craft glue, glue the ears in place.

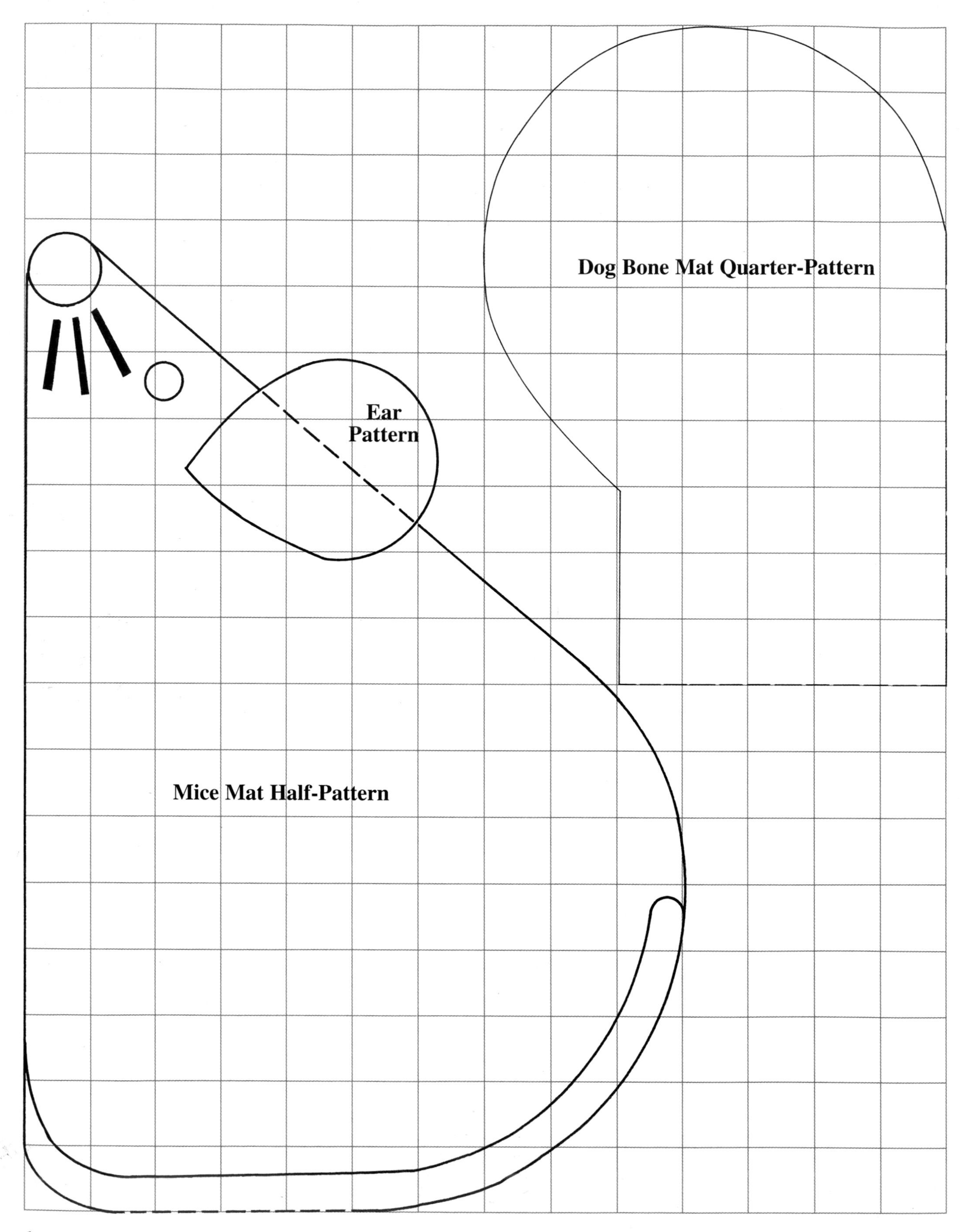
Dog Bone Mat Quarter-Pattern
Ear
Pattern
Mice Mat Half-Pattern
1 square = 1 inch
Enlarge 200%

# PERSONALIZED PET STOCKINGS

*Felt, glue, and fabric paint are all it takes to create special stockings for the furry, four-legged members of the family. Tabby hopes for miles of yarn to play with, while Butch's mind is fixed on treats. You'll have plenty of room for all sorts of toys and temptations in these oversized, easy-to-craft stockings.*

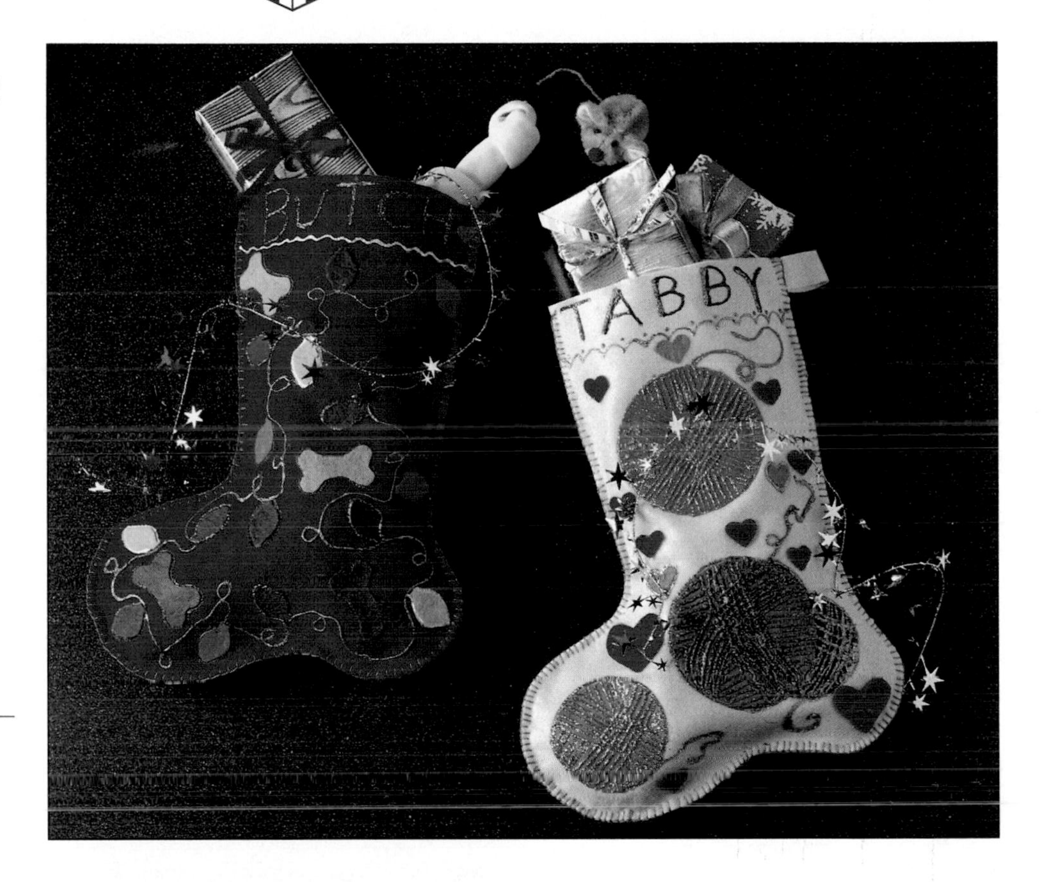


## Cat Stocking

**Size:** 16½ inches long

### Materials

- Tracing paper
- Pencil
- Scissors
- ½ yard of cream felt and small amounts of red, candy pink, green, medium blue, and orange felt
- Thick white craft glue
- Dimensional glitter fabric paints in gold, raspberry, blue, orange, and green
- Dark green, dimensional shiny fabric paint
- Large-eyed embroidery needle
- Skein of medium green embroidery floss

### Directions

1 Enlarge as indicated and then carefully trace the **Stocking, Small Heart, Small Ball, Large Heart, Large Ball,** and **Partial Ball** patterns on page 157. Cut out all of the pattern pieces.

2 From the cream felt, cut two stockings and one 1 × 5-inch piece for the hanging loop. From the red felt, cut eight small hearts and two large hearts. From the pink felt, cut three small hearts and one small ball. From the green felt, cut one partial ball. From the blue and orange felt, cut one large ball of each color.

3 Refer to the **Cat Stocking Placement Diagram** for the position of the appliqué pieces. Use the craft glue to glue the pieces in place on one stocking piece. Let the glue dry thoroughly.

**Cat Stocking Placement Diagram**

4 Use the matching color dimensional glitter paint to paint the strands of "wound yarn" on each felt ball. Paint six to eight strands in one direction, curving the lines slightly for the wound-yarn effect, as shown in **Diagram 1.** Let the paint dry thoroughly before painting the next group of yarn strands.

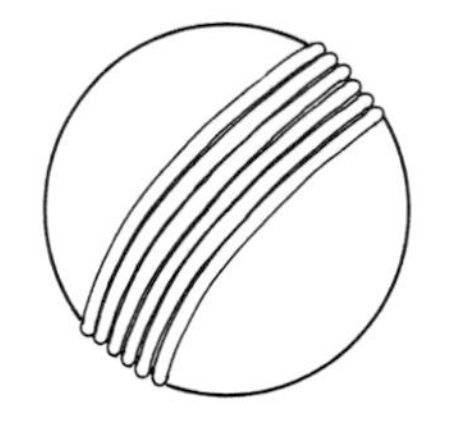

**Diagram 1**

5 Paint the next group of strands in another direction, working over the existing strands as needed. Continue to paint groups of strands until the entire ball is covered, as shown in **Diagram 2.**

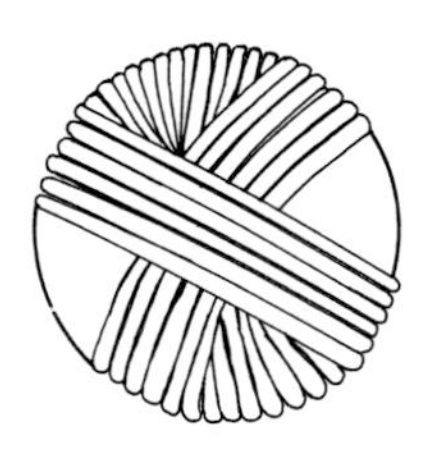

**Diagram 2**

6 With a slightly thinner line of paint, outline the yarn ball. Add the loose yarn tail as a curved line of paint, spreading the paint slightly for a thicker strand.

7 Referring to the photograph on page 155, use the gold paint to outline two of the pink hearts. Paint a scalloped and dotted gold line about 2 inches from the top edge of the stocking. Use the shiny green paint to paint the pet's name across the space above the scalloped line. Use the green glitter paint to highlight the left edge of each letter, as shown in **Diagram 3.** Let the paints dry for 48 hours.

**Diagram 3**

8 Place the two stocking pieces together with the wrong sides facing. Fold the felt hanging loop in half and insert it between the stocking pieces at the upper back edge. Referring to **Diagram 4,** use a blanket stitch and the embroidery floss to sew the sides and lower edges of the stocking together, catching the hanging loop in the stitching.

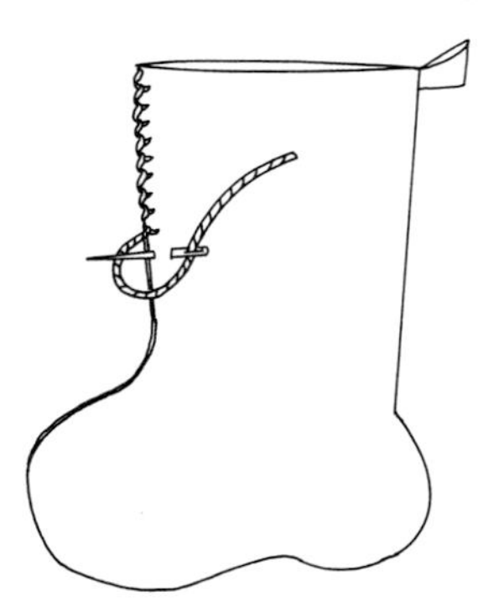

**Diagram 4**

# Dog Stocking

**Size:** 16½ inches long

## Materials

- ❄ Tracing paper and pencil
- ❄ Scissors
- ❄ ½ yard of red felt and small amounts of camel, medium brown, royal blue, green, orange, and bright yellow felt
- ❄ Air-soluble marking pen
- ❄ Thick white craft glue
- ❄ Dimensional glitter fabric paints in gold, blue, and orange
- ❄ Large-eyed embroidery needle
- ❄ Dimensional shiny fabric paints in green, brown, pink, and pearl
- ❄ Skein of pink embroidery floss

## Directions

1 Enlarge and trace the **Stocking, Dog Bone,** and **Tree Light** patterns on the opposite page. Cut out all the pattern pieces.

2 From the red felt, cut two stockings and one 1 × 5-inch piece for the hanging loop. From the camel felt, cut two dog bones. From the brown felt, cut three dog bones. From the blue, green, and orange felt, cut four tree lights each. From the yellow felt, cut three tree lights.

3 Refer to the **Dog Stocking Placement Diagram** for the position of the appliqué pieces. Use the marking pen to draw the light cord on one stocking piece. Use the craft glue to glue the pieces in place on the stocking piece, arranging the tree lights along the light-cord line. Let the glue dry thoroughly.

**Dog Stocking Placement Diagram**

4 Use the dimensional glitter or shiny paint to outline the lights and bones. Use the gold paint for the light cord and the pearl paint to paint a wavy line 2 inches from the top edge of the piece. Use the blue glitter paint to paint the pet's name in the space above the wavy line. Use the shiny pink paint to paint a heart behind the pet's name. Let all of the paints dry for 48 hours. Assemble the stocking, referring to Step 8 of the "Cat Stocking" above.

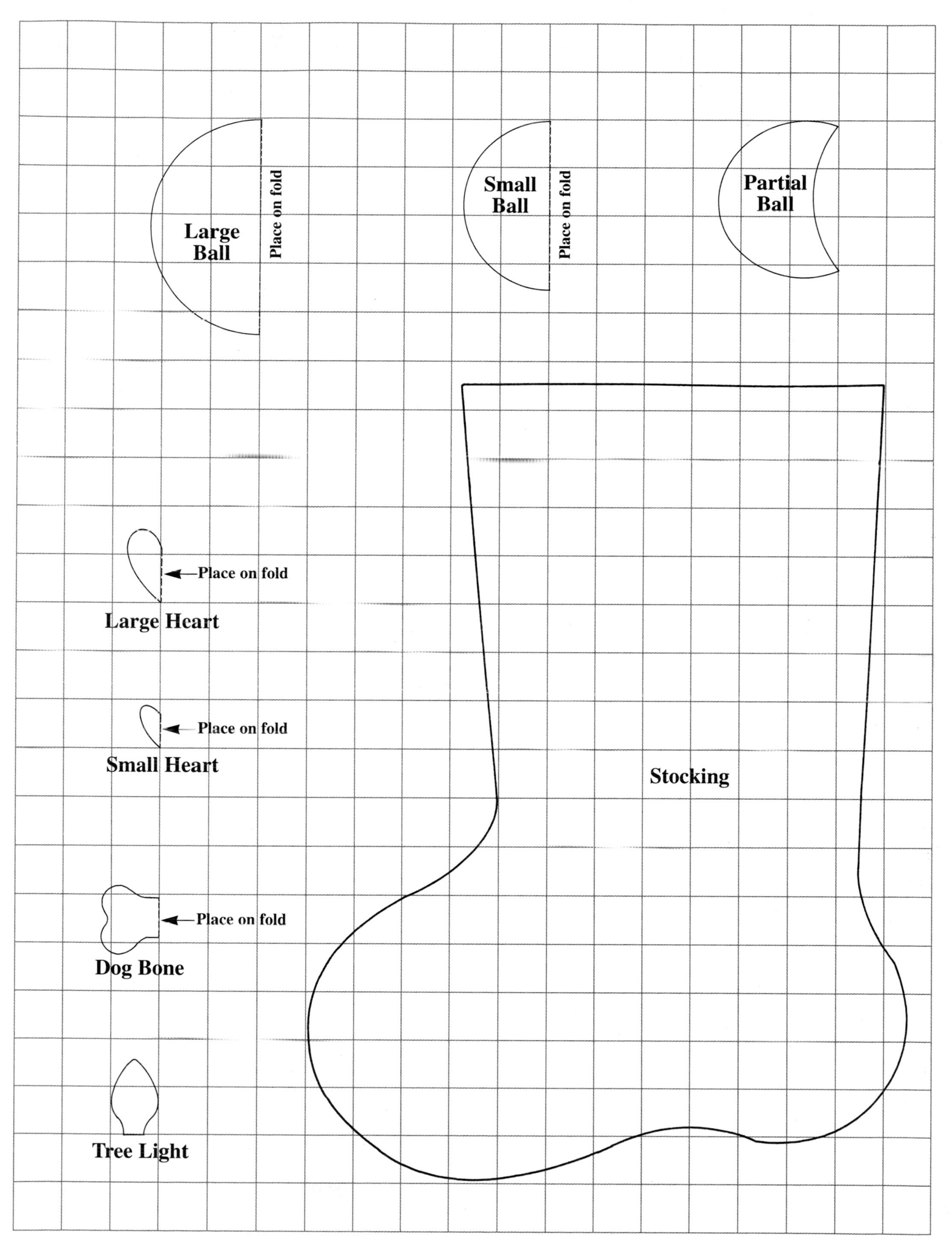


1 square = 1 inch

Enlarge 266%

*Chapter Seven*

# Favor-ite Gifts

*One of the greatest joys of the season is hosting friends and family. We've designed small gifts that can be used as place markers or souvenirs for special occasions. Fill simple herb bags with a mixture of herbs and spices, or craft a fabric game to have at each place setting. Your home-blended bath oils can be formulated to relax or energize. Easy hair scrunchies are ideal grab bag gifts. Involve the family in crafting shapes from polymer clays or in making angels from handkerchiefs as favors.*

# SWEET HANDKERCHIEF ANGELS

*Originally created to keep children quiet during church services, handkerchief dolls required only a few deft twists and a couple of knots. Our angels are beautifully embellished, but the original technique is still apparent. Angels have long been a part of Christmas; let these celestial messengers continue to warm your heart.*

## Lace-Winged Angel

**Size:** About 9 inches tall

### Materials

- Iron
- Two 12-inch-square handkerchiefs: 1 white with lace trim and 1 with colored appliqué
- Small amount of polyester fiberfill
- White thread
- Hand-sewing needle
- 12-inch length of ¼-inch-wide gold braid
- Small amounts of blue and rose embroidery floss and an embroidery needle
- Cosmetic blush and cotton swab
- Short lengths of cotton string or floss in different weights
- Thick white craft glue
- Gold metallic thread
- 12-inch length of gold star garland

### Directions

1 Press the handkerchiefs to eliminate any creases.

2 Fold the lace-trimmed hankie in half diagonally to form a triangle. Place a small, walnut-sized ball of fiberfill into the center of the folded hankie. Gather the hankie

below the ball to shape the angel's head. Then use the white thread to wrap and loosely tie the gathers together. Tie the gold braid around the neck to cover the thread wrap.

3 Fold the appliquéd hankie in half diagonally with the appliqué at the center front. Referring to **Diagram 1,** fold the two side points of this triangle to the back and tack with a few hand stitches. Knot the thread but do not cut it.

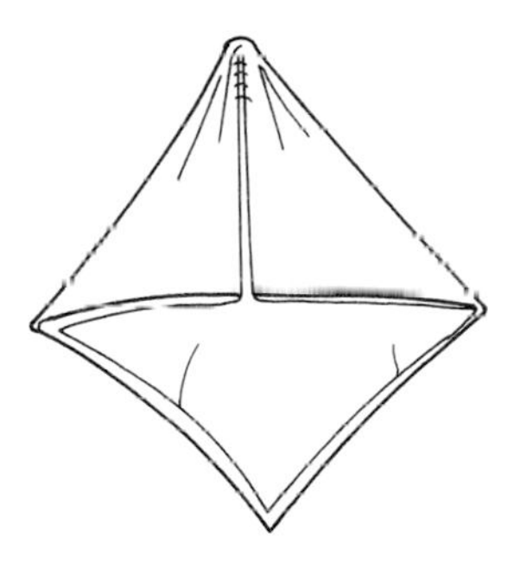

**Diagram 1**

4 Place the folded appliquéd hankie inside the lace-trimmed hankie angel and insert the folded point of the appliquéd hankie in the neck gathers of the angel. Use the thread still attached to the second hankie to tack it under the head, as shown in **Diagram 2.**

**Diagram 2**

5 Smooth the top hankie. Pull the two side points of the top hankie to the back of the angel, then pinch the ends close to the head to shape the wings, as shown in **Diagram 3.** Then tack the pinched area of the wings to the back of the angel's head to secure the gathers.

**Diagram 3**

6 Referring to the photograph on the opposite page, use three strands of floss to embroider the angel's face as follows: Stitching from the back of the head through to the front, work blue French knots for the eyes and two rose straight stitches for the mouth, as shown in the **Stitch Details.** Apply the blush to the cheeks with a cotton swab.

7 Untwist the plies of the cotton string or floss to make tresses of wavy hair. Spread a small amount of craft glue on the top and sides of the angel's head and glue the hair on the head. After the glue has dried, use the gold thread to hand stitch a center "part" in the angel's hair. Twist the star garland into a halo and tack it to the head with gold thread.

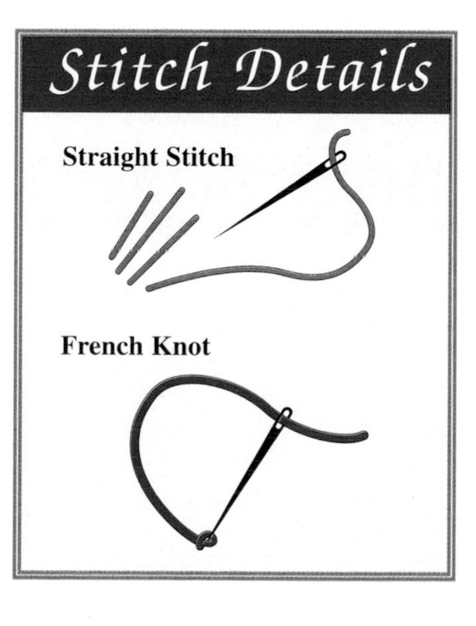


## *Treasuring Yesterday's Hankies*

❄

**Handkerchief dolls and angels are a delightful way to display fine old handkerchiefs. You will find most vintage handkerchiefs have a main design in one corner; use that area for the front of the angel's "skirt." The lace edging of the handkerchief trims the "hem" of the angel's top. Hide any stained or discolored spots with strategic tucking and stitching—or the addition of a little embroidery.**

❄

**While handkerchiefs from the early 1900s were usually made of linen fabric, embroidered and lace-trimmed handkerchiefs from the 1930s and 1940s were more frequently made of cotton fabric with brightly colored floral patterns. You will find that each type of handkerchief will produce a beautiful angel with a different look.**

❄

**How wonderful it would be to present every granddaughter with a pretty little angel made from one of Grandmother's prized handkerchiefs as a family remembrance. Attach a note saying that the recipient should display her angel in a miniature chair, on a keepsake shelf, or floating angelically from nylon fishing line in a china cabinet.**

## Print Hankie Angel

**Size:** About 9 inches tall

### Materials

- ❄ Two 12-inch-square handkerchiefs: 1 embroidered and lace-trimmed, and 1 floral print
- ❄ Polyester fiberfill
- ❄ White thread
- ❄ Hand-sewing needle
- ❄ 12-inch length of ⅛-inch-wide green ribbon
- ❄ Thick white craft glue
- ❄ Small amounts of dried craft artemisia, tiny acorns, and dried flowers
- ❄ 6-inch-diameter Battenberg lace doily
- ❄ 6-inch length of artificial pine branch

### Directions

1 Repeat Steps 1 through 5 of the "Lace-Winged Angel" on pages 160 and 161 to shape and join the two hankies together; use the embroidered hankie for the head triangle and the floral print for the second hankie. At the neck, tie the ribbon instead of the braid.

2 Twist the tacked "wing" points to form the arms, as shown in the **Arm Diagram,** then pull them to the front and tack the ends of the arms together. Tack the arms to the front of the embroidered hankie.

**Arm Diagram**

3 Glue on the artemisia for hair, then add acorns and dried flowers for accents, referring to the photograph on page 160.

4 Gather the center of the Battenberg lace doily and pull up the gathers to shape the wings. Tack the wings to the angel's back.

5 Twist the pine branch into a circular halo and tack it to the back of the angel's head.

## Sunflower Angel

**Size:** About 9 inches tall

### Materials

- ❄ Two 12-inch-square white handkerchiefs with embroidery
- ❄ Small amount of polyester fiberfill
- ❄ Small amount of raffia
- ❄ Scissors
- ❄ White thread
- ❄ Hand-sewing needle
- ❄ 2 green velvet leaves
- ❄ Embroidery needle and small amounts of blue and rose embroidery floss
- ❄ Cosmetic blush and cotton swab
- ❄ Gold thread
- ❄ Spanish moss
- ❄ Thick white craft glue
- ❄ 1½-inch-diameter silk sunflower

### Directions

1 Repeat Steps 1 and 2 of the "Lace-Winged Angel" on pages 160 and 161 to form the head; use the raffia instead of the white thread to tie the gathers.

2 Fold the second hankie in half diagonally. Referring to the **Twisting Diagram,** pull out the side points and twist to make the arms. Tie 3-inch lengths of raffia at the ends of the arms for "wrists."

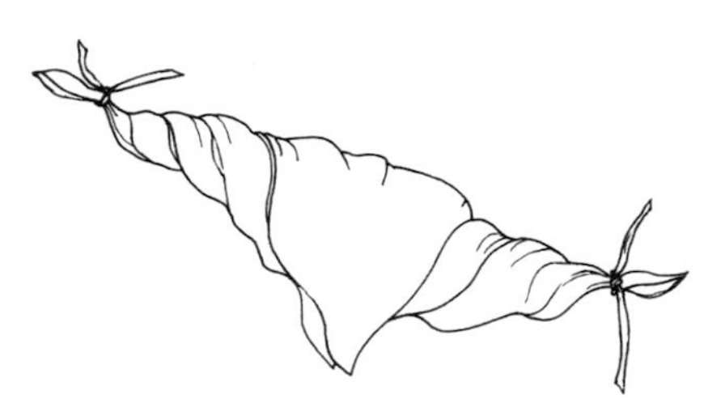

**Twisting Diagram**

3 Cut a small slit just below the head on each side of the first hankie. Slip the second hankie inside the first, then pull the arms through the slits. Pull the points down to form an underskirt.

4 Shape the angel's bodice by wrapping a length of raffia around the body as follows: Beginning at the front of the waist, wrap each raffia end around to the back and then back to the front. Continue wrapping up across the chest and over the shoulders to the back, then around to the front, tying it in the center.

5 Use the white thread to tack the two velvet leaves to the angel's back for wings, slightly angling the leaves, so they show from the front.

6 Repeat Step 6 of the "Lace-Winged Angel" on page 161 to embroider the face of the angel and apply the blush.

7 Cut the gold thread into short lengths. Glue the lengths of thread, along with the moss, onto the angel's head for hair. Cut the stem off the sunflower and glue the flower to the top of the head.

# HOLIDAY HAIR SCRUNCHIES

*Make heads turn! Scrunchies make perfect favors, gifts, and stocking stuffers because they are easy to craft and only require a few yards of opulent ribbon to complete. Add glimmering trinkets and buttons for fashionable accents. You'll create many variations of these "little something extras" for girls of all ages on your list.*

# GOURMET HERB BAGS

*Do friends adore your cooking skills and look forward to dining at your home? Why not give them a taste of your special herbs as a little Christmas favor when they come to visit? Share the recipe—or keep it a secret so they will come back to you for more!*

**Size:** 3½ × 6 inches

## Materials

- ❄ Fabric paints in several shades of green
- ❄ Saucer or palette
- ❄ Sprigs of various fresh herbs
- ❄ Paper towels
- ❄ 4 × 10-inch piece of tightly woven muslin for each bag
- ❄ Scissors
- ❄ Sewing machine
- ❄ 8-inch length of 1½-inch-wide eyelet lace for each bag
- ❄ Herb mixture
- ❄ 10-inch length of ⅛-inch-diameter gold cord for each bag

## Directions

1 Working with one shade of paint at a time, squirt a small amount of paint onto the saucer or palette and spread it around evenly. Lightly touch the largest sprig into the paint. Press the sprig onto the paper towel to remove the excess paint, then touch it to the muslin, centering it on one-half of the length. Repeat for the other bags. Allow the paint to dry thoroughly.

2 Repeat with the remaining shades of paint and sprigs, arranging them into a pleasing design. Use the darkest paint first, then the lightest, then as desired. Allow the paint to dry thoroughly between each touching.

3 Cut the lace in half. With right sides facing, sew one piece to each short end of the bag. Sew the side seams, using a ¼-inch seam allowance. Clip the corners; trim the seams and turn the bag right side out.

4 Fill the bag two-thirds full with the "Herb Recipe" on this page or your own mixture. Tie the neck closed with a length of gold cord.

## *Herb Recipe*

❄

**The herbs used in the featured blend are an approximation of Herbes de Provence. Mix the herb blend in large quantities during the summer when the herbs are inexpensive and easy to come by. You might even grow your own! You will have plenty for gifts and for use throughout the year.**

❄

**Combine equal parts of dried thyme, rosemary, basil, and marjoram, and blend the mixture evenly. If desired, add a small amount—not more than a quarter of the amount of the other spices—of anise. Store in an airtight container.**

# PAMPERING BATH OILS

*The gift of aromatherapy can reduce stress, revitalize, and refresh. Create bath oils specifically balanced to create energy or calm by blending fragrant oils with herbs, spices, and flowers. These luxurious bath treats are composed of two different types of oil—a base oil for a foundation and a fragrant essential oil.*

**Size:** As desired

## MATERIALS

- ❄ Glass mixing bowl
- ❄ Spoon
- ❄ Base oil, such as sweet almond, safflower, sunflower, or soy
- ❄ Essential oil
- ❄ Dried herbs, spices, fruits, or flowers, as desired
- ❄ Decorative glass bottle with a cork stopper
- ❄ Funnel
- ❄ Sealing wax
- ❄ Ribbon or raffia, as desired

## DIRECTIONS

1 In the mixing bowl, combine three parts of any base oil with one part of any essential oil to make each bath oil. Stir the mixture thoroughly with a spoon.

2 Place herbs, spices, fruits, or flowers in the glass bottle. Be sure the pieces you have chosen will complement the scent of the selected essential oil.

3 Using the funnel, pour the bath oil into the bottle.

4 Replace the cork stopper and seal with sealing wax, following the manufacturer's directions.

5 Accent the bottle with ribbon or raffia and dried flowers or spice sticks, as desired.

## *Pleasure Scents*

❄

**Base oils are light and unobtrusive, supporting the essential oils without confusing or overpowering any of the stronger scents. Essential oils, by comparison, are extracted by a distillation process and embody the very essence of a particular plant. Take the time to search out the true essential oils—the more readily available perfume oils have been greatly diluted and will not produce the desired fragrance strength.**

**Match your essential oil to the results you desire. Notice that a number of different scents have similar properties. If you wish to blend different essential oils together, try the mixes in small quantities first and allow them to meld for several minutes before sniffing.**

- ❄ **ACHING MUSCLES: eucalyptus, lavender, and rosemary**
- ❄ **ANTISEPTIC: eucalyptus, juniper, lavender, peppermint, and tea tree**
- ❄ **REFRESHING: lemon, lime, pepper mint, pine, and spearmint**
- ❄ **RELAXING: chamomile, clary, cypress, frankincense, lavender, lemon verbena, sandalwood, sassafras, rose, rose geranium, thyme, and vanilla**
- ❄ **SOOTHING: aloe vera, calendula, catnip, rose, sassafras, tangerine, tansy, and ylang-ylang**
- ❄ **STIMULATING: bay, hops, jasmine, juniper, lemon balm, marjoram, patchouli, peppermint, rosemary, and rosewood**
- ❄ **UPLIFTING: bergamot, geranium, jasmine, lemongrass, orange, patchouli, and rosemary**

# CLAY CHRISTMAS JEWELRY

*Some of the simplest polymer-clay techniques have been used to create these timely party favors. Your guests will love them so much, they'll want to wear their gifts home. Just be careful—everything looks good enough to eat!*

## MATERIALS

For all the jewelry:
- ❄ Craft knife
- ❄ Clay blocks as indicated for individual projects*
- ❄ Plastic food-storage bags
- ❄ White-paper work surface covering for each project
- ❄ 6-inch length of ½-inch-diameter Plexiglas rod
- ❄ Ruler
- ❄ Baking sheet
- ❄ Wire cooling rack

**See the "Buyer's Guide" on page 176.*

## DIRECTIONS

### CONDITIONING THE CLAY

**1** Use the craft knife to cut the clay block into small pieces, as you would dice a vegetable. Knead a few pieces together until soft. (The clay is soft when, after being rolled into a rod, it can be folded in half without cracking.) Add additional pieces of the cut clay into the softened clay and knead until it is incorporated into the mix. Continue adding and softening pieces of clay until the entire block of clay has been softened. Place the clay in a food-storage bag to keep it soft.

**2** Repeat the softening process for each color of clay. Store each color in a separate bag until you are ready to work with it.

### MAKING THE SHAPES

**1** *To make a slab:* Flatten the clay slightly with your fingers, poking the point of the craft knife into any bubbles that appear. Next, place the clay on a paper-covered work surface and use the Plexiglas rod to gently roll out the clay. After a few rolls, lift and turn the slab to keep it from sticking to the surface and to correct for uneven pressure. Use the ruler to check the thickness of the slab. To make a slab of a certain size, roll the slab to a size slightly larger than the desired finished size. Use a ruler and the craft knife to cut the slab to the correct size and to give it an even edge.

**2** *To make a basic rod:* Place the clay on a flat, paper-covered surface and use the palm of the hand to stretch and roll the clay into a rod. Roll from the center out to the ends with light, even pressure. Press the ends in to keep them from narrowing. After a few rolls, lift and turn the rod to keep it from sticking to the work surface. Use a ruler to measure the rod diameter.

**3** *To make a triangle rod:* Roll a basic rod following Step 2 above. With the rod placed on a flat, paper-covered surface, squeeze the top between two fingers to shape the top curve of the triangle, as shown in the **Triangle Rod Diagram.** Press from the center out to the ends. Roll the rod onto a flattened side and squeeze the new top edge as before. Roll once more and repeat on the third side for a triangle rod with three equal sides.

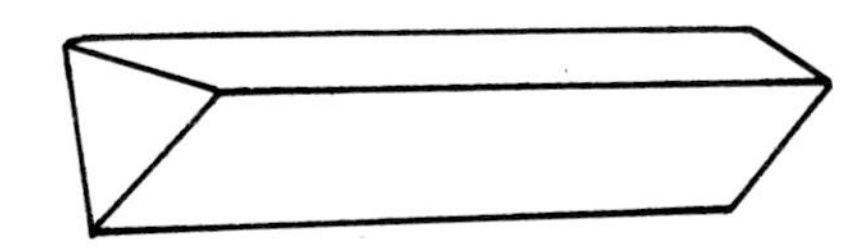

**Triangle Rod Diagram**

**4** *To make a candy cane rod:* Roll two or more contrasting color rods, each about ¼-inch diameter. Place the rods together and, holding them at the ends, twist them once or twice to begin spiraling the rods. Roll the rods once or twice to help them mesh, then twist them together a little more. Continue to twist and roll the rods until the color stripes are as wide as desired. Finish the rod by rolling it until the outer surface is smooth.

# CANDY CANES PIN

**Size:** 5 inches high

## MATERIALS

- ❄ Polymer clays in 58-gram blocks: 1 block each of red and white
- ❄ 1-inch pin back
- ❄ ¼ yard of ¼-inch-wide bright green picot-edged ribbon
- ❄ Strong crafter's glue for metal and china
- ❄ ½ yard of ⅛-inch-wide gold metallic ribbon

## DIRECTIONS

**1** Prepare the clay following the directions under "Conditioning the Clay" on this page.

**2** Referring to Step 3 under "Making the Shapes" on this page, form eight red and eight white ¼ × 6-inch clay triangle rods.

**3** To shape one candy cane, press eight triangle rods (four each of white and red) together with the narrow points in the center and alternating the colors, as shown in the **Candy Cane Diagram.** Roll the candy cane once or twice to round the surface slightly.

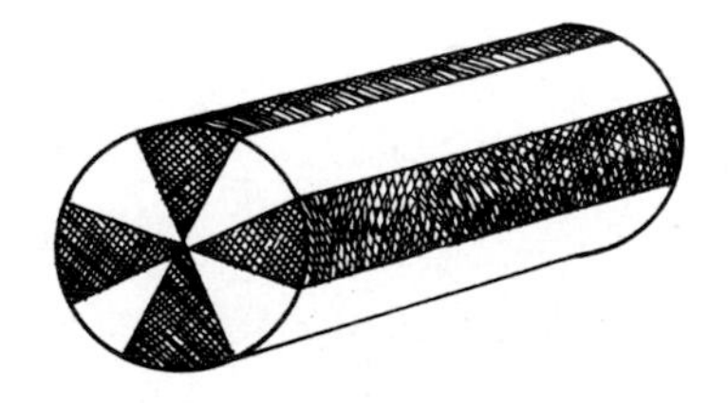

**Candy Cane Diagram**

4 Refer to Step 4 of "Making the Shapes" on page 171 to twist the candy cane. Roll the twisted cane on a flat surface until it is ⅜ inch in diameter. Measuring from the center out, cut it into a 5-inch-long piece. Trim the ends.

5 Repeat Steps 3 and 4 on page 171 with the remaining eight triangle rods to shape a second cane.

6 Bend each cane into a candy-cane shape, as shown in the photograph on page 170. Place one cane on a baking sheet. Position the second cane across the first, pressing them together where they cross.

7 Following the manufacturer's directions, bake the canes and let them cool on a wire rack.

8 Use the crafter's glue to glue the pin back to the bottom cane. Tie the ribbon around the middle of the pin, making a small bow. Trim the ends of the ribbon.

## Lollipop Pin

**Size:** 5½ inches high

### Materials

- Polymer clays in 58-gram blocks: 1 block each of red, white, and green
- Bamboo skewer
- Paintbrush
- Accent Jewelry Glaze Diamond Bright acrylic glitter glaze*
- 1-inch pin back
- Strong crafter's glue for metal and china
- ½ yard of ⅜-inch-wide picot-edged bright green ribbon

*See the "Buyer's Guide" on page 176.*

### Directions

1 Prepare the clay following the directions under "Conditioning the Clay" on page 171.

2 Referring to Step 2 under "Making the Shapes" on page 171, roll one ¼ × 12-inch rod each with the white, green, and red clays. Refer to Step 4 under "Making the Shapes" to twist and roll the three rods together to shape the cane. Roll the twisted cane once or twice to smooth the surface.

3 On a flat surface, roll the twisted cane into a spiral lollipop shape, as shown in the **Lollipop Diagram,** blending the outer end of the cane into the edge of the spiral. Cut a 3-inch length of bamboo skewer. Insert the 3-inch skewer into the side of the clay spiral, pushing it in about 1 inch.

**Lollipop Diagram**

4 Bake the lollipop and let it cool thoroughly on the wire rack, following the manufacturer's directions for baking.

5 Brush the glitter glaze on the spiral with the paintbrush. Let the glaze dry thoroughly.

6 Use the crafter's glue to glue the pin back in place. Tie the ribbon around the middle of the pin, making a small bow. Trim the ends of the ribbon.

## Peppermint Candy Earrings

**Size:** About 2 inches high

### Materials

- Polymer clays in 58-gram blocks: 1 block each of red and white
- Wire cutters
- Jewelry findings: 2 fishhook earring backs, four 7mm jump rings, and 2 eye pins
- Needle-nose pliers
- ½ yard of ¼-inch-wide picot-edged bright green ribbon

### Directions

1 Prepare the clay following the directions under "Conditioning the Clay" on page 171.

2 Referring to Step 3 under "Making the Shapes" on page 171, form four ⅜ × 2-inch triangle rods each with the white and red clays. To shape the cane, press the triangle rods together with the narrow points in the center and alternating colors, as shown in the **Candy Cane Diagram** on page 171. Roll the cane on a flat surface until it is about 1 inch in diameter.

3 With the craft knife, carefully cut the cane into two ¼-inch-thick slices.

4 Use the wire cutters to cut two eye pins each ½ inch long. Press one eye pin into the side of each slice. Reshape the slices on a flat surface, if necessary.

5 Following the manufacturer's directions, bake the slices and let them cool on a wire rack.

6 Using the needle-nose pliers, attach a jump ring to each eye pin. Tie a 7-inch length of ribbon to each attached ring, making a small bow. Attach a second jump ring to each of the first rings. Attach a fishhook to each of the second jump rings. Trim the ends of the ribbon.

## Star Necklace

**Size:** 1 to 2 inches high

### Materials

- Pencil
- Tracing paper
- Scissors
- One 58-gram block of yellow polymer clay
- Bamboo skewer
- Assorted colored seed beads
- Paintbrush
- Accent Jewelry Glaze Diamond Bright acrylic glitter glaze*
- Needle-nose pliers
- Five 7mm jump rings
- 1 yard of black rattail cording
- Fabric glue

*See the "Buyer's Guide" on page 176.*

### Directions

1 Use the pencil and tracing paper to trace the star patterns on the right. Cut out the shapes and use them for pattern templates.

2 Prepare the clay following the directions under "Conditioning the Clay" on page 171.

3 Referring to Step 1 under "Making the Shapes" on page 171, roll out a ¼-inch-thick clay slab large enough to fit the five star-pattern templates. Then place the templates on the clay slab and use the craft knife to cut out one large star, two medium stars, and two small stars. Use the tip of the knife to cut the clay, pressing the knife straight down into the clay. Do not drag the knife through the clay.

4 Use a skewer to pierce a hole in the top point of each star. Press seed beads into the clay surface of each star.

5 Bake the stars and cool them thoroughly on the wire rack, following the manufacturer's directions for baking.

6 Use the paintbrush to brush the glitter glaze on the stars. Let the glaze dry thoroughly.

7 Using the needle-nose pliers, attach a jump ring in the hole of each star. Fold the rattail cording in half. Pull the folded end of the cording through the jump ring of the large star. Pull the cut ends of the cord through the folded end and tighten to knot the star in the center of the cord, as shown in the **Necklace Diagram.**

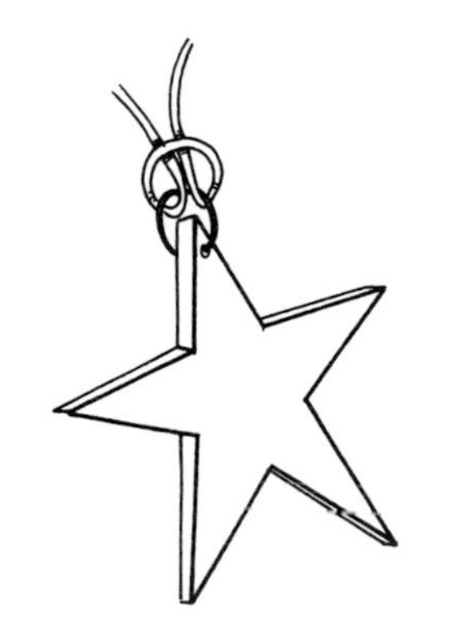

**Necklace Diagram**

8 Knot a medium star onto one end of the cording, spacing this star about 2 inches from the center knot. Knot a small star onto the cording, spacing it about 2 inches from the medium star. Knot the two remaining stars on the other half of the cording to match the first side.

9 Use the ends of the cording to tie the necklace to the desired length. Place a dab of glue on the ends of the cording to prevent fraying, and on each knot to secure it.

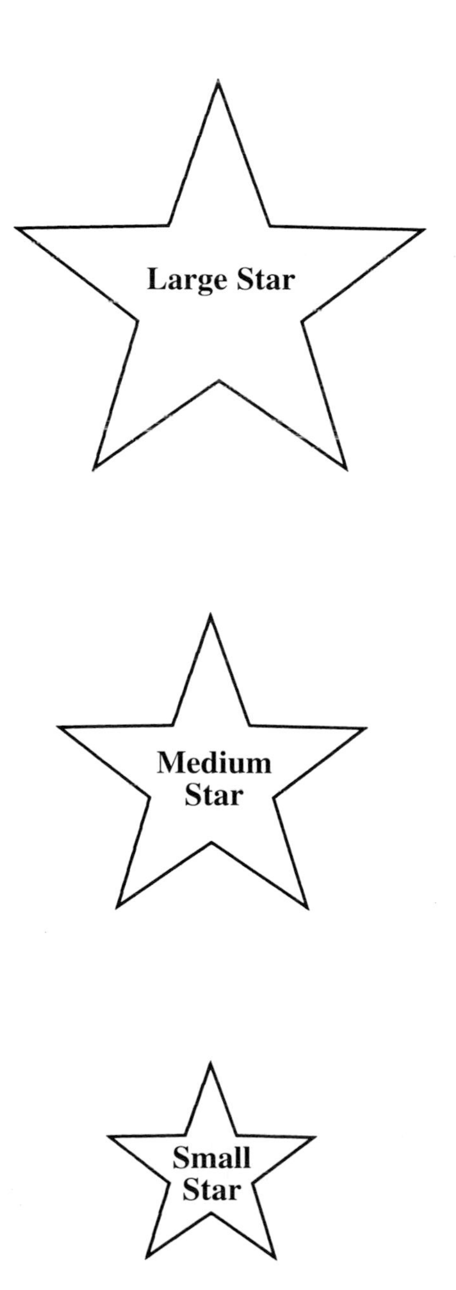

# PRINCESS TIC-TAC-TOE GAME

*Gold and velvet and jewels—all the grown-up trimmings girls love—make this a pretty favor for young party guests. The heart-shaped acrylic gem markers store right in the drawstring pouch, making this game a perfect accessory to take along on overnights and trips to Grandma's house.*

**Size:** 11-inch diameter

## Materials

- Compass and paper
- 12-inch square each of dark rose velveteen and fine, white cotton
- Air-soluble marking pen
- Scissors
- Pencil
- Ruler
- Pointed paintbrush
- Plum iridescent and white paint, such as Duncan Scribbles fashion paint*
- Sewing machine
- J. & P. Coats gold metallic machine sewing thread
- Matching sewing thread
- Hand-sewing needle
- 1 yard of ¼-inch-diameter decorative gold cord
- Two 2-inch gold tassels or gold thread to make tassels (See "How to Make a Tassel" on the opposite page.)
- Thick white craft glue
- Large, faceted acrylic rhinestones: 4 each of 2 colors (Here we used Dark Fuschia and Aurora Borealis from The Beadery.*)

*See the "Buyer's Guide" on page 176.

## Directions

1 Using the compass, mark a 12-inch circle on a piece of paper for a pattern. Use this pattern to cut out one circle each from the velveteen and cotton fabrics.

2 Using the compass, mark a 4¾-inch circle on a piece of paper. Cut out the circle and fold it in half, then in half again so it is in quarters. Unfold the paper. Draw a solid line across the circle ¾ inch on

both sides of each fold line, as shown in **Diagram 1,** to mark the game's crossbars.

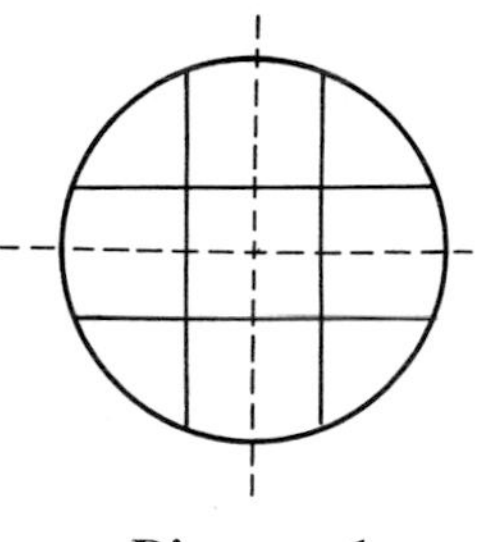

**Diagram 1**

*3* Center the small paper pattern on the large cotton circle and mark the outline of the small circle on the fabric, using the air-soluble marking pen. Also mark the ends of the crossbar lines—where the lines meet the circle's outline—onto the fabric. Remove the paper pattern from the fabric and draw the pattern of crossbar lines on the fabric by connecting the end marks of the crossbar lines, as shown in **Diagram 2.**

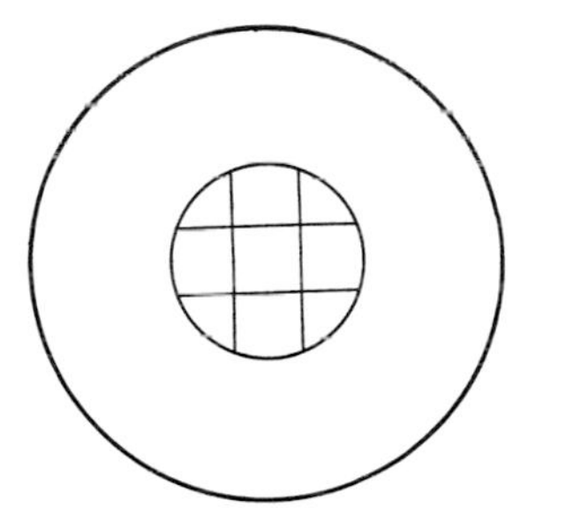

**Diagram 2**

*4* Paint the center square and the four alternate outside spaces of the inner circle with the plum iridescent, as shown in the photograph on the opposite page. Add white to the plum color to make a lighter shade and use it to paint the remaining spaces of the circle. Let the paint dry thoroughly before you proceed.

*5* With the metallic sewing thread and sewing machine, stitch a line of narrow satin stitch along each marked crossbar, widening and narrowing the stitch width at each end to make a diamond shape just outside the circle, as shown in **Diagram 3.**

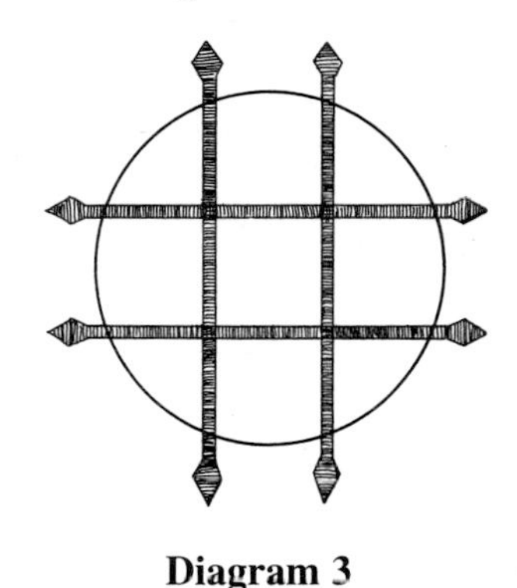

**Diagram 3**

*6* With right sides facing, and using a ¼-inch seam allowance, sew the cotton and velveteen circles together with matching sewing thread, leaving a small opening for turning. Clip the seam allowance along the curve and turn the circles to the right side. Tuck in the remaining seam allowance and slip stitch the opening closed. Then with matching sewing thread, machine topstitch along the outer edge of the circle.

*7* Mark the circle for eight pairs of buttonholes, 1 inch from the outer edge of the fabric and centered above a space on the crossbar circle. Use the metallic thread to sew a pair of ⅝-inch buttonholes at each mark (16 buttonholes in all), spacing each buttonhole in a pair ½ inch apart from the other, as shown in **Diagram 4.**

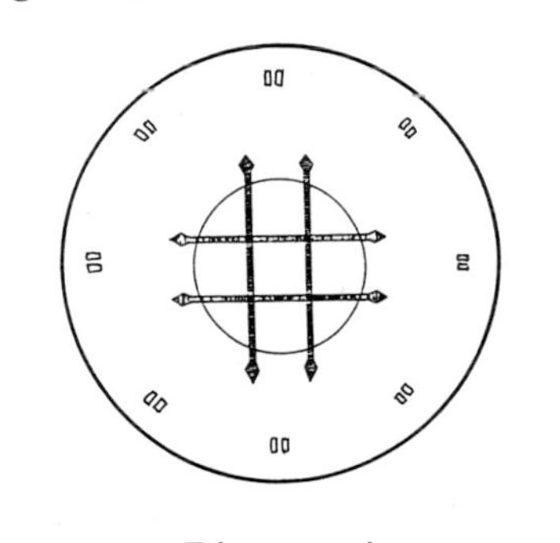

**Diagram 4**

*8* Cut each buttonhole open and lace the gold cord through the pairs of buttonholes on the velveteen side. Tie a tassel 1 inch from each end of the cord. Fold up the end of the cord on itself and glue it in place, as shown in **Diagram 5.**

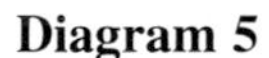

**Diagram 5**

*9* Referring to **Diagram 6,** wrap metallic gold thread around the cord to cover the end. Trim the length of the cord to fit the circle when it is flat, leaving several inches at the ends for tying. Attach the second tassel to the other end of the cord in the same way.

**Diagram 6**

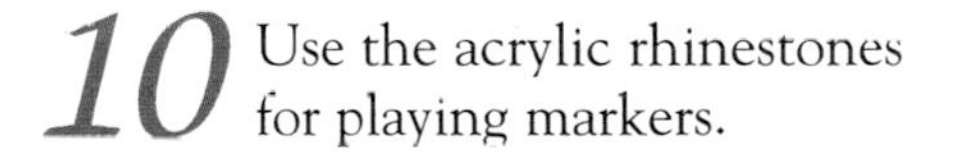

*10* Use the acrylic rhinestones for playing markers.

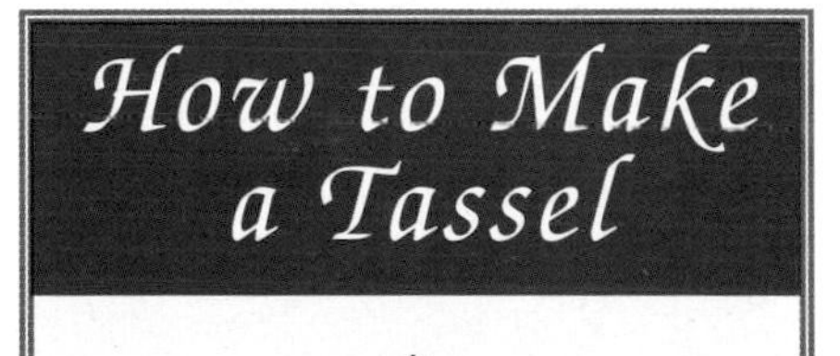

## *How to Make a Tassel*

❄

**Wrap thread or embroidery floss multiple times around a 2-inch piece of cardboard. Use a length of thread to tie the loops together at one end; cut the loops apart at the other end. Then remove the cardboard and wrap the strands together with another piece of thread, about ½ inch from the tied end. Trim the ends of the tassel even.**

# BUYER'S GUIDE

*We would like to thank the following suppliers for providing us with the products and support that were instrumental in the completion of this book.*

**American Art Clay Co., Ltd.**
4717 West 16th Street
Indianapolis, IN 46222
*Polymer clays, including Fimo and Night Glow*

**The Beadery**
105 Canonchet Road
Hope Valley, RI 02832
*Beads and findings*

**Charles Craft, Inc.**
P.O. Box 1049
Laurinburg, NC 28353
*Cross-stitch fabrics, including KitchenMates terry towel and Linaida 14-count cross-stitch fabric*

**Dalee Book Co.**
267 Douglass Street
Brooklyn, NY 11217
*Canvas-covered stationery accessories*

**DecoArt**
P.O. Box 360
Stanford, KY 40484
*Acrylic paints*

**Delta Technical Coatings**
2550 Pellissier Place
Whittier, CA 90601
*Paints and finishes, including Ceramcoat Acrylic Paint*

**Design Originals**
2425 Cullen Street
Fort Worth, TX 76107
*Rug braiding tools*

**Duncan Enterprises**
5673 East Shields Avenue
Fresno, CA 93727
*Paints, including Scribbles fashion paint, dimensional writer, acrylic paint, and textile medium*

**Fiskars**
7811 West Stewart Street
Wausau, WI 54402-8027
*Scissors*

**J. & P. Coats**
P.O. Box 27067
Greenville, NC 29616
*Yarns and threads, including Red Heart 4-ply Super Saver and Classic 4-ply worsted-weight yarns, and gold metallic thread*

**Lion Brand Yarn Co.**
34 West 15th Street
New York, NY 10011
*Yarns, including Wool-Ease Sprinkles worsted-weight yarn and Jiffy yarn*

**Mundial Inc.**
50 Kerry Place
Norwood, MA 02062
*Scissors*

**Nancy's Notions, Ltd.**
333 Beichl Avenue
P.O. Box 683
Beaver Dam, WI 53916
*Ultrasuede*

**C. M. Offray & Son**
P.O. Box 601
Chester, NJ 07930
*Ribbons*

**Plaid Enterprises**
1649 International Boulevard
Norcross, GA 30091
*Paints and accessories, including Royal Coat Decoupage Finish acrylic sealer, Mod Podge glue-type finishing sealer, and Metallic Acrylic Paints*

**Singer Sewing Company**
135 Raritan Center Parkway
Edison, NJ 08837
*Sewing machines*

**Therm O Web**
770 Glenn Avenue
Wheeling, IL 60090
*Heat n Bond vinyl*

**V.I.P. Fabrics**
1412 Broadway
New York, NY 10018
*Assorted cotton prints*

**Walnut Hollow Farm**
Route 2
Dodgeville, WI 53533
*Birdhouses, including Large Cloud Cabin and Medium Cloud Cabin*

**Westrim Crafts**
9667 Canoga Avenue
Chatsworth, CA 91311
*Craft foam sheets*